Exercising Human Rights in Armenia

GESELLSCHAFTEN UND STAATEN IM EPOCHENWANDEL

SOCIETIES AND STATES IN TRANSFORMATION

Herausgegeben von / Edited by
Dittmar Schorkowitz / Stefan Troebst

Mitbegründet von / Co-founded by
René Ahlberg/Lawrence Krader/Klaus Meyer

BAND 24

PETER LANG

Liana Geghamyan

Exercising Human Rights in Armenia

Interactions between governmental and non-state actors

PETER LANG

Bibliographic Information published by the Deutsche Nationalbibliothek
The Deutsche Nationalbibliothek lists this publication in the Deutsche Nationalbibliografie; detailed bibliographic data is available online at http://dnb.d-nb.de.

Library of Congress Cataloging-in-Publication Data
A CIP catalog record for this book has been applied for at the Library of Congress.

Zugl.: Leipzig, Univ., Diss., 2019

Printed by CPI books GmbH, Leck

15
ISSN 0941-7389
ISBN 978-3-631-81459-8 (Print)
E-ISBN 978-3-631-82323-1 (E-Book)
E-ISBN 978-3-631-82324-8 (EPUB)
E-ISBN 978-3-631-82325-5 (MOBI)
DOI 10.3726/b17016

Peter Lang – Berlin · Bern · Bruxelles · New York · Oxford · Warszawa · Wien

This publication has been peer reviewed.

www.peterlang.com

Acknowledgements

This research project would not have been possible without the support of those people I have encountered throughout the course of my studies. The many exchanges, conversations and discussions I have had with them have in different ways contributed to this project as well as to my understanding of the subject matter. I wish to extend my gratitude first and foremost to my supervisor Professor Stefan Troebst for giving me the opportunity to conduct my PhD study under his guidance and for his patient, understanding and supportive supervision throughout this research. I owe him many thanks for his encouraging and motivating feedback as well as insightful comments that made sure I stayed on the right track. I am also very grateful to Professor Gert Pickel for his time and efforts spent on reading my write-ups and pinpointing the gaps that needed to be filled. My time at Leipzig University and my stay in the city of Leipzig have been facilitated by Dr. Martina Keilbach who has been of great help and assistance during times of difficulty and uncertainty. She has been an advisor, a confidant, a wonderful listener, interlocutor and a friend. And last but not least I owe appreciation and thanks to my colleagues and friends, in particular Hakob Matevosyan with whom I have many a time discussed Armenian-ness and tried to make sense of what it means to be one, along with sharing the hurdles of doing a PhD and the theoretical and practical challenges we found ourselves in; to Altynay Kulmyrzaeva for her always positive and optimistic outlooks on the future, much cherished friendship and memorable talks beyond human rights; as well as Xue Wang, Lobsang Tenpa and others to whom I am immensely grateful for making this journey worthwhile. Finally, my research would not have been complete if not for those respondents who confided their thoughts in me, shared their struggles with me and revealed a different reality to me. It is their relentless efforts this PhD project is dedicated to.

Table of contents

1 Introduction

"By calling our actions sabotage, you insult us. Your comments undermine and devalue our struggle for such fundamental rights as are the right to life, the right to access water, and the right to live in a healthy environment".
Aharon Arsenyan[*]

Civic activism, manifest in locally termed civic initiatives and outbreaks of protests, has marked the public places in Armenia prominently since 2007/2008[1]. Comprising groups of young people determined to make their voices heard about issues ranging from the environmental and the social sectors all the way to the political, activism headed by conscious citizens has overshadowed both the political parties and the non-governmental organizations in its modus operandi, perceptions and practices related to human rights, democratic governance, rule of law and state-society relations. Environmental or ecological activism, the most pronounced confrontation involving active citizens and the government, has been the cornerstone of active citizenship. It has highlighted common problem areas linked to environmental crime including Armenia's vast mining sector, the logging industry and the hydroelectric sector[2].

The manner in which mining is conducted in Armenia causes damage not only to the country's environment but also harms the well-being of its citizens. Mining has resulted in widespread deforestation and the destruction of arable

---

* Peter Liakhov and Knar Khudoyan, "How Citizens Battling a Controversial Gold Mining Project Are Testing Armenia's New Democracy," *openDemocracy*, 7 August 2018, accessed 14 February 2019, https://www.opendemocracy.net/od-russia/peter-liakhov-knar-khudoyan/citizens-battling-a-controversial-gold-mining-project-amulsar-armenia.

1 Armine Ishkanian, *Democracy Building and Civil Society in Post-Soviet Armenia* (Routledge, 2008).

2 Christoph H. Stefes and Katherine Weingartner, "Environmental Crime in Armenia: A Case Study on Mining," January 2015, accessed 14 February 2019, https://efface.eu/sites/default/files/EFFACE_Environmental%20crime%20in%20Armenia_A%20case%20study%20on%20mining.pdf.

land[3]. Furthermore, it has led to contamination of lakes, rivers and soil, also causing air pollution putting the health and subsistence of Armenian citizens at risk[4]. Citizens involved in struggles to save the environment have pointed to the violation of such rights as the right to life, the right to access water and the right to live in a healthy environment. They have confronted the government and the mining companies with documentary evidence affirming that mining violates both Armenian and international legislation. Moreover, they have cited a number of documents as well as aerial pictures of mines indicating that certain mines are operated illegally[5].

Environmental or ecological activism has achieved some success in Armenia. However, it is still ongoing and has, over the years, extended to other sectors beyond nature protection and to other rights, emphasising the interconnectedness and indivisibility of human rights. The civic initiatives and protests that have followed since 2007/2008 have reflected the gradual rise in civic, rights and legal consciousness among Armenian citizens, the youth in particular. Moreover, for the past ten years human rights language has increasingly been employed by Armenian citizens when interacting with state actors, assembling in public spaces to protest wrongdoings, oppose government decisions and press for change – social or political. Opposition to government decisions, whether formally (through institutions) or informally (in the streets), have revealed tension with regard to the ways in which universal human rights are enacted, debated, practiced, violated, envisioned, and experienced in Armenia. The protesters have referred to domestic laws and constitution as failing to protect their interests and have also sought justice via human rights treaty bodies and the European Court of Human Rights.

The human rights discourse in the Armenian context has evolved around specialized language used by NGO representatives to protect the rights of the citizens vis-à-vis the state as well as around a more 'native/local language', that is, a 'thicker sense of the moral vernacular' revealing tension between the Armenian citizens and the state (the "rights holder" and the "rights withholder"[6]). Informal non-state actors in Armenia have come to speak on their own behalf and make

3 Ibid.
4 Ibid.
5 Armine Ishkanian (2016), "Challenging the Gospel of Neoliberalism? Civil Society Opposition to Mining in Armenia," In Thomas Davies, Holly Eva Ryan, Alejandro Milcíades Peña (ed.) *Protest, Social Movements and Global Democracy Since 2011: New Perspectives* (Research in Social Movements, Conflicts and Change, Volume 39) Emerald Group Publishing Limited, pp. 107–136.
6 Gerard A. Hauser, "The Moral Vernacular of Human Rights Discourse," *Philosophy & Rhetoric* 41, no. 4 (2008): 446.

their cause heard, valid and justified 'in order to restore the rights that have been withheld'[7]. The human rights language that has been used during confrontations, resistances and interactions in "the Street" has transformed the perceptions as well as the practices of the notion of 'the citizen' in the Armenian context.

1.1 Problem statement

Human rights is a diverse and challenging field of study and has been written about from the perspective of more than one discipline. All these various accounts have attempted to shed light on rights as aspirational principles[8], ethical dilemmas[9], contested universal norms[10], political tools[11], legal entitlements[12] and culturally embedded values[13]. A prominent discourse particularly in the 20th century and at the threshold of the 3rd Millennium, human rights have played

7 Ibid.

8 Michael Ignatieff, *Human Rights as Politics and Idolatry* (Princeton University Press, 2003); Mitchell N. Berman, "Aspirational Rights and the Two-Output Thesis," Harvard Law Review Forum 119 (2005): 220; Ellen Wiles, "Aspirational Principles or Enforceable Rights? The Future for Socio-Economic Rights in National Law," *American University International Law Review* 22, no. 1 (2006): 35–64.

9 Daniel Bell and Joseph H. Carens, "The Ethical Dilemmas of International Human Rights and Humanitarian NGOs: Reflections on a Dialogue between Practitioners and Theorists," *Human Rights Quarterly* 26, no. 2 (2004): 300–329.

10 Abdullahi Ahmed An-Na'im, "An Inclusive Approach to the Mediation of Competing Human Rights Claims," *Constellations* 20, no. 1 (2013): 7–17; Abdullahi Ahmed An-Na'im, *Human Rights in Cross-Cultural Perspectives: A Quest for Consensus* (Philadelphia: University of Pennsylvania Press, 1995).

11 Paul Gready, "The Politics of Human Rights," *Third World Quarterly* 24, No. 4 (2003): 745–757; Laura Valentini, "Human Rights, Freedom, and Political Authority," *Political Theory* 40, No. 5 (2012): 573–601; Neil Stammers, "Human Rights and Power," *Political Studies* 41, no. 1 (1993): 70–82.

12 Ed Sparer, "Fundamental Human Rights, Legal Entitlements, and the Social Struggle: A Friendly Critique of the Critical Studies Movement," *Stanford Law Review* 36 (1984): 509–574; Guglielmo Verdirame, "Human Rights in Political and Legal Theory," *Routledge Handbook of International Human Rights Law*, pp. 41–64. Routledge, 2014.

13 Ajnesh Prasad, "Cultural Relativism in Human Rights Discourse," *Peace Review: A Journal of Social Justice* 19 (2007): 589–596; Katherine Brennan, "The Influence of Cultural Relativism on International Human Rights Law: Female Circumcision as a Case Study," *Law & Inequality: A Journal of Theory and Practice* 7 (1989): 367–398.

the role of moral and ethical deterrents[14] and have been an essential part of people's lexicon in different parts of the world. They have put forward definitions of rights and wrongs, acceptable or condemnable ways of state treatment of citizens, in other words, established a contract, a so-called modus vivendi for peaceful co-existence. Nonetheless, the concept has not been void of controversies and contradictions. "The problem of universals", "the limits of particularism", "gender-neutral or gender-specific"[15], "the sovereignty discourse"[16], "economic and military interventions"[17] along with questions arising from globalization are some of the notable dilemmas surrounding the concept of human rights and presenting challenges to date.

The complexity becomes more apparent when the global meets the local, making it difficult for universally and internationally established 'should' and 'ought to' to proceed unhindered. Rony Brauman, former President of Médecins sans Frontières (MSF), in a lecture delivered at the Carnegie Council on 14 February 2001 stated[18]:

> In a number of cases [during the war in Mogadishu] we had to amputate because of massive infections that could not be treated properly. In our experience, the decision to amputate was a medical, technical diagnosis, which doesn't incur any criticism because it poses a solution to a life-and-death situation. Thus we were surprised to find that most of the young people we wanted to operate on refused to be amputated. They preferred – and this took us some time to understand - to die with their entire body than to live with a visible mutilation.

---

14 Romuald R. Haule, "Some Reflections on the Foundation of Human Rights – Are Human Rights an Alternative to Moral Values?" *Max Planck Yearbook of United Nations Law Online* 10, no. 1 (2006): 367–395.

15 Linda M. G. Zerilli, "This Universalism Which Is Not One," *Diacritics* 28, no. 2 (1998): 3–20. *Project MUSE*, doi:10.1353/dia.1998.0013.

16 Mahmood Monshipouri and Claude E. Welch, "The Search for International Human Rights and Justice: Coming to Terms with the New Global Realities," *Human Rights Quarterly* 23, no. 2 (2001): 370–401.

17 Ibid.

18 Rony Brauman, "Controversies Within Health and Human Rights, Address at the Carnegie Council on Ethics and International Affairs," (February 14, 2001), available at: https://www.carnegiecouncil.org/studio/multimedia/20010214-controversies-within-health-and-human-rights, cited in Daniel A. Bell and Joseph H. Carens, "The Ethical Dilemmas of International Human Rights and Humanitarian NGOs: Reflections on a Dialogue between Practitioners and Theorists," *Human Rights Quarterly* 26, no. 2 (2004): 305.

Tensions have evolved around other cultural and religious practices such as Female Genital Mutilation (FGM) – 'a ritual commonly practiced in many African countries as well as many Islamic communities and deemed by many as a form of religious purity'[19]. While different versions of this practice 'pose serious health risks that inevitably violate a female's intrinsic right to life, dignity and health, simply abolishing the practice without pragmatic remedies would also be in violation of Article 18 which states that everyone has the right to freedom of thought, conscience and religion'[20]. Furthermore, it would also be in breach of Article 27 of the Universal Declaration providing the right 'to freely participate in the cultural life of a community. Respect for the rights of culture is imperative when seeking potential remedies for the long-standing cultural practice'[21].

1.2 Rationale for research

Human rights is a relationship between the state and its citizens. That relationship is more contested in some countries than others. Democratically governed states tend to respect the rights of their citizens more than autocracies. Human rights instruments – treaties, covenants and conventions are designed to protect citizens against the abuses of states. The abused comprise different groups of individuals, such as victims of domestic violence, political prisoners, refugees and so on. Advocacy on behalf of these groups often takes place by those who 'speak by deputy for those whose faces we do not see, whose voices we do not hear, and whose pain we do not witness'[22]. On the other hand, human rights discourse 'comes from the abused and, by showing us their human face, gives presence to their pain and immediacy to their plea for help'[23]. Claims to rectify injustice and provide redress for human rights violations are put up against states that bear the obligation to both refrain from breaching the human rights of their citizens and actively engage to investigate or punish human rights abuses should the latter occur.

Human rights is best placed to demonstrate the relationship between the government and non-state actors since abuses bring the "rights holder" and the

19 Sandra Danial, "Cultural Relativism vs Universalism: Female Genital Mutilation, Pragmatic Remedies," *The Journal of Historical Studies* 2, no. 1 (2013): 1.

20 Ibid.

21 Ibid.

22 Gerard A. Hauser, "The Moral Vernacular of Human Rights Discourse," *Philosophy & Rhetoric* 41, no. 4 (2008): 441.

23 Ibid.

"rights withholder"[24] into a conflict the settlement of which requires negotiation, recognition and eventual rectification of a wrongdoing. Moreover, 'human rights discourse can propel mobilization since it helps social groups reanalyze issues that society initially considered to be 'problems' and rename them as 'violations'; that is, something that should not be accepted or endured'[25]. In the words of Michael Ignatieff, 'human rights is the only universally available moral vernacular that validates the claims of women and children against the oppression they experience in patriarchal and tribal societies; it is the only vernacular that enables dependent persons to perceive themselves as moral agents and to act against practices – arranged marriages, purdah, civic disenfranchisement, genital mutilation, domestic slavery, and so on – that are ratified by the weight and authority of their cultures. These agents seek out human rights precisely because it legitimizes their protests against oppression'[26].

Whereas it is challenging to reconcile cultural practices and universal absolutes, some scholars have proposed to 'go beyond the polarities' and 'inform the cross-fertilisation of ideas'[27] across various cultures. They have attempted to break the impasse between universals and particulars and bridge the two, noting the usefulness in 'calling attention to the ways in which the notions of liberty and individualism can be, and have been used to rationalise the abuses of capitalism'[28]. In a similar vein, 'notions of equality and collectivism can be, and have been used as excuses for arbitrary and authoritarian governance'[29]. Therefore, and rightly so, 'the object of human rights discourse should be the quest for a reasonable and balanced approach to human rights that recognises the interplay between various cultural factors in the construction and constitution of human rights'[30].

---

24 Michael Ignatieff, *Human Rights as Politics and Idolatry*, ed. Amy Gutmann. With commentary by K. Anthony Appiah, David A. Hollinger, Thomas W. Laqueur, and Diane F. Orentlicher (Princeton: Princeton University Press, 2001), 67.

25 Neve Gordon, and Nitza Berkovitch, "Human Rights Discourse in Domestic Settings: How Does It Emerge?" *Political Studies* 55, no. 1 (2007): 244.

26 Michael Ignatieff, *Human Rights as Politics and Idolatry*, ed. Amy Gutmann. With commentary by K. Anthony Appiah, David A. Hollinger, Thomas W. Laqueur, and Diane F. Orentlicher (Princeton: Princeton University Press, 2001), 68.

27 Bonny Ibhawoh, "Cultural Relativism and Human Rights: Reconsidering the Africanist Discourse," *Netherlands Quarterly of Human Rights* 19, no. 1 (2001): 43–62.

28 Ibid., 61.

29 Ibid.

30 Ibid.

Such an approach places actors at the centre, researching their 'interpretations and strategies and how these interlock through processes of negotiation and accommodation'[31]. Moreover, it 'rejects linear, determinist and simple empiricist thinking and practice. . . [A]n actor-oriented perspective entails recognizing the "multiple realities" and diverse social practices of various actors, and requires working out methodologically how to come to grips with these different and often incompatible social worlds'[32]. This research is embedded in the latter approach. It aims to demonstrate the ways in which human rights ideas are appropriated, encouraged and resisted in Armenia. Through studies of key human rights actors, or as Sally Engle Merry terms them 'translators'[33], this research pursues the objective of finding out the perceptions and practices of both state and non-state actors in claiming, exercising, as well as negotiating about human rights in the Armenian context.

Translators are critical in that they 'move between local and global sets of cultural understandings, helping each to make sense of the other'[34]. These intermediaries, be they Non-Governmental Organizations (NGOs) or social movement activists, play a crucial role 'in interpreting the cultural world of transnational modernity for local claimants. They appropriate, translate, and remake transnational discourses into the vernacular, at the same time taking local stories and framing them in national and international human rights language'[35]. These intermediaries or translators (NGOs, activists, academics, local politicians, journalists or lawyers) lie at the centre of this research. Nonetheless, I acknowledge that taking their words or actions at face value invites a good amount of naiveté and runs the risk of separating them from the rest of the citizenry, thereby making them elitist. I bear this in mind as I explore their role in aiding the translation of human rights in the Armenian context, conveying human rights ideas to ordinary citizens as well as the ways they are perceived by one another and the population at large. I view the appropriation and/or resistance of human rights in the Armenian setting as a process that is evolving, gradually extending and incrementally transforming.

Since the 2010s Armenian citizens have increasingly interacted with governmental actors in public spaces through human rights language and domestic

31 Ann-Belinda S. Preis, "Human Rights as Cultural Practice: An Anthropological Critique," *Human Rights Quarterly* 18, no. 2 (1996): 312.

32 Ibid.

33 Sally Engle Merry, "Human Rights and Transnational Culture: Regulating Gender Violence through Global Law," *Osgoode Hall Law Journal* 44, no. 1 (2006): 53–75.

34 Ibid., 55.

35 Ibid., 58.

laws to question, oppose and protest government decisions and seek redress. These interactions have not been unhindered, rather, civic protests have at times been curtailed by force, and activists have been detained while journalists have become targets of police interference. It is not my aim to provide an in-depth study of the exercise and enjoyment of one particular right in Armenia. Instead, I examine the citizens' exercise of their civil and political rights to voice concerns or put up claims in regard to their social and economic as well as other rights. I look at civic protests, collective struggles and resistances as platforms wherein 'personal agency, laden with collectively produced differences of power is implicated'[36]. The terms 'civic protests', 'collective struggles' and 'resistances' are used interchangeably throughout this research.

1.3 Research questions

Democratization efforts, democracy building projects, NGOs, the civil society as well as relationships and differences between them in Armenia are well documented. However, the link between human rights, civic and legal consciousness, interactions between the state and non-state actors, extension of human rights ideas or their disruption thereof is understudied in the Armenian setting, and it is these themes among others that this research explores. It looks at human rights and its key actors through the lens of sociology to discover the ways in which 'universal human rights, believed to be entailed by a common human nature, are enacted, debated, practiced, violated, envisioned, and experienced'[37]. In this regard, the present research attempts to answer the following questions:

- What are the human rights perceptions and practices of non-state actors in Armenia?
- What is the role of non-state actors in improving the human rights situation in Armenia?
- In what ways do non-state actors interact with each other, as well as with the government and the citizenry at large?

36 William H. Sewell, Jr., "A Theory of Structure: Duality, Agency, and Transformation," *American Journal of Sociology* 98, no. 1 (1992): 21.

37 Mark Goodale, "Introduction: Locating Rights, Envisioning Law between the Global and the Local," In *The Practice of Human Rights: Tracking Law between the Global and the Local*, eds. Mark Goodale and Sally Engle Merry (Cambridge University Press, 2007), 133.

1.4 Thesis outline

The research project is organized in the following order:

This introductory chapter is followed by *Chapter 2* that underscores the role of the state as an important actor in relation to compliance with internationally recognized human rights norms. Human rights, after all, 'are a profoundly national- not international –issue. States are the principal violators of human rights and the principal actors governed by the regime's norms; international human rights are concerned primarily with how a government treats inhabitants of its own country. . . .'[38] Whether states comply with established human rights standards is a different matter and indeed, despite the existence of a large number of human rights instruments, their implementation leaves much to be desired. The softness of the international human rights system is partly to blame for this, allowing states to get away with violations. More often than not, states make careful economic and political calculations with regard to both respecting as well as violating human rights norms and it is these key points that lie at the core of this chapter.

Chapter 3 lays out the theoretical considerations that inform this research and act as the lens through which human rights are approached. The chapter argues for a sociological understanding of rights, emphasising the key actors and the process within which human rights are negotiated, contested, constructed and reproduced. It reveals a process that is uneven, prone to disruption and contingent upon intersubjective as well as idiosyncratic factors and embedded in power dynamics. *Chapter 4* presents the methodological steps taken and followed to conduct the fieldwork and collect the necessary data to answer the research questions as well as the methods of data interpretation and analysis.

Chapter 5 outlines Soviet and post-Soviet human rights practices, looking at the different stages Armenia has gone through following the break-up of the Soviet Union, including 3 presidents, switching to a parliamentary system of government with a 4th president, increase in the number of NGOs as well as protest groups. The aim of the chapter is to trace the perceptions of human rights in the course of the above-mentioned periods starting with Soviet conceptions of human rights up to and including the ways key human rights actors in Armenia perceive and negotiate them with the Armenian state.

Chapter 6 presents the research findings, detailing the roles of both formal and informal civil society actors, issues and [mis]perceptions with regard to

38 Henry J. Steiner and Philip Alston, *International Human Rights in Context: Law, Politics, Morals* (Clarendon Press, 1996), 452.

both, conceptual distortions, nuances between the ways the actors are defined and perceived, as well as the manners in which both interact with one another, the government and the citizenry at large. Through the study of different protests and civic initiatives as the latter are termed locally, this chapter reveals the ways in which activism manifests itself in the Armenian context and the role it plays in claims-making, voicing disagreement with government decisions and the functioning of the domestic laws and constitution.

Chapter 7 concludes this research project with reflections on whether the research questions have been answered sufficiently, broader implications of the research and findings as well as suggestions for further research.

2 Contesting human rights

2.1 Overview

This chapter focuses on top-down approaches of human rights, highlighting the role of the state as an important actor and the main implementer of internationally recognized human rights norms. External as well as internal factors affecting the success and/or failure of installing human rights in any particular domestic setting are extensively discussed. Despite the existence of a large number of international human rights instruments, their implementation has been far from absolute. This is to an extent due to the softness of the international human rights system and the states' ability to get away with violations through the loopholes of that very system. More often than not states make careful economic and political calculations with regard to both respecting as well as violating human rights norms and it is these key points that lie at the core of this chapter.

2.2 Human rights: An aspirational model

In 1948 the UN General Assembly, by adopting the Universal Declaration of Human Rights (UDHR), aspired to prevent atrocities like the Nazi Holocaust from happening again. The adoption of UDHR was followed by other international human rights instruments, some of which are legally binding for states that have become parties to them. Soon the human rights regime would evolve into a promotion, protection, monitoring and prevention mechanism making sure human rights violators would be brought to justice and remedy the wrongs done to the victims. Since the state is both the guarantor and the perpetrator of human rights of its citizens, human rights regime acts as an organ which citizens can turn to for protection and remedy where domestic remedies have been exhausted without success. Despite the existence of a large number of human rights documentation, human rights remain a relationship between the state and the citizens with the state being the guarantor of rights. However, that relationship bears positive and negative implications. The former is about setting up provisions for citizens to enjoy their rights, while the latter 'prohibits a wide range of state interferences in the personal, social, and political lives of citizens, acting both individually and collectively'[39].

---

39 Jack Donnelly, *Universal Human Rights in Theory and Practice* (Cornell University Press, 2003), 35.

The International Covenant on Civil and Political Rights (ICCPR, 1976) calls on states to 'respect and to ensure to all individuals within its territory and subject to its jurisdiction the rights recognized in the present Covenant, without distinction of any kind, such as race, colour, sex, language, religion, political or other opinion, national or social origin, property, birth or other status' (Article 2). Moreover, states are called on to make changes to domestic laws to incorporate the rights recognized in the Covenant (Article 2, para. 2). The language of this international human rights instrument like that of the others includes 'all peoples', 'any person', 'every human being', 'anyone', 'all persons', meaning that everyone is entitled to the same rights regardless of characteristics that differentiate them as well as irrespective of the state whose citizen they happen to be. Despite the 'everyone', 'all persons', 'anyone' language of the ICCPR, human rights practices and domestic implementation vary tremendously across states and societies. It has been argued that proper implementation of social and economic rights requires financial resources which poor states lack. Cranston posits that 'if we insist on the standards of, say, Sweden, it may not be false to say that realizing most economic and social rights is "impossible" in most countries. But Northern European standards for civil and political rights would be nearly as "impossible"'[40]. The implementation of basic economic and social rights is a matter of feasibility, that is, do states have the capacity to effectively implement these rights? Feasibility presents a challenge given that 'some of the world's countries are too impoverished, troubled and disorganized to respect and implement them effectively'[41].

While there is an element of truth in the above claim, failure to implement social and economic rights is also a matter of poor governance and political economy rather than that of natural scarcity. For instance, although 'Africa's grim economic situation remains a significant constraint on the financial abilities of African states, the lack of political will and the corruption of the ruling elite' as well as 'maldistribution, inequitable allocation of resources and provision of government controlled benefits' play a large role in the lack of enforcement of the International Covenant on Economic, Social and Cultural Rights (ICESCR)[42].

---

40 Ibid., 29; Maurice Cranston, *What Are Human Rights?* (New York: Taplinger, 1973), 65–69.

41 James W. Nickel, "Poverty and Rights," *The Philosophical Quarterly* 55, no. 220 (2005): 399.

42 Shedrack C. Agbakwa, "Reclaiming Humanity: Economic, Social and Cultural Rights as the Cornerstone of African Human Rights," *Yale Human Rights and Development Journal* 5 (2002): 189–191; see also James Thuo Gathii, "Defining the Relationship between Human Rights and Corruption," *University of Pennsylvania Journal of International*

In a similar vein, in order to provide protection against torture (ICCPR, 1976, Article 7), major programmes are required to train, supervise and control the state and security forces[43]. According to Article 10 of the Convention against Torture (1987), 'each state party shall ensure that education and information regarding the prohibition against torture are fully included in the training of law enforcement personnel, civil or military, medical personnel, public officials and other persons who may be involved in the custody, interrogation or treatment of any individual subjected to any form of arrest, detention or imprisonment'[44]. However, achieving compliance with the Convention is quite difficult given that 'states have vastly different political and institutional capacities' and that 'there are political realities on the ground'[45]. In addition, the Convention against Torture suffers from a major difficulty in that 'it has no official "teeth" '[46]. Should a state refuse 'to comply with its provisions, the Committee against Torture cannot impose sanctions'[47]. Enforceability still remains a lingering weakness in all human rights systems[48].

Human rights' global appeal is their protection against 'domination and oppression, the arbitrary or unwarranted use of power to control or interfere in people's lives'[49]. Should such unwarranted interference occur human rights enable people to challenge power and hold power-holders to account[50]. Civil

---

Law 31 (2009): 125; Anne Peters, "Corruption as a Violation of International Human Rights," (2016), accessed 15 November 2018, http://www.mpil.de/files/pdf4/Peters_Corruption_and_Human_Rights20151.pdf; Herman Schwartz, "Economic and Social Rights," *American University International Law Review* 8 (1992): 551.

43 Jack Donnelly, *Universal Human Rights in Theory and Practice* (Cornell University Press, 2003).

44 UN General Assembly, *Convention Against Torture and Other Cruel, Inhuman or Degrading Treatment or Punishment*, 10 December 1984, United Nations, Treaty Series, vol. 1465, p. 85, available at: https://www.refworld.org/docid/3ae6b3a94.html (accessed 15 January 2018).

45 Tobias Kelly, "The UN Committee against Torture: Human Rights Monitoring and the Legal Recognition of Cruelty," *Human Rights Quarterly* 31, no. 3 (2009): 794.

46 Ronagh McQuigg, "How Effective Is the United Nations Committee against Torture?" *The European Journal of International Law* 22, no. 3 (2011): 827.

47 Ibid.

48 Andreea Vesa, "International and Regional Standards for Protecting Victims of Domestic Violence," *Journal of Gender, Social Policy and the Law* 12 (2011): 360.

49 Michael Goodhart, "Neither Relative nor Universal: A Response to Donnelly," *Human Rights Quarterly* 30, no. 1 (2008): 190–191.

50 Ibid.

liberties such as the 'freedoms of speech, press, and assembly, empower citizens to participate in politics and exercise some control over the state'[51]. In autocratic states with authoritarian regimes where power does not belong to the people, elections are fraudulent and leaders hold office through neutralizing opponents, civil liberties are a threatening force to those in power, therefore, in such states civil and political rights are curtailed to limit citizen participation in politics as much as possible[52]. Under the ICCPR states may make derogations, that is, 'deviation from many of the stated conditions declared by the Covenant'[53]. The ICCPR 'contains two types of provisions on limitations – permitting State Parties under closely stated conditions to restrict or condition to varying degrees the exercise of the rights enshrined therein'[54]. Temporary derogation is permitted under Article 4 'in time of public emergency which threatens the life of the nation, provided that those rights are not abridged on a discriminatory basis'[55].

States have the power, under the Covenant, 'to limit, in exceptional circumstances, certain rights otherwise protected'[56]. For instance, Article 21 of the ICCPR permits restrictions on the right to peaceful assembly and Article 22 (2) on the right to freedom of association whereas 'somewhat narrower restrictions are permitted regarding the right to a fair and public hearing, Article 4 (1); freedom of religion, Article 18 (3), and the right to freedom of expression, Article 19 (3)'[57]. A number of rights, thus, include asterisks, that is limitation

---

51 Jack Donnelly, *Universal Human Rights in Theory and Practice* (Cornell University Press, 2003), 32.

52 Freedom House, *Freedom in the World 2018: Democracy in Crisis*, 16 January 2018, available at: https://freedomhouse.org/sites/default/files/FH_FITW_Report_2018_Final_SinglePage.pdf (accessed 5 January 2019) (the report claims that political rights and civil liberties around the world deteriorated to their lowest point in more than a decade in 2017, extending a period characterized by emboldened autocrats, beleaguered democracies, and the United States' withdrawal from its leadership role in the global struggle for human freedom); also see Amnesty International, *Will Human Rights Survive Illiberal Democracy*, 21 October 2015, available at: https://www.amnesty.nl/content/uploads/2015/10/illiberal-democracy-PDF-20mrt.pdf?x65409 (accessed 17 February 2018).

53 Henry J. Steiner and Philip Alston, *International Human Rights in Context: Law, Politics, Morals* (Clarendon Press, 1996), 125.

54 Roza Pati, "Rights and Their Limits: The Constitution for Europe in International and Comparative Legal Perspective," *Berkeley Journal of International Law* 23 (2005): 243.

55 Ibid.

56 Ibid.

57 Ibid.

clauses – 'provisions indicating that a given right cannot be absolute but must be adapted to meet a state's interest in protecting public safety, order, health or morals, or national security'[58].

Protection of civil and political rights is closely linked to the type of government; the more democratic the government the more the citizens of that particular state enjoy and exercise their political rights and civil liberties. Collier and Levitsky define democracy by a 'procedural minimum', presuming 'fully contested elections with full suffrage and the absence of massive fraud, combined with effective guarantees of civil liberties, including freedom of speech, assembly, and association'[59]. Furthermore, liberal democracies follow the principle of accountability, that is, 'upholding important civil freedoms, including the freedom of speech, assembly and the press'[60]. The institutional arrangement in these types of governments is 'arriving at political decisions in which individuals acquire the power to decide by means of a competitive struggle for the people's vote'[61].

A number of characteristics qualifying a polity as fully democratic have been put forward: 'allocation of power that is inclusive, a scope of power that is liberal, a balanced and dispersed distribution of power, elite recruitment that is egalitarian and open, a sense of widely diffused self-responsibility and decisions that are challengeable'[62]. A genuine human rights regime requires 'the authority that has jurisdiction over the working and implementation of a rights regime' to also 'be accountable to the people whose rights it administers'[63]. In contrast to 'a non-democratic system in which the authority determines what "rights" a citizen has,' democratic systems allow 'the citizens themselves to engage in this process of determination'[64]. Human rights and democracy are embedded in that both 'are

58 Henry J. Steiner and Philip Alston, *International Human Rights in Context: Law, Politics, Morals* (Clarendon Press, 1996), 125.

59 David Collier and Steven Levitsky, "Democracy with Adjectives: Conceptual Innovation in Comparative Research," *World Politics* 49, no. 3 (1997): 433–434.

60 Tony Evans, "If Democracy, then Human Rights?" *Third World Quarterly* 22, no. 4 (2001): 624.

61 Tom J. Farer, "Elections, Democracy, and Human Rights: Toward a Union," *Human Rights Quarterly* 11, no. 4 (1989): 509.

62 Bruce Bueno De Mesquita, George W. Downs, Alastair Smith and Feryal Marie Cherif, "Thinking inside the Box: A Closer Look at Democracy and Human Rights," *International Studies Quarterly* 49, no. 3 (2005): 440.

63 Anthony J. Langlois, "Human Rights without Democracy? A Critique of the Separationist Thesis," *Human Rights Quarterly* 25, no. 4 (2003): 1016.

64 Ibid., 1017.

about getting authorities to rule in the name of and for the interests of the people, rather than merely serving their own interests'[65].

Liberal democracy 'makes the protection of human rights not merely politically desirable but also a moral and social priority that applies to all citizens'[66]. In states with no such tradition rulers pursue accumulation of resources or holding on to power through loyalty to certain elites[67]. Through human rights abuses power and personal security are preserved[68]. Liberal democracies are built upon transparency and accountability allowing citizens 'to sanction their rulers for inappropriate or undesirable behaviour by voting them out of office'[69]. Rulers in such systems, therefore, are keen on satisfying their voters by protecting their rights or at least refraining from violating them. Autocratic systems and other forms of illiberal and non-democratic governments, on the other hand, are not wary of being voted out of office since they come to power through fraudulent elections rather than transparent voting, and so 'they are more likely to scare citizens into obedience by at least occasionally resorting to abuses'[70].

Democratic or democratizing states are less prone to repression and demonstrate a more relaxed and tolerant attitude towards the civil liberties and political rights of their citizens[71]. The human rights situation in democratic states is directly related to the institutions and norms underlying democracy – 'compromise,

---

65 Ibid.

66 Emilie M. Hafner- Burton, *Making Human Rights a Reality* (Princeton University Press, 2013), 23–24.

67 Ibid.

68 Tom Ginsburg and Tamir Moustafa, *Rule by Law: The Politics of Courts in Authoritarian Regimes* (Cambridge University Press, 2008); Thomas O'Brien, "Shifting Patterns of Governance in Authoritarian Regimes," *Australian Journal of Political Science* 52, no. 2 (2017): 303–316.

69 Emilie M. Hafner- Burton, *Making Human Rights a Reality* (Princeton University Press, 2013), 23–24.

70 Ibid.

71 Samantha Besson, "Human Rights and Democracy in a Global Context: Decoupling and Recoupling," *Ethics and Global Politics* 4, no. 1 (2011): 19–50; David Beetham, *Democracy and Human Rights* (Polity Press, 1999); Neil J. Mitchell and James M. McCormick, "Economic and Political Explanations of Human Rights Violations," *World Politics* 40, no. 4 (1988): 476–498 (The authors offer an understanding of the conditions that precipitate human rights violations); Freedomhouse.org (2017), *Freedom in the World 2017| Populists and Autocrats: The Dual Threat to Global Democracy*, available at: https://freedomhouse.org/sites/default/files/FH_FIW_2017_Report_Final.pdf (accessed 7 December 2018).

toleration, and facilitation' and it is these norms that 'influence the decisions that rulers make with regard to state-societal relations, increasing the costs of human rights violations as well as decreasing the value of quiescence'[72]. The role of democratic governance in the context of human rights protection is noteworthy. First, 'democracy will decrease a government's use of political repression'[73]. Under democratic governance, 'people have a chance to acquire their goals and will not become so restive as to attract restraint'[74] on the part of the state. Second, democracy enables citizens to resist repressive leaders and get to it that the latter are removed from office 'before they are able to become a serious threat'[75]. This is facilitated by both 'popular elections and an independent judiciary which may act both as a preventative and corrective mechanism against this abuse'[76].

In contrast to democratic polities, authoritarian leaders usually attempt to hold strong control over the independent media and resort to methods such as 'bribery, the selective allocation of state advertising, the manipulation of debts and taxes owed by media outlets, the fomentation of conflicts among stockholders, and restrictive press laws that facilitate the prosecution of independent and opposition journalists'[77]. The way illiberal states handle human rights is through careful political calculations designed to benefit the powerholder and reduce resistance as much as possible. Hence, 'the definition, development and application of international human rights standards' become "political ends," and 'humanity's life on earth and the development of international human rights standards have yet to transcend social conflict and politics'[78].

---

72 Christian Davenport, "Human Rights and the Democratic Proposition," *The Journal of Conflict Resolution* 43, no. 1 (1999): 96.

73 Linda C. Keith, "The United Nations International Covenant on Civil and Political Rights: Does It Make a Difference in Human Rights Behavior?" *Journal of Peace Research* 36, no. 1 (1999): 107.

74 Conway W. Handerson, "Conditions Affecting the Use of Political Repression," *The Journal of Conflict Resolution* 35, no. 1 (1991): 133.

75 Steven C. Poe and C. Neal Tate, "Repression of Human Rights to Personal Integrity in the 1980s: A Global Analysis," *American Political Science Review* (1994): 855, quoted in Linda C. Keith, "The United Nations International Covenant on Civil and Political Rights: Does It Make a Difference in Human Rights Behavior?" *Journal of Peace Research* 36, no. 1 (1999): 107.

76 Ibid.

77 Steven Levitsky and Lucan Way, "The Rise of Competitive Authoritarianism," *Journal of Democracy* 13, no. 2 (2002): 58.

78 Mahmood Monshipouri and Claude E. Welch, "The Search for International Human Rights and Justice: Coming to Terms with the New Global Realities," *Human Rights Quarterly* 23, no. 2 (2001): 370.

Since 1948 the concept of human rights and the theories within which it has been examined and developed have multiplied, with each theory shedding light on certain aspects of human rights as an ideology and practice. The first question which needs to be answered before going in depth with regard to all those theories and concepts surrounding human rights is 'what is a human right?' Stating that one has a right only by virtue of being human has been the core argument of natural rights theorists. However, it has not come without criticism. One possesses a human right only by virtue of being human is a matter of moral rather than an empirical enquiry. As Messer notes; 'all these discussions of "what are rights" and which rights take precedence in any society also raise serious discussion of who is included in the category "human" modifying the rights concept'[79]. That we all possess human rights because of our common humanity is not common practice in all countries and all societies of the world. It is the category "human" mentioned by Messer that conditions the perception and practice of the "rights" concept in different societies.

Moreover, human rights are intended to facilitate human life, make it one of quality and are, thus, 'understood in both its biological and existential sense'[80]. It is the conditions of human existence rather than the human being that make the case for human rights, since these rights 'make an individual life possible. We have these rights not by virtue of being a certain kind of creature or agent or having a certain moral status, but by virtue of sharing the human condition'[81]. Framed narrowly, human rights signify 'a high-priority claim, or authoritative entitlement, justified by sufficient reasons, to a set of objections that are owed to each human person as a matter of *minimally decent treatment* [italics added]'[82].

---

79 Ellen Messer, "Anthropology, Human Rights, and Social Transformation," in *Human Rights: An Anthropological Reader*, ed. Mark Goodale (Oxford: Blackwell, 2009), 108.

80 Serena Parekh, "Resisting Dull and Torpid Assent: Returning to the Debate over the Foundations of Human Rights," *Human Rights Quarterly* (2007): 775, quoted in Annabelle Mooney, "Human Rights: Law, Language and the Bare Human Being," *Language & Communication* 32, no. 3 (2012): 179.

81 Ibid.

82 Brian Orend, *Human Rights: Concept and Context* (Guelph, Ontario, Canada: Broadview Press, 2002), quoted in Christopher J. Anderson, Aida Paskeviciute, Maria Elena Sandovici and Yulia V. Tverdova, "In the Eye of the Beholder? The Foundations of Subjective Human Rights Conditions in East-Central Europe," *Comparative Political Studies* 38, no. 7 (2005): 774.

2.3 Universal, relative or relatively universal/universally relative?

The notion of human rights has been conceptualized from various perspectives – as a universal concept whose application worldwide will ensure a life with dignity and quality[83], as positive liberties and negative freedoms[84], as entitlements and/or claims[85] and as values whose applicability needs to be tested within particular cultural settings[86].

To start with, 'human rights authorize and empower citizens to act to vindicate their rights; to insist that these standards be realized; to struggle to create a world in which they enjoy (the objects of) their rights. Human rights claims express not merely aspirations, suggestions, requests, or laudable ideas, but rights-based demands for change'[87]. Change must stem from below, from within

---

83 Mary Ann Glendon, "The Forgotten Crucible: The Latin American Influence on the Universal Human Rights Idea," *Harvard Human Rights Journal* 16 (2003): 27–39; Max Du Plessis, "The Universal Aspirations of the International Criminal Court," *African Security Review* 11, no. 4 (2002): 115–118; Rhoda E. Howard-Hassmann, *In Defense of Universal Human Rights* (Polity Press, 2018); Johannes Morsink, *The Universal Declaration of Human Rights: Origins, Drafting, and Intent* (University of Pennsylvania Press, 1999); Paul Gordon Lauren, *The Evolution of International Human Rights: Visions Seen* (University of Pennsylvania Press, 3rd edition, 2011).

84 Isaiah Berlin, *Two Concepts of Liberty: An Inaugural Lecture Delivered before the University of Oxford on the 31st of October 1958* (Clarendon, 1959); Stephen Cohen, "The Significance of 'In the Name of Civil Liberties,'" *Law and Philosophy* 7, no. 3 (1988–1989): 375–394; UN General Assembly, *International Covenant on Civil and Political Rights*, 16 December 1966, United Nations, Treaty Series, vol. 999, p. 171, available at: https://www.refworld.org/docid/3ae6b3aa0.html (accessed 19 January 2017).

85 Marco Antonio Oliveira, "Rights as Entitlements and Rights as Claims," *Veritas (Porto Alegre)* 55, no. 1 (2010); Jack Donnelly, "Human Rights as Natural Rights," *Human Rights Quarterly* 4, no. 3 (1982): 391–405; United Nations (6 November 2012). *Universal Recognition of Inalienable Right to Self-Determination Most Effective Way to Guaranteeing Fundamental Freedoms, Third Committee Told.* Retrieved from https://www.un.org/press/en/2012/gashc4051.doc.htm.

86 Colleen Good, "Human Rights and Relativism," *Macalester Journal of Philosophy* 19, no. 1 (2010): 4; Katherine Brennan, "The Influence of Cultural Relativism on International Human Rights Law: Female Circumcision as a Case Study," *Law & Ineq.* 7 (1988): 367; Michael J. Perry, "Are Human Rights Universal? The Relativist Challenge and Related Matters," *Human Rights Quarterly* 19, no. 3 (1997): 461–509; Tracy E. Higgins, "Anti-Essentialism, Relativism, and Human Rights," *Harvard Women's Law Journal* 19 (1996): 89.

87 Jack Donnelly, *Universal Human Rights in Theory and Practice* (Cornell University Press, 2003), 12.

a society or a community within which an individual is located and in which he/she functions as a member. Rights-based demands for change are grievances that are set forward to the state. It is the state, which is the duty holder and must guarantee and ensure the exercise of human rights by the rights-holder, that is, its citizens. However, human rights have been subjected to controversy since their creation. Controversies have circulated around individualistic and communitarian notions of rights, private and public spheres, religious foundations etcetera. Kausikan observes that 'the Asian tradition is less confrontational and more consensus-seeking, less concerned with checks against the power of the state (rights) and more with obligations toward society and community. Many East and Southeast Asians tend to look askance at the starkly individualistic ethos of the West'[88].

Criticism is often directed at the fact that individualistic human rights are egoistic and self-centred with the individual avoiding any duty to family and community[89]. Whereas in Asian societies individual autonomy gives in to communal duties and the harmony of the society, or as Williams claims: '"The Asian values" debate asserts that Asian peoples have distinct values which are incompatible with the human rights focus on individual autonomy, as these people come from a tradition where community and ruler were both elevated above the interests of the individual'[90]. Thus, through submission to authority social order and harmonious society are maintained while directly challenging it may disturb the already established social order. This is one of the reasons that at the inception of human rights the West prioritized civil and political rights while the Communist World attached significance to social and economic rights with the latter tied to subsistence and basic human rights such as food, shelter and healthcare.

Although the Universal Declaration (1948) has a near universal acceptance, communitarian third world societies view human rights as 'an imperialist liberal agenda emanating from the Western-dominated United Nations'[91]. Interestingly, the United States that is considered one of the champions of human rights is yet to

---

88 William Korey, *NGOs and the Universal Declaration of Human Rights: A Curious Grapevine* (New York: St. Martin's Press, 1998), 474.

89 Rhoda E. Howard, "Human Rights and the Culture Wars: Globalization and the Universality of Human Rights," *International Journal* 53, no 1 (1998): 94–112.

90 Craig Williams, "International Human Rights and Confucianism," *Asia-Pacific Journal on Human Rights and the Law* 7, no. 1 (2006): 38.

91 Rhoda E. Howard, "Cultural Absolutism and the Nostalgia for Community," *Human Rights Quarterly* 15 (1993): 315.

ratify the International Covenant on Social, Economic and Cultural Rights (1976) as well as the Convention on the Rights of the Child (1990) amongst others. Is there then such a notion as 'American childhood', 'Vietnamese childhood', 'Indian childhood', 'Chilean childhood', 'Armenian childhood' etcetera? If the reason for not ratifying the Convention on the Rights of the Child (1990) has to do with the concept of 'childhood', in similar fashion 'torture', 'liberty', 'security' and other human rights concepts could be defined differently across the globe as well.

With reference to Article 5 of the Universal Declaration Donnelly writes: 'no one shall be subjected to torture, cruel, inhuman or degrading treatment or punishment'[92]; he highlights the controversy surrounding the definitions of terms such as "cruel". In most European states death penalty is considered cruel, inhuman or degrading but not in the United States[93]. Provided that human rights are universal and applicable to all members of the human family with a shared morality, life shall be sacred in every society. However, such moral principles endorsed by universalists 'tend to be sufficiently abstract that they flirt with triviality, as "societies everywhere hold that human life is sacred and cannot be taken without justification" '[94]. While such a statement is not necessarily wrong, it is not helpful either in view of the fact that diverse cultural settings justify taking life owing to a range of circumstances[95]. Application of natural law based on those circumstances is the opposite of universalism – relativism.

The rights enshrined in international human rights treaties/instruments are stated at a high level of abstraction and generality and in that way many appear indisputable. It is when they must be particularized to be implemented in concrete settings that contradiction arises[96]. Two important issues need to be distinguished; do we agree that everyone is entitled to human rights by virtue of the unique moral status of human dignity and by their 'being rational, autonomous and free'[97] and disagree on the universalism of human rights when it comes to their applicability or do we reject all universalism of human rights in general? The answer to this question will solve the issue of agreeing on the foundations of human rights in

92 Jack Donnelly, *Universal Human Rights in Theory and Practice* (Cornell University Press, 2003).

93 Ibid.

94 Michael Brown, "Cultural Relativism 2.0," *Current Anthropology* 49, no. 3 (2008): 368.

95 Ibid., 363–383.

96 Randall Peerenboom, "Beyond Universalism and Relativism: The Evolving Debates about Values in Asia," *Indiana International & Comparative Law Review* 14 (2003): 1.

97 John D'Arcy May, "Human Dignity, Human Rights, and Religious Pluralism: Buddhist and Christian Perspectives," *Buddhist-Christian Studies* 26, no. 1 (2006): 51–52.

terms of morality that entitles each human being regardless of national, social, cultural and religious characteristics to human rights while their application continues to be non-universal in which case the focus should be on the state.

It is noteworthy that 'demonstrating that human rights are not universal would significantly damage the philosophical case for, and therefore also the political cause of, human rights'[98]. It is the legitimacy of human rights that is at stake. Furthermore, 'theoretical or analytical arguments for the universality of human rights are crucially relevant to the work of human rights advocates'[99]. In other words, universality matters when human rights need to be translated from theory into practice. Put more elaborately, relativists assert that individuals are shaped by the society and culture of which they form part; they are the bearers of the modes and beliefs of that culture, thus they are unable to reflect critically upon that culture[100]. Moreover, it is assumed under relativism that any single society is founded on different bodies of belief and the means of judging them do not overarch[101]. Conversely, under universalism it is assumed that 'one conception of the good can be applicable across all cultures'[102]. This assumption is based on the conception of human nature which is said to be universal and has its roots in natural law. These two assumptions stand at odds with one another, with relativism maintaining a unique cultural stance while universalism maintaining that it is possible to apply human rights across all cultures regardless of differences and uniqueness.

Further to this point, the Universal Declaration itself is often argued to be distinctively Western and thus not really universal[103]. This claim is problematic in view of the fact that although the principal drafters of the UDHR (1948) were Canadian (John Humphrey) and French (Rene Cassin), and Eleanor Roosevelt played a leading role in ushering the Declaration through the UN machinery, important contributions in the drafting were also made by Charles Malik from Lebanon, P.C. Chang from China, Hernan Santa Cruz from Chile and Alexi Pavlov from USSR[104]. The Universal Declaration was voted for by twenty Latin

98 Michael Goodhart, "Neither Relative nor Universal: A Response to Donnelly," *Human Rights Quarterly* 30 (2008): 184–185.

99 Ibid.

100 Lydia Morris, *Human Rights and Social Theory* (Macmillan International Higher Education, 2013).

101 Ibid.

102 Ibid., 111.

103 Jack Donnelly, *Universal Human Rights in Theory and Practice* (Cornell University Press, 2003).

104 Ibid.

American States and thirteen "non-Western" countries: Afghanistan, Burma, China, Egypt, Ethiopia, India, Iran, Iraq, Lebanon, Pakistan, Philippines, Syria and Turkey[105]. This evidence in regard to voting would provide a good answer to the West versus the Rest split when it comes to human rights were it not overshadowed by subsequent reservations made to certain articles of later covenants and conventions as states found fit. In 1966, the two core Covenants came into being; the International Covenant on Civil and Political Rights and the International Covenant on Social, Economic and Cultural Rights. Together with the UDHR (1948) they comprise the International Bill of Rights. However, unlike the UDHR, the two core covenants are legally binding.

Civil and political rights are negative in nature, meaning that they require the state to refrain from interfering with the citizens' exercise of these rights. In other words, 'civil and political rights ("first generation") are understood as freedom from interference'[106]. Conversely, social economic and cultural rights are positive rights, with the state required to act to ensure its citizens make full use of these rights. "Positive rights" 'include freedom to act in a positive way – entailing the provision by some individual or institution of a valued service'[107]. Interestingly, at the time of their creation, the two Covenants were a bone of contention between the countries of the West and those of the Soviet Bloc which 'wanted greater emphasis on economic and social rights'[108]. Civil and political rights empower citizens to actively participate in the political life of their states and they are in themselves tools that can be used to defy political authority. Positive rights, on the other hand, consist of 'social rights such as the universal right to services meeting basic human needs (e.g., health care, basic housing, education, social security and welfare, and an adequate standard of living)'[109]. Unlike negative rights, these positive rights 'require the state to act positively to promote the well-being of its citizens, rather than merely refraining from acting'[110].

105 Ibid.

106 Ran Hirschl, "'Negative' Rights vs. 'Positive' Entitlements: A Comparative Study of Judicial Interpretations of Rights in an Emerging Neo-Liberal Economic Order," *Human Rights Quarterly* 22 (2000): 1071.

107 Ibid.

108 Jack Donnelly, *Universal Human Rights in Theory and Practice* (Cornell University Press, 2003), 22.

109 Ran Hirschl, " 'Negative' Rights vs. 'Positive' Entitlements: A Comparative Study of Judicial Interpretations of Rights in an Emerging Neo-Liberal Economic Order," *Human Rights Quarterly* 22 (2000): 1071.

110 Ibid.

The International Covenant on Economic, Social and Cultural Rights, while providing for progressive realization and acknowledging the constraints due to the limits of available resources, also imposes various obligations which are of immediate effect[111]. In particular, states are obligated to 'take steps' and 'adopt legislative as well as administrative, financial, educational and social measures' for the realization of the rights recognized in the Covenant[112]. The implementation of the rights enshrined in the Covenant varies and gaps exist even in countries with good and democratic governance. The UN Committee on Economic, Social and Cultural Rights that oversees the implementation of the Covenant, in its sixth Periodic Report of Germany found the following problems resulting from the implementation of the International Covenant on Economic, Social and Cultural Rights in Germany – persistence of gender-specific role stereotypes, poverty issues affecting many different groups in Germany, different forms of violence against women (35 % in 2015) and so on[113].

The concept of 'universalism' has received one of its strongest criticisms in the paper issued by the American Anthropological Association in June of 1947[114]. The question posed was as follows: 'How can the proposed declaration be applicable to all human beings and not be a statement of rights conceived only in terms of the values prevalent in the countries of Western Europe and America?'[115]. In a similar vein, Mutua terms universalism of human rights as the 'impulse to universalise Eurocentric norms and values by repudiating, demonizing, and "othering" that which is different and non-European'[116]. A lot of such

---

111 UN Committee on Economic, Social and Cultural Rights (CESCR), *General Comment No. 3: The Nature of States Parties' Obligations (Art. 2, Para. 1, of the Covenant)*, 14 December 1990, E/1991/23, available at: https://www.refworld.org/docid/4538838e10.html (accessed 1 November 2018).

112 Ibid.

113 UN Economic and Social Council, Forum Menschenrechte, *UN Report Shows Inadequate Implementation of Economic, Social and Cultural Rights by Germany (Concluding Observations by the UN Committee on Economic, Social and Cultural Rights on the Sixth Periodic Report by Germany)*, 31 October 2018, available at: https://www.forum-menschenrechte.de/wp-content/uploads/2017/10/List-of-Issues-FMR-GERMANY_TERRITORIAL_FINAL.pdf (accessed 9 December 2018).

114 The Executive Board, American Anthropological Association, "Statement on Human Rights," *American Anthropologist* (1947): 539–543.

115 Mark Goodale, *Human Rights: An Anthropological Reade*r (Oxford: Blackwell, 2009), quoted in Lydia Morris, *Human Rights and Social Theory* (Macmillan International Higher Education, 2013), 112.

116 Makau Mutua, *Human Rights: A Political and Cultural Critique* (Philadelphia: PA: University of Pennsylvania Press, 2002), quoted in Lydia Morris, *Human Rights and Social Theory* (Macmillan International Higher Education, 2013), 113.

kind of criticism of universal rights stems from viewing culture as static. The new cultural theorists view culture as contested, fluid, unstable and adaptable to change, with 'cultural practices routinely outliving their usefulness, and cultural values changing either through internal dialogue within the cultural group or through cross-cultural influences'[117].

It is noteworthy that cultural relativist arguments often reveal political realities. Why would economic or political elites make arguments of cultural relativism in the case when they have long abandoned traditional culture?[118]. By relativizing human rights they disguise political repression, corruption and other social and political ills and justify failure to internalize human rights standards[119]. Accusations of universality of human rights usually come from countries outside the West which is seen to impose its values on others. A notable example has been China by asserting that its people's right to subsistence and livelihood as well as the right to sovereignty are its core priorities. In Steiner and Alston's words; 'China has always maintained that human rights are essentially matters within the domestic jurisdiction of a country. Respect for each country's sovereignty and non-interference in internal affairs are universally recognized principles of international law, which are applicable to all fields of international relations, and of course applicable to the field of human rights as well'[120]. By maintaining such a stance on universality of human rights China has taken the opposite direction from what human rights are meant to be.

---

117 Jack Donnelly, *Universal Human Rights in Theory and Practice* (Cornell University Press, 2003), 102.

118 Ibid.

119 Ajnesh Prasad, "Cultural Relativism in Human Rights Discourse," *Peace Review* 19, no. 4 (2007): 589 (The author claims that prior to the mid-1950s, 'cultural relativism was a construct employed by both Western anthropologists and indigenous peoples to resist European initiatives for cultural hegemony'. However, following decolonization, 'third world bourgeois-nationalist elites have appropriated the concept to undermine pre-colonial rights of members of various non-Western communities.' Prasad illustrates this point through his study of homophobia in Zimbabwe and reveals how 'political elites of postcolonial states are exploiting the constructive ethos of cultural relativism to persecute individuals who fall outside the socio-religious purview of "compulsory heterosexuality"'; see also Jane Krishnadas, "The Sexual Subaltern in Conversations 'somewhere in Between': Law and the Old Politics of Colonialism," *Feminist Legal Studies* 14 (2006): 53–77; Saba Mahmood, "Feminist Theory, Embodiment and the Docile Agent: Some Reflections on the Egyptian Islamic Revival," *Cultural Anthropology* 16, no. 2 (2001): 202–236.

120 Henry J. Steiner and Philip Alston, *International Human Rights in Context: Law, Politics, Morals* (Clarendon Press, 1996), 233.

Since their creation human rights were intended to oppose the arbitrary power of the state and mistreatment and abuse of its citizens by the state by being above the state. However, the historic, economic, political and cultural realities of any country must be carefully examined in order to explain why they have succeeded or failed in their efforts to realize and protect human rights. The latter statement is a case for arguments of human rights relativism. The concept and ideal of human rights is universal, based on morality and dignity of the human being and everyone possesses rights by virtue of their humanity. Asserting that morality and dignity are Western means to excuse 'abominable acts against populations using relativism as a useful available ideology which facilitates international acquiescence in state repression'[121]. Indeed, local realities, be they social, cultural, economic or political, shall be considered in trying to explain successes or failures of domesticating human rights, but in no way shall an argument about a unique culture resistant to change be used to reject the universality of human rights norms. As Howard argues, 'knowledge and ideas can transcend racial, religious, and geographic boundaries'[122]. What human rights reflect is one particular philosophy: liberalism, which may have originated in the West, but can be applied elsewhere[123]. This philosophy strongly emphasizes the 'individual human being', that is, the 'individualistic and secular understanding of human nature and human rights'[124]. Hence, the emphasis is placed on 'a free, independent rational agent, capable of building and maintaining social structures based on free contracts between supposedly equal rational subjects/agents endowed with similar rational capacity and common sense'[125].

It would appear that despite this specific world-view and trajectory of the concept of human rights, their appeal should be universal owing to 'contemporary social, political and economic conditions'[126]. But is that so? The answer to this question is most likely to be negative, provided that even in European countries there is a 'different interpretation of the same Judeo-Christian tradition' in

121 Richard A. Wilson, *Human Rights, Culture and Context: Anthropological Perspectives* (Pluto Press, 1997), 8–9.

122 Rhoda E. Howard, "Human Rights and the Culture Wars: Globalization and the Universality of Human Rights," *International Journal* 53, no. 1 (1998): 98.

123 Ibid.

124 Silviu E. Rogobete, "Morality and Tradition in Postcommunist Orthodox Lands: On the Universality of Human Rights, with Special Reference to Romania," *Religion, State & Society* 32, no. 3 (2004): 275.

125 Ibid.

126 Ibid.

addition to the 'unprecedented trauma of the political totalitarianism of communist regimes'[127]. These varying interpretations of human rights are demonstrated in the study of 'Orthodox understandings of humanity and otherness, nationality, and tradition' conducted by Silviu Rogobete[128]. The study reveals that countries of Orthodox religion 'find it hard to implement a human rights regime', in view of 'a different anthropology and a different perspective on church, tradition and national and religious identity from those of the churches of the West'[129].

Some scholars have proposed to tackle the stalemate between universalists and relativists by taking the middle ground, that is, a 'weak cultural relativist' – 'strong universalist' position[130]. From this perspective deviations from international human rights norms are permitted but at the level of form and implementation. Furthermore, according to Donnelly, human rights are both universal and relative; they possess a certain 'limited relativity'[131], particularly with regard to forms of implementation. His proposition of the relative universality of internationally recognized human rights is best suited to settle the debate about relativism versus universalism. Indeed, human rights are universal since all the members of the human family are endowed with human nature, dignity and morality and they all want to live a quality life. Nobody wants to be subjected to xenophobia, discrimination, hatred, be arbitrarily deprived of their freedom, put on an unfair trial, be deprived of access to a lawyer when incarcerated or any of their rights breached. To claim that adherents of any particular culture will deny having the same rights as people from other cultures only because there are certain differences is a weak argument. As Zechenter puts it: 'culture is far more effectively characterized as an ongoing adaptation to a changing environment rather than as a static superorganic entity. In a changing environment, cultural practices routinely outlive their usefulness, and cultural values change either through internal dialogue within the cultural group or through cross-cultural influences'[132]. According to Cowan et al., universalism and relativism represent a changing relationship between the global and the local rather than one

127 Ibid.

128 Ibid., 275–297.

129 Ibid., 293.

130 Jack Donnelly, *Universal Human Rights in Theory and Practice* (Cornell University Press, 2003).

131 Ibid., 98.

132 Elizabeth Zechenter, "In the Name of Culture: Cultural Relativism and the Abuse of the Individual," *Journal of Anthropological Research* 53, no. 3 (1997): 332–333, quoted in Jack Donnelly, *Universal Human Rights in Theory and Practice* (Cornell University Press, 2003), 102.

of opposition[133]. Since the world has become more interconnected and cultures interact, no one state is an island but rather we all live in a web of interconnectedness. It is important to bear in mind that speaking of human rights and cultural relativism in 1948 or 1958 is not the same as speaking about them in 2010 or 2016. True, human rights have their roots in Western liberal-legalist thought, but in nowadays world they are no longer the exclusive ownership of the West[134].

Global human rights system serves as a tool that facilitates local people's struggles for human rights. It is by reinterpreting and transforming Western law in compliance with their own local legal conceptions that locals construct a new law by using the old one as a medium[135]. Therefore, the culture or the context, within which human rights are shaped or fought for, do not merely exist but keep being reshaped through social processes[136]. Universalism and relativism or the global and the local, thus, are often in tension for the fact that 'in every human rights situation and in every human rights activist, there will necessarily be mutually constitutive global and local dimensions'[137]. Those who insist that universalism of human rights is blind to cultural specificities, fail to recognize that culture is simply brought forward as an argument for failure or reluctance to apply universal human rights norms in domestic settings. It is to that discussion that I now turn.

2.4 Committing to comply?

As was mentioned above, human rights have not lacked any controversy since they were created. In addition to the heated debates between universalists and relativists, the role of the state as the human rights implementing force has received no less academic writing. An-Na'im suggests analysing the meaning of human rights within the statist framework[138]. Questions to ask in that context

---

133 Jane K. Cowan, Marie-Bénédicte Dembour and Richard A. Wilson, eds. *Culture and Rights: Anthropological Perspectives* (Cambridge: Cambridge University Press, 2001), cited in Lydia Morris, *Human Rights and Social Theory* (Macmillan International Higher Education, 2013).

134 Lydia Morris, *Human Rights and Social Theory* (Macmillan International Higher Education, 2013).

135 Ibid.

136 Richard A. Wilson, *Human Rights, Culture and Context: Anthropological Perspectives* (Pluto Press, 1997).

137 Steve J. Stern and Scott Straus, *The Human Rights Paradox: Universality and Its Discontents* (University of Wisconsin Press, 2014), 4.

138 Abdullahi Ahmed An-Na'im, "Toward a Cross-Cultural Approach to Defining International Standards of Human Rights: The Meaning of Cruel, Inhuman, or Degrading Treatment or Punishment," in *Human Rights: An Anthropological Reader*, ed. Mark Goodale (Oxford: Blackwell, 2009).

refer to the relationship between the universal human rights doctrine and national mores and rules of behaviour, state government behaviour with regard to the universal framework, and acceptance of that framework in its entirety by the states etcetera[139]. States sign and ratify international human rights instruments for various reasons. Socio-cultural and political-economic rationales underpin those reasons.

To start with, human rights regime consists of a number of instruments, namely, treaties, covenants and conventions that states sign and ratify, thereby accepting their jurisdiction and committing themselves to comply with the norms and standards ascribed therein. However, the gap between commitment and compliance remains rather big. States are expected to behave in a certain way when signing and ratifying binding human rights instruments; specifically, 'they are bound to *respect* (not directly violate the treaty), *protect* (prevent others, such as private corporations, from violating the rights defined in the treaty through the rule of law), and *fulfill* (create an environment in which people can reasonably enjoy their rights) the rights defined in the instrument'[140]. These instruments serve as legal obligations for member states, 'subject to the ability, will, and resources of states and state actors (governments) to fulfill these international legal obligations'[141].

Despite the expectation that states should theoretically comply with human rights instruments they have committed themselves to, in practice, especially for less democratic states 'the ratification of human rights instruments does not seem to have a "normative" effect'[142]. This reflects the reality of inconsistent human rights practice universally. As a matter of fact, states, usually those with power and repressive practices, prioritize dominant national agendas over international law and standards when the two come into conflict[143]. In case states do not comply with or abide by the norms and standards there is no power that can call them to order or demand that they comply with what they have committed themselves to. As a rule, it is presumed that 'the state is capable and governments are willing to abide by their international human rights agreements and that the state is the only institution of power affecting human rights'[144]. Sanctions against

139 Ibid.

140 William T. Armaline, Davita S. Glasberg and Bandana Purkayastha, *The Human Rights Enterprise: Political Sociology, State Power, and Social Movements* (Polity Press, 2015), 5.

141 Ibid.

142 Ibid., 7.

143 Ibid.

144 Ibid., 24.

powerful states yield no effect, whereas monitoring reports by UN bodies and their partner NGOs have limited ability to intervene when violations occur.

It is not the case that states either comply with a norm or violate it[145]. In fact, state leaders can act in a variety of ways depending on which choice they consider more to their advantage. The violation of a norm can either be increased or state leaders can engage in lip service. Furthermore, they can respect some aspects of a norm but not others[146]. In other words, 'when norms conflict, compliance is not an all-or-nothing outcome; it takes different forms and occurs to varying degrees'[147]. In the absence of societal groups or lack of consciousness and action thereof, as well as poorly functioning human rights institutions and the lack of will and interest on the part of national leaders, external sources such as foreign governments, international institutions, and international non-state actors can do little to force compliance especially for less democratic states. For the latter, commitment to human rights instruments is 'insincere'[148]. According to Smith-Cannoy, following the break-up of the Soviet Union, the newly independent states found themselves in poor economic conditions[149]. As a result, 'their need for global partners with the resources to rescue their economies increased'[150] and they took account of the recommendations of Western states and institutions purely for economic purposes.

States tend to comply with human rights obligations to build reputation 'when they are seeking foreign assistance from political entities that include human rights observance as a condition for aid'[151]. The US and the European Union both 'have specific provisions in their laws stipulating that human rights obligations be met by countries receiving their foreign assistance'[152]. In particular, Article

---

145 Sonia Cardenas, *Conflict and Compliance: State Responses to International Human Rights Pressure* (University of Pennsylvania Press, 2007).

146 Ibid.

147 Ibid., 1.

148 Heather Smith-Cannoy, *Insincere Commitments: Human Rights Treaties, Abusive States, and Citizen Activism* (Georgetown University Press, 2012).

149 Ibid.

150 Ibid., 22.

151 Dana Zartner and Jennifer Ramos, "Human Rights as Reputation Builder: Compliance with the Convention Against Torture," *Human Rights Review* 12, no. 1 (2011): 78.

152 Ibid.; Jan Wouters et al., *A Comparative Study of EU and US Approaches to Human Rights in External Relations*, November 2014, available at: http://www.europarl.europa.eu/RegData/etudes/STUD/2014/534981/EXPO_STU(2014)534981_EN.pdf (accessed 22 January 2019); Daniel J. B. Hofrenning, "Human Rights and Foreign Aid: A Comparison of the Reagan and Carter Administrations," *American Politics Quarterly* 18, no. 4 (1990): 514–526.

22 of the United States Code 2004 requires that '[n]o assistance may be provided ... to the government of any country which engages in a consistent pattern of gross violations of internationally recognized human rights ...'[153]. The decrease in human rights violations in Latin America has been partly attributed to the U.S. policy under the Carter administration in Latin America to deny aid to governments that violated human rights[154]. Likewise, human rights violations in Kenya decreased following a threat by the U.S. congress to cut off aid[155]. Kenya was forced to adopt multiparty elections and access the Convention against Torture and Other Cruel, Inhuman or Degrading Treatment or Punishment in 1997.

Smith-Cannoy sums up six implications for commitment and compliance – governments ratify in response to human rights policy recommendations from Western actors during periods of acute economic weakness, ratification is a modest strategy employed by leaders to attract assistance of external actors, newly independent states ratify human rights treaties when pressured by Western states and institutions, NGOs enhance the costs of noncompliance by teaching domestic populations how to complain to the UN, NGOs enhance levels of domestic compliance by using individual petitions before the UN as focal points, drawing attention to the omission of specific human rights policies in domestic law and governments that accept the UN oversight will not comply with their commitment to respect the human rights of their citizens in the short term[156].

Committing to a certain human rights treaty does not mean that states automatically comply with the norms enshrined therein. In fact, 'for most states, ratifying these covenants is like paying dues to a club, and they are easy to ratify precisely because they confer membership without conferring onerous obligations'[157]. Moreover, when ratifying treaties, states are guided more by

---

153 Dana Zartner and Jennifer Ramos, "Human Rights as Reputation Builder: Compliance with the Convention against Torture," *Human Rights Review* 12, no. 1 (2011): 78.

154 Ellen L. Lutz and Kathryn Sikkink, "Internaitonal Human Rights Law and Practice in Latin America," *International Organization* 54, no. 3 (2000): 633–659.

155 Hans Peter Schmitz, "Transnational Activism and Political Change in Kenya and Uganda," in *The Power of Human Rights: International Norms and Domestic Change*, eds. Thomas Risse, Steve Ropp & Kathryn Sikkink (Cambridge University Press, 1999).

156 Heather Smith-Cannoy, *Insincere Commitments: Human Rights Treaties, Abusive States, and Citizen Activism* (Georgetown University Press, 2012).

157 Nicholas Owen, *Human Rights, Human Wrongs: Oxford Amnesty Lectures 2001* (Oxford University Press on Demand, 2003), 59.

self-interest as well as image and prestige rather than by genuine willingness to internalize international human rights norms. Acceptance of regime norms and procedures is usually faster when no immediate threat is perceived by states[158]. Furthermore, the largely promotional function of the human rights regime serves as a loophole for most non-democratic states that commit without complying for the very fact that an enforcement power of the regime is absent.

Naming and shaming may work for states that are dependent on cooperation, foreign funding, trade agreements etcetera but 'recalcitrant states can ignore international committees with impunity, and they regularly do'[159]. It has already been mentioned in this chapter that human rights ideas are moral norms in and of themselves and that distances them from state behaviour. States are the main if not only actors charged with human rights implementation. Since human rights are meant to tame the state when the latter breaches the rights of their citizens, conflicts between human rights norms and the state/s, as well as citizens and the state/s take place more often than not as human rights ideas, that is, the morality upon which they are based is in constant conflict with state behaviour. As a matter of fact, human rights norms have diminished sovereignty, but 'have they seriously affected state behaviour? That's where the "no" answer comes in'[160].

States commit to international human rights treaties more or less voluntarily and compliance with those treaties is also the 'prerogative' of states, provided that there is no power to compel compliance. Thus, states 'participate in an international regime only to achieve national objectives in an environment of perceived international interdependence, to address national problems caused by the existing international state of affairs'[161]. Were the burden of commitment perceived to be too much and the international regime stronger than it is now states would not get away with simple ratification and voluntary compliance. Although in theory one would expect the international human rights regime to bring

158 Jack Donnelly, *Universal Human Rights in Theory and Practice* (Cornell University Press, 2003); Natalie Baird, "To Ratify or Not to Ratify – An Assessment of the Case of Ratification of International Human Rights Treaties in the Pacific," *Melbourne Journal of International Law* 12 (2011): 249; Richard A. Nielsen and Beth A. Simmons, "Rewards for Ratification: Payoffs for Participating in the International Human Rights Regime?" *International Studies Quarterly* 59, no. 2 (2015): 197–208.

159 Jack Donnelly, *Universal Human Rights in Theory and Practice* (Cornell University Press, 2003), 177.

160 Henry J. Steiner and Philip Alston, *International Human Rights in Context: Law, Politics, Morals* (Clarendon Press, 1996), 165.

161 Ibid., 451.

states together to agree on the meaning of human rights and their subsequent obligations in guaranteeing them, the situation is not the same on the ground[162]. On the contrary, it appears 'the ratification of human rights instruments has no "normative" effect on human rights practices within the member state, particularly for less democratic states'[163]. This does not mean that ratification is nonsensical; simply that ratification shall not be the final step. There exists a big gap between human rights theory and practice, with the latter being far from consistent.

Regime type and the rule of law are the two significant and necessary prerequisites for a strong compliance with international human rights norms. It stands to reason that political regimes such as stable autocracies make treaties largely irrelevant[164]. The opposite is true about stable democracies, where treaties are 'readily accepted, but they are often redundant'[165]. Indeed, a government that respects the rights of its citizens, does not interfere with the judicial decisions delivered by domestic courts and already has got well-established human rights institutions and mechanisms has little to gain from treaties which in a way are reflection of its constitution and domestic laws. Whereas in the case of autocratic states human rights violations abound and are a constant reminder that the force of treaties to bring about a change is weak and non-functional.

For the sake of comparison democratic regimes are often juxtaposed to autocratic ones in terms of treaty ratification and compliance to demonstrate that human rights will work best in practice through internalization, strong commitment to constitutionalism, rights and the rule of law and establishment of institutions to nurture that commitment. Internalization shall not only be in the form of amendments to domestic laws in order to continue receiving benefits without a genuine intention to respect human rights norms. In other words, human rights shall not serve as 'utility maximizers'[166] whereby 'norm-violating governments pursue primarily material interests and change their behaviour in order to reach their goals without necessarily believing in the validity of the

162 William T. Armaline, Davita S. Glasberg and Bandana Purkayastha, *The Human Rights Enterprise: Political Sociology, State Power, and Social Movements* (Polity Press, 2015).

163 Ibid., 7.

164 Beth A. Simmons, *Mobilizing for Human Rights: International Law in Domestic Politics* (Cambridge University Press, 2009).

165 Ibid., 16.

166 Thomas Risse, Stephen C. Ropp and Kathryn Sikkink, *The Power of Human Rights: International Norms and Domestic Change* (Cambridge University Press, 1999), 12.

norms'[167]. This means that the soft nature of the international human rights system allows states to selectively respect human rights norms and feel free to violate them when they so wish. Amos may have a point in arguing that 'once the concept of "human rights" stood for the power of law; now it stands for the power of the loophole'[168].

Steiner and Alston rightly note the paradox surrounding 'the installation of human rights in the international constitution after 1945'[169]. Human rights were soon enough taken up by governments, put into treaties and formed part of international relations. However, the high morality and intention with which human rights were created would not be appropriated with as much morality and sincerity. Instead, 'from being a source of ultimate anxiety for usurping holders of public social power, they were turned into bureaucratic small-change'[170]. In Eleanor Roosevelt's view, the Universal Declaration '"set up a common standard of achievement of all peoples and all nations" and "might well become an international Magna Carta of all mankind"'[171]. The problem with regard to referring to "all peoples and all nations" and "all mankind" has been discussed in more details elsewhere in this chapter. Evidence from various countries has revealed that appropriation and internalization of human rights norms does not happen instantly and at the same time across the world. The latter is far too diverse.

The concept of human rights is not static. It evolves over time with states and citizens going through processes of social learning and experience in their relationship with one another as well as the rest of the world. In the words of Heather Smith-Cannoy: 'norms such as democracy, capitalism, and human rights emerge and evolve as states interact with each other and with other international actors. These global norms are not unlike fashion trends. In some years respect for women's rights is fashionable, while in other years respect for the rights of social minorities is more popular'[172]. As citizens learn to call abusive states to order,

---

167 Ibid.

168 Owen Amos, "Rights and Wrongs," (The Northern Echo, 2008): 18, quoted in Annabelle Mooney, "Human Rights: Law, Language and the Bare Human Being," *Language & Communication* 32 (2012): 176.

169 Henry J. Steiner and Philip Alston, *International Human Rights in Context: Law, Politics, Morals* (Clarendon Press, 1996), 454.

170 Ibid.

171 Thomas Risse, Stephen C. Ropp and Kathryn Sikkink, *The Power of Human Rights: International Norms and Domestic Change* (Cambridge University Press, 1999), 1.

172 Heather Smith-Cannoy, *Insincere Commitments: Human Rights Treaties, Abusive States, and Citizen Activism* (Georgetown University Press, 2012), 26–27.

responsibility and remedy, states themselves (particularly autocratic ones) learn new ways to carry on with abuse and violations and more importantly, to get away with them. Moreover, they aptly slip through the loopholes of international human rights regime which lacks enforcement power and turn to human rights largely as a result of careful cost-benefit analysis. Once 'a reservoir of unlimited power in all the self-creating of society' human rights 'have become a plaything of governments and lawyers', a game which has been played 'in international statal organizations by diplomats and bureaucrats, and their appointees, in the setting and the ethos of traditional international relations'[173].

Norms make human rights instruments what they are – a list of common standards that should be adhered to and followed by states. In other words, norms relate to state behaviour with regard to duties and obligations towards citizens within their jurisdiction. According to the legal philosopher Hart, 'norms become authoritative when there exists critical reflection upon behaviour with reference to a common standard'[174]. Hart further holds that 'such reflection may be displayed in "criticism ... demands for conformity, and in acknowledgments that such criticism and demands are justified, all of which find their characteristic expression in the normative terminology of 'ought', 'must', and 'should', 'right' and 'wrong'"'[175]. Human rights norms are checks on states' treatment of their citizens and as such, they have the potential to alter sovereign practices. For this reason, external comments on, let alone external interference in internal governing practices are not welcome by governments[176]. More often than not it is the older norm of non-interference that weakens implementation of global human rights norms. Under sovereignty states imply that whatever they do to their citizens within their own territory is their business alone and as a matter of fact, 'sovereignty is typically the mantle behind which rights-abusive regimes hide when faced with international human rights criticism'[177].

---

173 Philip Allott, *Eunomia. New Order for a New World* (New York: Oxford University Press, 1990), quoted in Henry J. Steiner and Philip Alston, *International Human Rights in Context: Law, Politics, Morals* (Clarendon Press, 1996), 454.

174 H.L.A. Hart, *The Concept of Law* (Oxford: Clarendon Press, 1961), quoted in Ann Marie Clark, *Diplomacy of Conscience: Amnesty International and Changing Human Rights Norms* (Princeton: Princeton University Press, 2001), 16.

175 Ibid.

176 Ibid.

177 Jack Donnelly, *Universal Human Rights in Theory and Practice* (Cornell University Press, 2003), 108.

2.5 Human rights monitoring

Despite internalization of human rights norms and their global appeal, implementation remains almost exclusively the duty and obligation of the state, thus national. The existing international as well as regional human rights regimes function as supervisory mechanisms to monitor state and citizen relationships. They cannot replace the role the state plays in incorporating human rights in domestic settings[178]. In order to internationally observe the implementation of human rights, monitoring procedures have been put in place. These procedures ensure that states submit regular reports to human rights monitoring bodies regarding their performance and/or any progress/improvement in terms of earlier recommendations. Such monitoring procedures have the aim of international promotion including encouraging or assisting the state to implement international norms on a national level[179]. Human rights monitoring bodies include the UN Commission on Human Rights, the Human Rights Committee and the High Commissioner for Human Rights amongst others[180]. Each of these bodies is charged with monitoring the implementation of certain core human rights treaties. For instance, Human Rights Committee was established to monitor compliance with the International Covenant on Civil and Political Rights. Its function includes reviewing periodic reports on compliance submitted by parties[181].

The United Nations High Commissioner for Human Rights, created in 1993, 'may deal directly with governments to seek improved respect for internationally recognized human rights – but with the added advantage of an explicit mandate to deal with all governments on all issues'[182]. Although the global human rights regime comprises widely accepted substantive norms and authoritative multilateral standard-setting procedures, activity wise it continues to be considerably

178 Ibid.

179 Ibid.

180 Hellen Keller and Geir Ulfstein, *UN Human Rights Treaty Bodies: Laws and Legitimacy* (Cambridge University Press, 2012); Kerstin Mechlem, "Treaty Bodies and the Interpretation of Human Rights," *Vanderbilt Journal of Transnational Law* 42 (2009): 905; Thomas Buergenthal, "The U.N. Human Rights Committee," *Max Planck YBUNL* 5 (2001): 341; Andrew C. Byrnes, "The Other Human Rights Treaty Body: The Work of the Committee on the Elimination of Discrimination against Women," *The Yale Journal of International Law* 14 (1989):1.

181 Jack Donnelly, *Universal Human Rights in Theory and Practice* (Cornell University Press, 2003).

182 Ibid., 135.

promotional with limited international implementation that 'rarely goes beyond mandatory reporting procedures'[183]. International enforcement is lacking. Consequently, there exists a global human rights regime endowed with normative strength but procedural weakness which, interestingly enough, is not accidental but 'the result of conscious political decisions'[184].

The procedural weakness of the human rights regime also weakens the pressure a supervisory committee is able to exert on a particular state after the latter has been found violating human rights norms. A supervisory committee, therefore, can either 'appeal to the good will and shared concerns of the state or to (threaten to) embarrass it by drawing international attention to apparent violations or inadequacies in reports that seem to be attempts to cover up questionable or culpable practices'[185]. In certain cases such pressure may work since some states have both domestic and international reasons to be concerned with how their human rights practices feature internationally. However, shame and embarrassment, in the end, is dependent upon some kind of good faith on the part of the violator[186]. The effect of reporting-questioning procedures in respect of human rights is likely to be marginal and even with a marginal effect it can only be an additional aid to positive national efforts. In order to truly protect citizens against the arbitrary breaches of human rights by the state, fundamental national political changes are essential. Absent such changes, international monitoring can be nothing but a peripheral factor. To take, for example, reports that should be submitted to committees for review regarding country performance; committees cannot force countries to submit reports on time.

Furthermore, even if a state submits pro-forma reports along with extracts from its constitution and statues, its reporting obligation is formally fulfilled[187]. Inadequacies in reports cannot be addressed until the next scheduled report since there are no follow-up procedures in place. If anything, states themselves should initiate such a procedure with reports of additional information in which case those reports will not be reviewed on a formal basis[188]. Some countries, 'even those who are ardent promoters of human rights, ignore recommendations'[189].

183 Ibid.
184 Ibid.
185 Ibid., 174.
186 Ibid.
187 Ibid.
188 Ibid.
189 Emilie M. Hafner- Burton, *Making Human Rights a Reality* (Princeton University Press, 2013), 102.

Changes following recommendations have been made by some countries, although such reactions are unusual. More commonly governments opt to pay no attention to recommendations that clash with their interests or cultural practices[190]. Human rights monitoring also provides for individual complaints procedure which despite benefits to the complainants, suffers from limitations. The accused government should approve before an individual is able to file a complaint and still not all victims do, reasons being lack of knowledge and resources to access the system[191].

Human rights abuses are revealed through reports that are submitted to monitoring bodies overseeing the compliance with this or that core treaty; NGOs can also contribute to bringing the abuses 'to notice of what is called "world public opinion", but there are no explicit rules mandating sanctions or coercive measures if states fail to discharge their responsibilities'[192]. Any measures taken to punish a particular state for human rights abuses are usually soft in character ranging from 'diplomatic reproof, through public criticism in international forums, up to economic sanctions, aid cut-offs, withdrawal of military and other forms of co-operation, withdrawal of diplomatic recognition and finally full-scale blockade'[193]. Adoption of each of the stated measures against rights abusive states depends on the type of abuse or breach of the right, as well as the scale and severity of it. It also depends on what state is under question[194].

Amongst the existing human rights protection mechanisms the European Convention on Human Rights (ECHR) 'is widely regarded as the most successful

---

190 Ibid.

191 Ibid.

192 Nicholas Owen, *Human Rights, Human Wrongs: Oxford Amnesty Lectures 2001* (Oxford University Press on Demand, 2003), 72.

193 Ibid.

194 Stanley Cohen, "Government Responses to Human Rights Reports: Claims, Denials, and Counterclaims," *Human Rights Quarterly* 18 (1996): 517–543; James C. Franklin, "Shame on You: The Impact of Human Rights Criticism on Political Repression on Latin America," *International Studies Quarterly* 52, no. 1 (2008): 187–211; Lars Schoultz, *Human Rights and United States Policy toward Latin America* (Princeton: Princeton University Press, 1981); David Forsythe, *Human Rights and World Politics* (University of Nebraska Press, 1989); Darren G. Hawkins, *International Human Rights and Authoritarian Rule in Chile* (University of Nebraska Press, 2002); Susanne Jonas, *The Battle for Guatemala: Rebels, Death Squads, and U.S. Power* (Boulder: Westview Press, 1991).

experiment' both transnationally and judicially[195]. First established as an international treaty comprising mostly civil and political rights, 'making a largely symbolic statement of the liberal democratic identity of its ten founding members in the Cold War aftermath of the Second World War', it now 'embraces every state in Europe except Belarus, with a land mass stretching from Iceland to Vladivostok and a combined population of nearly 800 million'[196]. Yet, despite its widely acknowledged success, the European Convention on Human Rights whose overseeing body is the European Court of Human Rights is suffering from problems of its own. The latter have to do with low levels of compensation, few rewards, coupled with 'criticism for being too generous with national authorities seeking to derogate from the Convention'[197]. Moreover, unlike the European Court of Justice, 'whose rulings may have direct effect on domestic legal orders because of the supremacy of European Community law, the judgments of the ECHR constitute binding interpretations of the Convention for future cases only in a very broad sense (as precedents)'[198]. The applicants must first make use of the available domestic remedies before they can access the Court, so there is no direct access to that body[199]. This is because it is the states and not the Court that bear the responsibility for securing the Convention rights[200]. Respectively, 'the Court comes into play only as a subsidiary authority, when the States have not fulfilled their responsibility under Article 13'[201].

As was stated, the type of measures adopted against rights abusive states depends on the scale and severity of it. Thus, a massacre of its citizens by a state qualifies for a different stance from other states as compared to a clash

195 Steven Greer, "What's Wrong with the European Convention on Human Rights?," *Human Rights Quarterly* 30, no. 3 (2008): 680–681.

196 Ibid.

197 Ibid., 699.

198 Georg Ress, "The Effect of Decisions and Judgments of the European Court of Human Rights in the Domestic Legal Order," *Texas International Law Journal* 40 (2004): 374.

199 Janneke H. Gerards and Lize R. Glas, "Access to Justice in the European Convention on Human Rights system," *Netherlands Quarterly of Human Rights* 35, no. 1 (2017): 15.

200 Ibid.

201 Ibid.; also see Elizabeth F. Defeis, "Human Rights and the European Court of Justice: An Appraisal," *Fordham International Law Journal* 31 (2007): 1104; Murray Hunt, "The European Convention on Human Rights," *Yearbook of European Law* 22, no. 1 (2003): 483 – 497; Lee Hasselbacher, "State Obligations Regarding Domestic Violence: The European Court of Human Rights, Due Diligence, And International Legal Minimums of Protection," *Northwestern Journal of International Human Rights* 8 (2009): 190.

between protesters and the police during a rally that turns violent. This is not meant to justify police brutality towards rally participants, but merely to differentiate between types and scales of abuse. Moreover, it is a matter of terminology; a violation, an abuse and massacre are all different types and scales of disrespecting rights of humans. Those types and scales play a role in whether other states respond to what another state is doing to its citizens and if they do, what form that response takes. A human right violating or an abusive state could always use sovereignty as an alibi, though often an alibi is not even necessary since in the case of powerful states and even in high-profile cases, such as the 1989 Tiananmen massacre, double standards persist. Following the infamous events of 1989, 'most states that had substantial economic relations with China did adopt aid, trade, or investment sanctions. Japan did so with considerable reluctance, great inconsistency, and for the briefest possible period- yet with real costs to Japanese firms'[202]. The United States responded with enough vigor 'that economic sanctions were the central issue in the U.S. – Chinese relations until 1994 and a major irritant into 1997. Most European states took a middle course'[203]. Countries sharing a border with China were more constrained in their responses. India, for instance, was largely silent; Russia confined itself to verbal criticism while Japan's reluctance to pursue sanctions had important security as well as economic dimensions[204].

It is noteworthy that actions undertaken by states in response to human rights abuse by another state are usually of symbolic character such as 'recalling ambassadors, suspending cultural or sporting exchanges, endorsing international investigation, and voting for condemnatory resolutions in international organizations. Even aid sanctions often are largely symbolic'[205]. Although the notion of human rights has a universal appeal and everyone shall be treated with dignity and all humans shall be equal, human rights practice leaves much to be desired. Apart from states with democratic governance and relatively better performance with regard to human rights, there are few states where personhood is perceived in a way that everyone within the same jurisdiction is equal before the law, wealth and power are evenly distributed and moral norms prevail. In fact, 'as long as collective beliefs, perpetuated by basic disparities of wealth and power,

202 Jack Donnelly, *Universal Human Rights in Theory and Practice* (Cornell University Press, 2003), 163.

203 Ibid.

204 Ibid.

205 Ibid., 166.

support the view that some human beings are less equal than others, personal security will remain under the purview of the nation-state'[206].

Despite the existence of quite a comprehensive human rights regime comprising a number of treaties, "good" or "moral" norms do not prevail[207]. In effect, 'the norm of state sovereignty remains strong in spite of the emergence of competing norms of personal sovereignty'[208]. As key political forces of international relations, states more often than not strongly challenge the principles of the indivisibility and universality of human rights set by the UN[209]. In other words, 'states resist any ideology that puts in doubt their own definition of the national interest'[210].

The first step essential for human rights internalization is incorporating the norms enshrined in human rights instruments into domestic legislation. However, legislation alone is not enough to implement human rights. Legislation should be backed by enforcement for the right to be legally and politically secure[211]. Building human rights implementation strategies locally will ensure long-term commitment to human rights. Furthermore, a ground-up strategy of human rights fulfilment will reveal those groups which are more likely to contribute to desirable social and political change[212]. Since local activists are familiar with the obstacles hindering the appropriation of international human rights standards and values required to bring about a change, they are better placed to design mechanisms for rights protection. Nevertheless, the latter is more a practical statement rather than a theoretical one. Bell suggests 'operating with a plausible theory of culture and an accurate understanding of the culture in question and not assuming that culture trumps international norms'[213].

---

206 Sonia Cardenas, *Conflict and Compliance: State Responses to International Human Rights Pressure* (University of Pennsylvania Press, 2007), 133–134.

207 Ibid.

208 Ibid.

209 Jean-Philippe Thérien and Philippe Joly, "All Human Rights for All: The United Nations and Human Rights in the Post-Cold War Era," *Human Rights Quarterly* 36, no. 2 (2014): 373–396.

210 Ibid., 395.

211 Jack Donnelly, *Universal Human Rights in Theory and Practice* (Cornell University Press, 2003).

212 Ibid.

213 Lynda S. Bell, *Who Produces Asian Identity? Discourses, Discrimination, and Chinese Peasant Women in the Quest for Human Rights*, in *Negotiating Culture and Human Rights*, eds. Lynda Bell, Andrew J. Nathan and Ilan Peleg (New York: Columbia University Press, 2001), cited in Jack Donnelly, *Universal Human Rights in Theory and Practice* (Cornell University Press, 2003), 100.

Human rights implementation, curtailment, protection, violation, enforcement, denial, or enjoyment is largely within the remit of the state rather than beyond it[214]. Therefore, special emphasis should be laid on the national particularity as regards incorporating international norms into practice. National particularity would mean taking account of local circumstances, specifically, cultural beliefs, philosophical and religious traditions, the level of economic development, and the nature and level of development of political and legal institutions all of which are appropriate in terms of human rights implementation[215]. Further, morality of human rights, what they are, their nature and character go as far as explaining or justifying why one should be entitled to a right and why that right shall not be curtailed, in other words, the morally wrong and right aspects of rights, while when the 'beauty of the theory' is contrasted 'with its disfiguring implementation' it becomes 'a question of means, not goals'[216]. It is for the fact that rights are not simply moral concepts but legal instruments that their implementation in practice should be given as much consideration as has been given to the theory.

Human rights norms and standards are provided for in international treaties and covenants, however, 'parties seeking to invoke human rights must often rely on domestic legal systems' and 'domestic judges will need to interpret such rights in light of their constitution, domestic laws and other legal practices, including judicial practices'[217]. In addition to legal and judicial practices, human rights abuses may be prevented through 'well-reasoned cultural analyses as well as some transformation in political-economic structure and underlying conditions'[218]. Transformation in political-economic structure goes both ways; either the existing government is itself transformed through elections or, in case it fails to do so, civic action from below can force a government to respect human

214 Jack Donnelly, *Universal Human Rights in Theory and Practice* (Cornell University Press, 2003).

215 Randall Peerenboom, "Beyond Universalism and Relativism: The Evolving Debates about Values in Asia," *Indiana International & Comparative Law Review* 14, no. 1 (2003).

216 Nicholas Owen, *Human Rights, Human Wrongs: Oxford Amnesty Lectures 2001* (Oxford University Press on Demand, 2003), 33.

217 Randall Peerenboom, "Beyond Universalism and Relativism: The Evolving Debates about Values in Asia," *Indiana International & Comparative Law Review* 14, no. 1 (2003): 59.

218 Ellen Messer, "Anthropology, Human Rights, and Social Transformation," In *Human Rights: An Anthropological Reader*, ed. Mark Goodale (Oxford: Blackwell, 2009), 115.

rights. To put it differently, a right must be earned. As Steiner and Alston state: 'a government that respects human rights is almost always the legacy of persistent national political struggles against human rights violations'[219]. Most human rights respecting governments have been created from the bottom up rather than the top down[220]. Rights that are taken are usually a more stable solution than rights that are given. Moreover, pressuring the government from below with domestic mobilization ensures a lasting impact in the sense that a ground-up domestic pressure acts as some kind of a watchdog to the government; every time a government fails in its duties to provide for and respect a right, domestic pressure 'reminds' it of its duties.

Traditionally fields of law and political science have dominated human rights scholarship. Ample writings have been produced in international law and international relations, humanitarian law as well as comparative politics. At the core of these fields lie formal legal definitions and realizations of human rights, various legal and philosophical traditions providing the foundation of what is understood as international human rights, as well as the relationships between state policy and politics at both national and international levels[221]. In sum, 'the story of human rights is often focused on the story of the United Nations (UN), and the origins and evolution of human rights as a legal concept and body of international law'[222]. Under law and political science, the state and its legitimate authority are somehow taken for granted and not critically questioned in real contexts[223]. What happens is a creation of legal rights and mechanisms lacking analysis as to how these legal concepts and accompanying mechanisms affect people's lives on the ground. It is in view of this fact that anthropologists approach human rights from a social perspective, that is, in order to better understand why human rights practices succeed or fail at local level, it is necessary to study how 'real people in real socio-cultural contexts come to interpret and then interact with state mechanisms and state policy'[224].

In a similar vein, since the 1990s sociologists have been intrigued by the gap between the legal discourse on human rights and social realities. The sociological

---

219 Henry J. Steiner and Philip Alston, *International Human Rights in Context: Law, Politics, Morals* (Clarendon Press, 1996), 452.

220 Ibid.

221 William T. Armaline, Davita S. Glasberg and Bandana Purkayastha, *The Human Rights Enterprise: Political Sociology, State Power, and Social Movements* (Polity Press, 2015).

222 Ibid., 4–5.

223 Ibid.

224 Ibid., 8–9.

approach to human rights has it that the concept and practice of human rights is constructed through social movements and social struggle[225]. Further to this point, while statist and legal approaches to human rights are important lenses through which one can perceive the role of the state in interacting with its citizens over human rights and either granting or denying them, as well as the legal do's and don'ts enshrined in international legal instruments and regimes, social movement approaches are just as important since they 'manifest as social struggles over power, resources, and political voice'[226].

Sociologically human rights are conceptualized as a terrain of social struggle, thus dynamic as opposed to the static, legal constructs offered by statist and legal approaches. The tension between these approaches becomes clearer when social movements oftentimes partnered with anti-globalization, anti-capitalist and environmental movements 'form against or in spite of the states (and often partnered private interest) charged with rights protection'[227]. It is scarcely the case that states respect human rights owing to compassion and good will. In fact, they serve human rights agreements to self-interest. The role of non-state actors involving NGOs, community organizations and social movements is to construct human rights from below by pressuring the state to comply with the standards it has agreed to guarantee and protect. The struggles taking place between non-state actors and the state can take different forms – ranging from direct action to open resistance and disobedience.

Each of the aforementioned forms of ground-up struggles presupposes the existence and availability of certain factors, such as number of participants, resources and networks to successfully challenge the state's human rights abuse. It goes without saying that attempts will be made by the state to repress and stifle protests, mass actions and disruptions, but 'the state resorts to the use of force and violence as a last resort, when its usual *hegemonic*, institutional mechanisms to coopt or otherwise mediate non-elite resistance become ineffective'[228]. A bottom-up approach to human rights protection in any particular country enables to explain the inconsistency as regards the role of the state in implementing human rights standards in compliance with international instruments. As was mentioned elsewhere in this chapter, sociological view on human rights has it that rights are taken in a terrain of social struggle over power, resources and

225 Ibid.

226 Ibid., 14.

227 Ibid.

228 Ibid., 35.

political voice. Furthermore, 'in action, human rights are not a thing that is given or taken away, that once won no longer requires vigilance to maintain'[229].

Human rights protection is a result of struggle wherein the status quo is challenged and a new status quo is created which has to continuously be checked vis-à-vis the state. Every time the latter fails in its duty to protect human rights of its citizens pressure is exerted from below through 'troubling the institutions, resisting and challenging the denial of rights by private interests and the state'[230]. However, resisting and challenging does not yet mean that the state will give in easily, make reforms and respect human rights to satisfy the demands of protesters. In other words, 'mere grievances against unjust systems do not lead people to mobilize for change'[231]. Not all types of organizing conclude successfully. In addition to mobilization required to be as massive as possible, persuasion, material and non-material resources involved in supporting any particular struggle as well as 'the context in which the struggle unfolds are germane to the understanding of the human rights enterprise'[232].

Struggles for human rights spring from collective action that brings together people who share similar concerns about injustice. Those struggles need to have continuity to have a lasting impact or at least to make sure that the initial grievance for which they were initiated is resolved. Since human rights violations are buried in unequal and unjust social, political and economic systems, struggles be they in the form of resistance or disobedience tend to focus on altering one or more elements of those systems[233]. As a rule, 'social movements attempt to wrest power to make and re-make institutions, to produce and disseminate ideologies to alter how people think of their concerns and options, to set agendas and policies, and to alter patterns of interactions that translate policy and law into everyday realities'[234]. Human rights struggles furthered by way of social movements should comprise three important aspects of mobilization: 'structures of opportunities, including the constraints on mobilization; resources and tactics that movement agents/actors command in order to mobilize others; and the

229 Ibid., 77.

230 Ibid.

231 William T. Armaline, Davita S. Glasberg and Bandana Purkayastha, *The Human Rights Enterprise: Political Sociology, State Power, and Social Movements* (Polity Press, 2015), 81.

232 Ibid.

233 Ibid.

234 Ibid., 81–82.

ways in which they frame their understanding of injustice'[235]. Last but not least, the conditions under which human rights struggles emerge are just as important as the above-mentioned components.

Tarrow defines political opportunity structures as 'consistent – but not necessarily formal, permanent or national – dimensions of the political environment that provide incentives for people to undertake collective action by affecting their expectations for success or failure'[236]. One could infer that political opportunity structures entail internal and external factors that one way or another impact the political environment thereby exposing the state as sensitive to pressure from below. Hence, bottom-up action against the state is most successful when the state is most sensitive. Amongst prerequisites for the success of human rights struggle are 'openness or closure of the institutionalized political system, stability or instability of elite alignments that typically undergird a polity, presence or absence of elite allies, and the state's propensity and capacity for repression'[237]. It stands to reason that human rights situation in a certain state is a result of political decisions; therefore, political actors play an important role in either engaging or disengaging in human rights struggles. Putting up human rights claims against the state is not sufficient ground to achieve change; laws need to be amended or adopted in parliaments, social, economic, political and judicial systems need to be reformed and this is all done at a government level; the more state actors join a human rights struggle, the stronger it will be and the higher the incentives will be for it to succeed.

Armaline et al. apply a critical sociological lens to the history of human rights struggles[238]. They call the emerging process 'the human rights enterprise' identified as 'a living, organic process of counter-hegemonic resistance that seeks to tip balances of power toward equality, shared resources, democracy, sustainability,

---

235 Ibid.

236 Sidney Tarrow, "Power in Movement: Social Movements, Collective Action and Politics" (New York: Cambridge University Press, 1994), quoted in William T. Armaline, Davita S. Glasberg and Bandana Purkayastha, *The Human Rights Enterprise: Political Sociology, State Power, and Social Movements* (Polity Press, 2015), 83.

237 Doug McAdam, "Conceptual and Theoretical Issues," In D. McAdam and D. Snow, "Social Movements: Readings on Their Emergence, Mobilization, and Dynamics" (Los Angeles: Roxbury Publishing Company, 1997), quoted in William T. Armaline, Davita S. Glasberg and Bandana Purkayastha, *The Human Rights Enterprise: Political Sociology, State Power, and Social Movement* (Polity Press, 2015), 83.

238 William T. Armaline, Davita S. Glasberg and Bandana Purkayastha, *The Human Rights Enterprise: Political Sociology, State Power, and Social Movements* (Polity Press, 2015).

peace, social stability with purpose, and personal liberty'[239]. In this living, organic process the engaged actors play an essential role; only few committed activists will not succeed in bringing about a change if human rights norms are not supported by a wide range of groups within civil society[240]. Here is when the role played by sociology in explaining successes or failures of non-state actors in human rights struggle proves indispensable.

Furthermore, human response is shaped by locality, that is, 'actors assert, mold, pull at, and change human rights destinies within their specific contexts of lived experience and struggle, always infecting human rights stories with their interpretation and their strategies'[241]. Thus, human rights are universally affirmed but fought for locally. A great deal of human rights discourse originates from political, cultural and intellectual figures whereas the words and actions of less visible people and movements have not received quite the attention. Human rights instruments are important tools to get to know the norms and standards on which the concept is based, however, 'the local sociology and politics in which they are embedded'[242] are better placed to illustrate why some societies embrace human rights norms faster and with more ease than others. Nevertheless, studies of domestic settings shall neither glorify local human rights heroes nor substitute general histories of human rights, but rather, aim to thoroughly examine in what ways less visible movements and actors have contributed to shaping and transforming national and international human rights ideas, actions, and strategies[243]. In brief, the story of human rights in particular local settings is better told from bottom up.

2.6 Conclusion

As has been argued throughout this chapter nothing is straightforward about human rights, starting from their origin, their universality or relativism, commitment to them or compliance with the established norms, as well as monitoring their protection or breaches. This is so because the field of human rights is fraught with paradoxes and entangled in politics and economy, the former in

239 Ibid., 165–166.

240 Sonia Cardenas, *Conflict and Compliance: State Responses to International Human Rights Pressure* (University of Pennsylvania Press, 2007).

241 Steve J. Stern and Scott Straus, *The Human Rights Paradox: Universality and Its Discontents* (University of Wisconsin Press, 2014), 9.

242 Ibid., 55.

243 Ibid.

particular. The factors that impact the success and/or the failure of human rights protection in any particular local settings are not only external but also internal in nature and can both facilitate as well as obstruct human rights implementation. That is why, interdisciplinary approaches have been favoured by some scholars in the study of human rights.

The role of the state, international as well as regional actors along with local non-state actors is important in demonstrating both successes as well as failures in the protection and implementation of human rights. However, since human rights signifies a relationship between the state and citizens, it is the latter that shall oppose ill treatment and conquer their rights by holding the state accountable whenever it fails in its duty to protect. It is these local non-state actors, the main beneficiaries of human rights in any state that are the focus in the following chapter. Throughout the upcoming chapters I maintain a questioning line with regard to the concept of human rights and demonstrate that related concepts are too intertwined to be ignored. I will reveal in the course of what follows that democratic governance, fluidity of culture, country specific characteristics as well as a 'burdened' monitoring and compliance system contribute to our understanding of human rights to an extent. Nonetheless, unless a bottom-up mobilization of actors most affected by human rights violations takes place, we shall look for change in vain elsewhere. I take up this line of inquiry in the next chapter.

3 Theoretical considerations

3.1 Overview

The previous chapter presented a largely statist framework emphasising the role of the state as the main guarantor of human rights and highlighted the difficulties related to that role as well as that of other actors involved in human rights realization and promotion. This chapter lays out the theoretical considerations that inform this research and act as the lens through which human rights are approached. Throughout the chapter human rights are viewed as contested claims that can either empower or constrain social actors as the latter seek for redress through collective action. The aim of the chapter is to bring together several scholarly perspectives to demonstrate the ways in which human rights can be applied and appropriated at the local level. The objective is a pursuit of a sociological understanding of rights emphasising the key actors and the processes through which human rights are negotiated, contested, constructed and reproduced. It reveals a process that is uneven, prone to disruption and contingent upon intersubjective as well as idiosyncratic factors and embedded in power dynamics.

3.2 Defining human rights

Discussions amongst scholars abound as to understanding rights in various ways: 'as a set of guiding principles which draw their inspiration from some notion of natural right; a body of positive law with accompanying systems of codification and implementation at both national and international level; and a dialectical movement involving both the assertion of political power from above and the expression of political agency from below'[244]. Locating rights in nature pursues the goal of neutralizing political influence; however, such pursuit naively dismisses the politicized nature of rights as well as somehow overlooks ordinary people as agents of change with responsibility to better their condition. Legal approaches to human rights, on the other hand, look to law and legal formulations of rights and wrongs to check for breaches and abuse. Furthermore, decisions regarding redress for victims or restoration of justice lie with judicial authorities and their interpretations of law. In this fashion, human rights become

244 Lydia Morris, *Human Rights and Social Theory* (Macmillan International Higher Education, 2013), 4.

confined to 'formulas contained in some abstract legal documents'[245]. While the concept of ' "legal right" can affirm and defend human autonomy and solidarity', it also can 'merely give the appearance of such autonomy and solidarity while in fact excusing oppression'[246]. In other words, 'various kinds of legal rights and entitlements may be used in a manner that helps to develop social movement, which in turns leads to expanded opportunities for a more humane society, or they may be used to help frustrate social movement by legitimating existing relationships'[247]. Therefore, one of the objectives of this chapter is to address the concept of 'legal consciousness' – ways, in which particular individuals think and act, interpret, 'construct, sustain, reproduce or amend the circulating (contested or hegemonic) structures of meanings concerning law'[248].

Human rights is a broad notion and can be understood in different ways, such as for instance, 'as a framework that encompasses human rights norms, principles, ideas, values, discourses and arguments'[249] on the one hand and as 'a set of principles contained in the Universal Declaration of Human Rights, along with the norms and standards developed by the International Covenant on Civil and Political Rights, and the International Covenant on Economic, Social and Cultural Rights, and subsequent treaties'[250] on the other. Rights consciousness

245 Ellen Messer, "Anthropology, Human Rights, and Social Transformation," In *Human Rights: An Anthropological Reader*, ed. Mark Goodale (Oxford: Blackwell, 2009), 127.

246 Ed Sparer, "Fundamental Human Rights, Legal Entitlements and the Social Struggle: A Friendly Critique of the Critical Legal Studies Movement," *Stanford Law Review* 36 (1984): 560.

247 Ibid.

248 Susan S. Silbey, "After Legal Consciousness," *Annual Review of Law and Social Science* 1 (2005): 334.

249 G. Oré Aguilar, "The Local Relevance of Human Rights: A methodological Approach," Institute of Development Policy and Management (IOB), Discussion Paper/2008.04, p. 13; Reidar Maliks and Johan Karlsson Schaffer, *Moral and Political Conceptions of Human Rights: Implications for Theory and Practice* (Cambridge University Press, 2017); Michael Freeman, "The Philosophical Foundations of Human Rights," *Human Rights Quarterly* 16, no. 3 (1994): 491–514; Anita Sophia Horn, "Moral and Political Conceptions of Human Rights: Rethinking the Distinction," *The International Journal of Human Rights* 20, no. 6 (2016): 724–743; Sarbani Guha Ghosal, "Human Rights: Concept and Contestation," *The Indian Journal of Political Science* 71, no. 4 (2010): 1103–1125; Joy Gordon, "The Concept of Human Rights: The History and Meaning of Its Politicization," *Brooklyn Journal of International Law* 23 (1998): 689.

250 Ibid.; See United Nations Human Rights Office of the High Commissioner, "The Core International Human Rights Treaties," (New York and Geneva, 2014), accessed 12 December 2018, https://www.ohchr.org/Documents/Publications/CoreInternatio

is an important concept and indicator in relation to how subjectivities shift as well as how the latter are contingent upon 'wider cultural understandings and individual experiences'[251]. However, measuring 'rights consciousness' in reality presents a big challenge, since it 'is a "slippery, unquantifiable concept"'[252]. One way to tackle this problem might be to look at the processes and stages the concept of human rights goes through in terms of formulating, presenting and resolving a particular problem at a particular time, in a particular place. Also, indicators of rights consciousness would be citizens' knowledge and awareness of international human rights instruments, references to the latter during protests, turning to human rights defenders/NGOs for assistance, appeals to the European Court of Human Rights, as well as follow-ups with regard to the procedures initiated after protests, that is, preservation of the pressure upon the state and its institutions until and unless the staked claim has been satisfied and the violation/abuse redressed. However, a lot will still depend on the context and the circumstances surrounding the violation as well as the interaction among various actors, both state and non-state and the power relations that are in play.

It is, therefore, befitting to adhere to Goodale's definition of human rights, which is a broad one, capturing 'the constellation of philosophical, practical, and phenomenological dimensions through which universal rights, believed to be entailed by a common human nature, are enacted, debated, practiced, violated, envisioned, and experienced'[253]. This definition moves beyond a mere

---

nalHumanRightsTreaties_en.pdf; for the core human rights instruments – Universal Declaration of Human Rights, International Convention on the Elimination of All Forms of Racial Discrimination, International Covenant on Economic, Social and Cultural Rights and its Optional Protocol, International Covenant on Civil and Political Rights and its Optional Protocols, Convention on the Elimination of All Forms of Discrimination against Women and its Optional Protocol, Convention on the Rights of the Child and its Optional Protocols, Convention against Torture and Other Cruel, Inhuman or Degrading Treatment or Punishment and its Optional Protocol, International Convention on the Protection of the Rights of All Migrant Workers and Members of Their Families, Convention on the Rights of Persons with Disabilities and its Optional Protocol and International Convention for the Protection of All Persons from Enforced Disappearance.

251 S. E. Merry, "Human Rights and Gender Violence: Translating International Law into Local Justice" (University of Chicago Press, 2006): 192, quoted in *The Local Relevance of Human Rights: A Methodological Approach*, G. Oré Aguilar (Institute of Development Policy and Management (IOB), 2008.04), 15.

252 Ibid.

253 Mark Goodale, "Introduction: Locating Rights, Envisioning Law between the Global and the Local," In *The Practice of Human Rights: Tracking Law between the Global and*

instrumental or legal level, while acknowledging that both are significant, and examines the 'coteries of concepts, practices, and experiences through which human rights have meaning at different levels'[254].

Human rights cannot be only local or only global; they are situated somewhere in between[255]. Human rights construction is a dynamic and continuous process the success of which is never assuredly guaranteed and the failures of which should necessarily make part of that very construction since the process involves intricacy in terms of relationships among different actors, the goals each is pursuing, the claims that are being staked and last but not least, the way the actors present themselves as opposed to the way the media presents them etcetera. For instance, 'competing conceptions of "victims" '[256] will bring forth varying ways of representation. Rights frames coexist with other competing frames and alternative frameworks and in between the global and the local. The universal and the particular are not situated on isolated planes, but are, instead, continuously opposed to one another and when 'the alleged universality of human rights is confronted with the contingency of their application in contexts informed by alternative normative frameworks, it initiates a process of cycling, which reinforms and destabilizes the unity of human rights as a monolithic discourse'[257].

Competing notions of human rights have surrounded academic scholarship for a long time. Debates have evolved among legal centralists, legal pluralists, political scientists, philosophers, anthropologists and increasingly sociologists. The key point of departure has to do with the definition of human rights. While legal centralists define human rights as those enforceable in a court of law, legal

the Local, eds. Mark Goodale and Sally Engle Merry (Cambridge University Press, 2007), 133.

254 Ibid.

255 Shannon Speed, "Exercising Rights and Reconfiguring Resistance in the Zapatista Juntas De Buen Gobierno," In *The Practice of Human Rights: Tracking Law between the Global and the Local*, eds. Mark Goodale and Sally Engle Merry (Cambridge University Press, 2007).

256 Sally Engle Merry, "Introduction: Conditions of Vulnerability," In *The Practice of Human Rights: Tracking Law between the Global and the Local*, eds. Mark Goodale and Sally Engle Merry (Cambridge University Press, 2007), 201.

257 Sari Wastell, "Being Swazi, Being Human: Custom, Constitutionalism and Human Rights in an African Polity," In *The Practice of Human Rights: Tracking Law between the Global and the Local*, eds. Mark Goodale and Sally Engle Merry (Cambridge University Press, 2007), 331.

pluralists adopt a more encompassing stance[258]. Political scientists tend to accord an essential role to the state and its institutions while anthropologists place themselves with and among the people most affected by human rights violations and their own perceptions of what rights are. Sociologists, in turn, examine the interactions between different actors and focus on human agency and power in the process of human rights construction. Definitional debates, while seemingly tiresome, are important in that they guide the scholars' understanding of and approach to human rights as a concept. Furthermore, they invite differing insights from other disciplines and those insights are important and necessary to not only complement and further add to the richness of the notion of human rights but to also 'enhance the field's meaning and global understanding'[259].

The view that the state is the main duty holder with regard to rights is prevalent in human rights literature. However, reliance on mere political will, especially in cases where it is absent, will scarcely allow citizens to exercise and enjoy the rights they are entitled to but denied. Claims-making in relation to rights implies continuous struggle and negotiation with the state, struggle that takes place in the realm of practice. The key negotiating actors, the state and civil society, would preferably need to be 'mutually balancing, each having a malign and benign potential'[260]. For the sake of neutrality and fairness, neither the state nor civil society rather not be idealized. Each of these actors pursues certain goals and may use rights to serve those. Furthermore, rights could be used as a façade to protect certain interests and last but not least, they could be 'constrained by the letter and practice of the law'[261].

Human rights come with moral requirements, rights and wrongs, do's and don'ts, determining what is morally right and wrong, how rational human beings should treat one another and what boundaries would be morally wrong to cross. Where the emphasis is on the vulnerability of individuals, 'the moral

---

258 Richard, A. Wilson, "Tyrannosaurus Lex: The Anthropology of Human Rights and Transnational Law," In *The Practice of Human Rights: Tracking Law between the Global and the Local*, eds. Mark Goodale and Sally Engle Merry (Cambridge University Press, 2007).

259 G. Oré Aguilar, "The Local Relevance of Human Rights: A methodological Approach," Institute of Development Policy and Management (IOB), Discussion Paper/2008.04, p. 23.

260 Frank Parkin, "Durkheim" (Oxford Paperbacks, 1992): 76, quoted in *Rights: Sociological Perspectives*, ed. Lydia Morris (Routledge, 2006), 3.

261 Lydia Morris, *Rights: Sociological Perspectives* (Routledge, 2006), 7.

requirement is to protect them from abuse'[262]. In the case of individuals as agents, the emphasis is on their capability of 'autonomously devising a life-plan and living it'[263]. The underlying moral requirement 'is to remove obstacles in the way of their autonomous action'[264]. Importantly, personal identity is constructed as individuals take part in social practice and reflect upon it[265]. Personal autonomy is also not a given, but achieved. Moreover, it is possible under certain conditions necessary for it to be achieved, such as, 'interpersonal, emotional-relational, cultural-linguistic, social structural and material-ecological conditions of life'[266]. When individuals devise life-plans, they necessarily include close others, people to whom they relate one way or another. This is so because an individual is not secluded from social life, but connected with the life of society. Therefore, 'others, when we start to give concrete form to the idea of a life-plan, figure not just as potential obstacles to our project, but, instead (or also) as indispensable partners, associates and conditions for it'[267]. Similarly, when one claims human rights, that claim includes others who might at one point be at the receiving end of a breach or abuse. The claimant is, on the one hand, affirming human rights as inclusive, while on the other hand, makes sure their claim acts as prevention for other members of the society not to be subjected to the same type of abuse. It is noteworthy that as much as individuals are able to exercise personal autonomy to devise life-plans, the latter 'are constrained and shaped both by their cultural horizons and actual placing in society, with its current pattern of fulfilments and frustrations'[268]. Moreover, life-plans are contingent upon 'our access or lack of access to resources'[269].

As we live out our life-plans, we enter into moral and political talk with regard to our rights, duties, responsibilities and entitlements. The underpinning moral argument is that we are entitled to x, y and z, the provision of which shall be guaranteed and the exercise and enjoyment of which shall be protected. Whenever we, as rational individuals, come to realize that we have been morally wronged,

262 Ted Benton, "Do We Need Rights? If so, What Sort?" In *Rights: Sociological Perspectives*, ed. Lydia Morris (Routledge, 2006), 21.
263 Ibid.
264 Ibid.
265 Lydia Morris, *Rights: Sociological Perspectives* (Routledge, 2006).
266 Ted Benton, "Do We Need Rights? If so, What Sort?" In *Rights: Sociological Perspectives*, ed. Lydia Morris (Routledge, 2006), 23.
267 Ibid., 24.
268 Ibid., 25.
269 Ibid.

we exercise our autonomy to take action to rectify the wrong. In this case, we actively 'engage in claims and counter-claims, animated by contesting interpretations, rationalisations and definitions of rights'[270]. Our role, then, becomes one of a conscious citizen driven by a vision of what the status quo should be, and our activity is aimed at 'convincing particular audiences of our legitimacy, and overcoming competition and conflict from those with other views'[271].

Rights are context-sensitive and specific, as well as relational. Exercise of one right shall not hamper that of others. The right to a peaceful protest shall not disrupt public order and safety, otherwise 'peaceful' will lose its meaning and turn into violence in which case police forces will be justified to intervene. Rights exist in relation to one another as well as in relation to the specific social, political and cultural contexts in which they are embedded. They are 'located in specific times and places, with their own historical and institutional legacies and with specific sets of norms and values, themselves more or less homogenous or pluralistic'[272]. Societies do not all subscribe to the same mentality and morality. In one place 'other moral considerations may exist alongside a commitment to rights, more or less equally, or they may exist as an alternative to rights-based thinking'[273]. For instance, some societies are guided by religious principles; others value communal solidarity over individual rights, whereas in others traditional systems of thought prioritize notions of virtuous conduct[274]. Where a society's moral worldview or practical philosophy is more or less plural and hybrid, rights-based morality is combined with alternative ways of thinking[275]. These specific characteristics are to be considered whenever rights are studied in different settings to find out why human rights realization succeeds in some parts of the world but fails in others. After all, 'a grassroots grounding is necessary if human rights are to be achieved in practice'[276]. Conceptualization of human rights takes place 'at different social levels and within multiple cultural contexts' and it is not only

---

270 Lydia Morris, *Rights: Sociological Perspectives* (Routledge, 2006), 130.

271 Ibid.

272 Rob Stones, "Rights, Social Theory, and Political Philosophy, a Framework for Case Study Research," In *Rights: Sociological Perspectives*, ed. Lydia Morris (Routledge, 2006), 136.

273 Ibid., 136–137.

274 Ibid.

275 Ibid.

276 Ellen Messer, "Pluralist Approaches to Human Rights," *Journal of Anthropological Research* 53, no. 3 (1997): 294.

the principle of universal human rights that matters but 'also the fact of cultural diversity in norms of behaviour'[277].

Perceptions of certain phenomena by the agent are guided by both the networks within which the agent finds themselves, as well as by 'the agent's grasp of the immediate circumstances, their perception of the specific conjuncture'[278]. Important questions with regard to autonomy are the extent to which an agent is capable of critically reflecting outside the conditions within which they have been socialized, as well as sufficiently distancing themselves from habits to re-examine them[279]. Furthermore, the agent may question the 'likely external social costs and sanctions associated with the exercise of autonomy' as well as how correct their beliefs are and what will happen if they obey or oppose[280]. It is possible for the agent to distance themselves from the routines, habits and beliefs once they are exposed to alternatives, otherness and ways of thinking and doing different from what they are accustomed to. In such cases the agent will be capable of drawing comparisons, reflecting on two different realities and drawing inferences regarding their society's 'historically fashioned social inheritance, that is, its historically situated ideals, customs, beliefs, institutions, and practices'[281].

The objective of human rights struggles is to achieve their guarantee and protection in the form of internalization, that is, incorporate rights in the domestic constitution and laws. The eventual stage of rights work is institutionalization, which, 'may... lead not to their more secure protection but to their protection in a form that is less threatening to the existing system of power'[282]. This does not mean that human rights institutionalization shall not take place, but that 'institutionalisation is a social process, involving power, and that it should be analysed and not assumed to be beneficial'[283]. Local demands are made in reference to universally affirmed principles, in terms of the gap between what is stated universally and what is absent locally. In addition, once the universal is internalised,

277 Ibid., 308.

278 Rob Stones, *Structuration Theory* (London: Palgrave Macmillan, 2005), quoted in *Rights: Sociological Perspectives*, ed. Lydia Morris (Routledge, 2006), 139.

279 Rob Stones, "Rights, Social Theory, and Political Philosophy, a Framework for Case Study Research," In *Rights: Sociological Perspectives*, ed. Lydia Morris (Routledge, 2006).

280 Ibid., 139.

281 Mark Sydney Cladis, *A Communitarian Defence of Liberalism: Emile Durkheim and Contemporary Social Theory* (Standford, CA: Stanford University Press, 1992), quoted in *Rights: Sociological Perspectives*, ed. Lydia Morris (Routledge, 2006), 140–141.

282 Michael Freeman, *Human Rights: An Interdisciplinary Approach, Key Concepts* (Cambridge: Polity Press, 2002), quoted in *Rights: Sociological Perspectives*, ed. Lydia Morris (Routledge, 2006), 179.

283 Ibid.

it becomes local and particular and 'its content historically contingent, an open series of demands, in the face of which "philosophy comes to an end and the realm of politics begins"'[284].

What happens to human rights locally must be examined within the scope of cultural and historical settings. Certainly, universally affirmed principles are of significance too, since they provide a reference point to local struggles. Claims-makers have as an objective to see to it that their human rights demands become internalised, constitutionalised and legalised. However, before that can be achieved, rights work has to go through several stages, starting from formulating a claim, directing it to the entity responsible for its guarantee as well as appealing to a wider audience for support. Throughout all of these stages what happens to human rights claims varies between morality and politics. The former justifies the claims, while the latter is responsible for their execution. Rights are a rich terrain to study, 'especially from the standpoint of sociology' since they have a 'multifaceted nature: as tools of governance, as expressions of moral responsibility, as elements in a status ranking, as components of belief systems, as elements of an economic system and as claims in a political engagement that makes the terrain so intellectually fascinating and challenging'[285].

3.3 Sociology and rights

Human rights scholarship has for long been dominated by political scientists, international relations scholars and the like who have come up with statist solutions to human rights problems. This is not surprising given the 'classically modernist definition of the state as "the legitimate monopoly over the use of violence within a recognized and bounded territory"'[286]. Stated otherwise, modern statehood comprises the 'principles of *territoriality, administrative and military monopoly*, including the use of violence, and the *legitimacy* to do so'[287]. It turns out then that 'there is no sovereign to force the sovereign'[288]. To make

284 Ernesto Laclau, "Emancipation(s)," In *Rights: Sociological Perspectives*, ed. Lydia Morris (Routledge, 2006), 242.

285 Lydia Morris, *Rights: Sociological Perspectives* (Routledge, 2006), 252.

286 Max Weber, "Economy and Society: An Outline of Interpretive Sociology," Vol. 1 (University of California Press, 1978): 904–905, quoted in Seyla Benhabib, "Political Geographies in a Global World: Arendtian Reflections," *Social Research* 69, no. 2 (Summer, 2002): 540.

287 Seyla Benhabib, "Political Geographies in a Global World: Arendtian Reflections," *Social Research* 69, no. 2 (Summer, 2002): 540.

288 Ibid., 561.

matters worse, the modern state cannot be tamed and it may treat its citizens in the manner it finds appropriate and it will often find violence the appropriate means with which to deal with its citizens. The latter statement almost reads as an unavoidable diagnosis that renders citizens as mere recipients of whatever treatment the state wishes to provide them. Furthermore, such statist approaches to human rights problems 'might have a negative effect, insofar as they might encourage a passive acceptance of state power'[289]. More than that, they are 'elitist and disabling and they constrain the potential for popular mobilization around human rights issues'[290].

It is popular mobilizations and the exercise of individual agency, amongst other aspects, that have drawn the attention of sociologists working in the field of human rights. Rights have been on the periphery of sociology for quite some time. It is as of late that the concept has been embraced by sociology, and attempts have been made by several scholars to locate human rights within sociology in terms of both theory and practice. Even prior to the embrace by sociology, human rights have been suffering from issues that are theoretical, phenomenological and practical[291]. The difficulty that sociology has faced in terms of human rights is their definition at a level of abstraction. It is due to that abstractness that sociologists have confronted the challenging task of transforming an abstract and universal concept into an empirical enquiry. Second, the division between civil and political rights on the one hand and social and economic rights on the other, has further complicated the matter which is studying human rights through a holistic approach or bearing the divisions between two generations of rights in mind. The focus on human rights in relation to the studies of citizenship, which almost always predetermines and assumes the presence of rights, suffers from its ties to the nation-state. One is entitled to rights owing to their being a citizen of this or that state. This makes the nation-state the sole guarantor of rights, turning human beings into passive recipients of rights rather than active claimants. The focus in the study of rights has been on legal institutionalization, that is, looking to law as protection. The criticism of this approach has to do with its normative legalism overlooking the process of abuse and the causes underlying the abuse. Rather, abuse has been explained by arguments on illegitimacy and state failure.

---

289 Neil Stammers, "A Critique of Social Approaches to Human Rights," *Human Rights Quarterly* 17, no. 3 (August, 1995): 507.

290 Ibid.

291 Mark Goodale, "Toward a Critical Anthropology of Human Rights," *Current Anthropology* 47, no. 3 (June, 2006): 485–511.

To close this gap, some scholars have proposed looking at human rights from a constructionist perspective, that is, the processes through which human rights bearers construct human rights for themselves in their communities. This approach attempts to move beyond normative conceptions of rights and whether they are supported in diverse communities; instead, it follows the reverse path of how human rights norms come into being in different local settings and what factors – social, economic, cultural, political and environmental stand in the way of that process[292].

Sociological approach to human rights looks to making them more concrete, tangible and within reach of ordinary people contesting rights in domestic settings. One way of achieving this has been through the lens of social theory 'whose principal strength lies in offering an understanding of the social and political dynamics which support or undermine the establishment and operation of a regime of rights'[293]. Instead of normative arguments about human rights, theoretical arguments in social theory look 'to a consideration of the necessary requirements for the full realisation of the human condition, an understanding of the dialectical dynamic of rights and controls, and a role for persuasion and imagination in the process of public reasoning'[294]. In this way, abstract and normative rights are transformed into details regarding their justification, implementation and impediment. To put it otherwise, social theory is concerned with the practice of human rights.

Viewed from a sociological perspective, human rights acquire a number of tools 'for both working through and moving beyond the customary categories of human rights'[295]. Furthermore, sociological study of human rights enables the examination of those conditions and circumstances – economic, political, social, cultural, and environmental – which compel 'under-represented, exploited, or marginalized groups to begin to mobilize to air their grievances'[296]. Instead of checking the local status of human rights in any particular setting across an already established normative framework, 'sociology of human rights offers a "bottom-up" approach to human rights'[297]. It examines human rights in their

292 Mathieu Deflem and Stephen Chicoine, "The Sociological Discourse on Human Rights: Lessons from the Sociology of Law," *Development and Society* 40, no. 1 (June, 2011): 101–115.

293 Lydia Morris, *Human Rights and Social Theory* (Macmillan International Higher Education, 2013), 14.

294 Ibid.

295 Mark Frezzo, *The Sociology of Human Rights* (Polity Press, 2015), xii.

296 Ibid., xiv.

297 Ibid., 24.

dynamism, in a process of change (if any) and transformation, construction and claiming with the view that 'without concerted citizen action to uphold them close to home, we shall look in vain for progress in the larger world'[298].

The sociological view on rights is much more dynamic; from a sociological standpoint rights are not a status allocated upon birth, or possessed by someone before they are born, but, instead, 'assembled through political (and moral) conflicts and eventually institutionalized into laws, ordinances and declarations'[299]. This view is easier to denounce since it puts human rights on a shaky ground by approaching them as entitlements to be fought for, conquered and achieved. It further underlines 'the central *social* aspect of human rights, namely, that when and where they have been claimed, it has been because the individuals concerned suffered from and protested against forms of oppression and/or exploitation that they believed disregarded their dignity as human beings'[300]. Whereas the view that human rights are inalienable and possessed by everyone by virtue of their being human reinforces their validity. However, people are not born equal, are not treated equally, and justice is not delivered upon request. Rather, rights can be assembled and lost; their meaning may change over time, and their status be renegotiated. Rights are created by agents involved in collective conduct. Collective agents, be it activists, philosophers, governments, social movements, academics, NGOs etcetera engage in interpretive and activist rights work which implies 'a continuous round of negotiated actions that attempt to interpret, rationalize and define both social identities and related rights'[301]. Rights work is not about claims made by one particular agent and uncritically accepted by other agents as well as the target audience. Instead, 'rights work entails claims makers involved in "claims" and "counter-claims", often animated by quasi-arguments and stories'[302]. Public sphere is the arena where rights work unfolds. Rights struggles are not only local, but intertwined with the global. Rights claims locally have a reference to the global. Finally, 'rights work takes place in morally grounded activities and political practices. It is a struggle over defining what it

298 Mary Robinson, "Taking Stock of the Human Rights Agenda Sixty Years On," *Maryland Journal of International Law* 24 (2009): 16.

299 Ken Plummer, "Rights Work, Constructing Lesbian, Gay and Sexual Rights in late Modern Times," in *Rights: Sociological Perspectives*, ed. Lydia Morris (Routledge, 2006), 152.

300 Rainer Forst, "The Justification of Human Rights and the Basic Right to Justification: A Reflexive Approach," *Ethics* 120, no. 4 (2010): 712.

301 Ken Plummer, "Rights Work, Constructing Lesbian, Gay and Sexual Rights in late Modern Times," in *Rights: Sociological Perspectives*, ed. Lydia Morris (Routledge, 2006), 153.

302 Ibid.

means to live a good life and to be human'[303]. Definitions of the latter will vary depending on who makes the claim and what moral background they hold.

To make it clear, sociology of rights shall not be understood as a specific disciplinary niche. Sociology in this context is used in 'broad terms to represent the social and relational conceptual tools necessary to construct a social theory of rights, which "refuses to separate rights from social life as a whole and issues of power in particular"'[304]. And rightly so, since 'the specific content, scope and form of human rights cannot be determined outside of a particular context which takes into account the actual processes and concrete mechanisms that are available and likely to be involved in its application'[305]. Negating the existence of power in the context of human rights would be naïve and short-sighted, if only for the reason that 'power is being held, developed, and exercised consciously by individual or collective social actors as well as manifests itself structurally through the patterning of social systems regardless of consciousness or intent'[306]. Moreover, 'power is always and necessarily embedded in a network of concrete social relations'[307].

Rights violations do not take place in a vacuum; they occur in particular social and political contexts which trigger collective action against the abuses and abusers. Collective action itself is not a straightforward road to victory and redress. Its successes as well as failure owe to a number of factors, ranging from perceptions of rights and violations, civic and legal consciousness, human rights consciousness, identity, knowledge and education of the actors coupled with the tools and resources they use to achieve their goals, etcetera. Claims of human rights may at first start as moral claims to equal recognition of individuals belonging to a certain political community. However, what is no less important is the tangibility of rights, rights as prerequisites for a life of quality, rights

---

303 Ibid.

304 Anthony Woodiwiss, "Making Human Rights Work Globally," (Routledge, 2003): 7, quoted in Margaret R. Somers and Christopher N. J. Roberts, "Toward a New Sociology of Rights: A Genealogy of "Buried Bodies" of Citizenship and Human Rights," *Annual Review of Law and Social Science* 4 (December, 2008): 391.

305 Tom Campbell, "The Political Approach to Human Rights: Matching Human Rights Morality with Human Rights Mechanisms," Undated https://www.scribd.com/document/111674326/Matching-Human-Rights-Morality-With-Human-Rights-Mechanisms-1 (accessed 5 June 2017).

306 Neil Stammers, "Social Movements and the Social Construction of Human Rights," *Human Rights Quarterly* 21, no. 4 (1999): 983.

307 Ibid.

as application of what is guaranteed and utilization of which is lacking. Rights and recognition, therefore, are linked, one aspect of that linkage being 'the argument that dissatisfaction in relation to entitlements has driven a variety of social movements in the quest for a fuller realisation of rights and the recognition that accompanies them'[308].

3.4 The quest for rights and 'legal consciousness'

The quest for recognition and realisation of rights may manifest in different forms, such as, protests, acts of civil disobedience, civic resistance, political dissent and social movements. While each of these expressions of disagreement regarding the lack of recognition and realization of human rights proceeds with differences as to resources, tools being used to achieve the intended goals, skills and potential of the individuals engaging in them, they all possess things in common as well. One such aspect where manifestations of disagreement might converge is "legal consciousness" – 'participation in the process of constructing "legality", the wide range of "meanings, sources of authority, and cultural practices that are commonly recognized as legal, regardless of who employs them or for what ends", and that operates both as an interpretive framework and a set of resources'[309]. Legal consciousness is revealed in people's speech and action[310]. Individuals may position themselves differently vis-à-vis the law, for instance, for some law may be the authority before which they all stand as equals, in which they engage in one way or another and which they oppose[311]. In other words, legal consciousness, with its current focus, emphasizes not the 'lawyer's law, that is, ideas, problems or situations of interest to legal practitioners and theorists or legal acts, that is, rules and regulations of the modern state, the processes of administrative governance, police behaviour or legal behaviour, that is, the unofficial as well as official work of legal professionals'[312]. Instead, research now focuses on 'the unofficial, non-professional actors – citizens, legal laymen- as they take account of, anticipate, imagine, or fail to imagine legal acts and ideas'[313].

---

308 Lydia Morris, *Human Rights and Social Theory* (Macmillan International Higher Education, 2013), 6.

309 Filipe Carreira da Silva, "Outline of a Social Theory of Rights: A Neo-Pragmatist Approach," *European Journal of Social Theory* 16, no. 4 (2013): 467.

310 Ibid., 457–475.

311 Ibid.

312 Susan S. Silbey, "After Legal Consciousness," *Annual Review of Law and Social Science* 1 (2005): 326–327.

313 Ibid.

The lifeworld and the everyday life of ordinary people have come to occupy the empirical focus[314]. Consciousness amongst ordinary people may be manifest in 'thinking and doing, telling stories, complaining, lumping grievances, working, playing, marrying, divorcing, suing a neighbour, or refusing to call the police'[315].

Studying legal consciousness involves searching for 'the forms of participation and interpretation through which actors construct, sustain, reproduce, or amend the circulating (contested or hegemonic) structures of meanings concerning law'[316]. That is, the way legality is collectively constructed is of significance for legal consciousness since forms of consciousness in tandem constitute ideological or hegemonic legality[317]. Legal consciousness has been differently defined. Those different definitions include the society's ideas about the nature, function and operation of law[318], ordinary citizens' experiences and conceptions of law[319], people's perceptions and usage of law[320], 'the ongoing, dynamic process of constructing one's understanding of, and relationship to, the social world through the use of legal conventions and discourses'[321] and the assumption 'that the distributed self continually evolves with experience, incorporating along the way multiple, sometimes contradictory elements and perspectives'[322]. All of the above-mentioned definitions of legal consciousness have at their core an actor

314 Ibid., 323–368.

315 Ibid., 334.

316 Ibid.

317 Ibid., 323–368.

318 David M. Trubek, "Where the Action Is: Critical Legal Studies and Empiricism," *Stanford Law Review* 36 (January, 1984): 592, quoted in Susan S. Silbey, "After Legal Consciousness," *Annual Review of Law and Social Science* 1 (2005): 323–368.

319 Sally E. Merry, "Concepts of Law and Justice among Working Class Americans: Ideology as Culture," *Legal Studies Forum* 11 (1985): 59–71, quoted in Susan S. Silbey, "After Legal Consciousness," *Annual Review of Law and Social Science* 1 (2005): 323–368.

320 Sally E. Merry, "Getting Justice and Getting Even: Legal Consciousness among Working Class Americans" (University of Chicago Press, 1990): 5, quoted in Susan S. Silbey, "After Legal Consciousness," *Annual Review of Law and Social Science* 1 (2005): 323–368.

321 Michael W. McCann, "Rights at Work: Pay Equity Reform and the Politics of Legal Mobilization" (University of Chicago Press, 1994): 7, quoted in Susan S. Silbey, "After Legal Consciousness," *Annual Review of Law and Social Science* 1 (2005): 334.

322 David M. Engel and Frank W. Munger, "Rights of Inclusion: Law and Identity in the Life Stories of Americans with Disabilities" (University of Chicago Press, 2003): 12, quoted in Susan S. Silbey, "After Legal Consciousness," *Annual Review of Law and Social Science* 1 (2005): 334.

who has a conception of law that he or she interprets in a certain way based on a self that continually evolves through a learned experience.

Rights consciousness is an important part of the aforementioned forms of legal consciousness. Rights consciousness is the 'ways in which people act towards and think about rights'[323]. Following this line of thought, 'rights emerge as discursive resources with multiple and varying meanings, as well as institutional resources. They are defined as "practices", a concept that captures cultural representations and brings in social relations'[324]. Dissenting actors who possess rights consciousness also have perceptions of legality and the latter's failure to regulate relations between the state and the citizens as well as amongst citizens themselves triggers dissatisfaction which manifests in different acts of dissent, resistance, disobedience and opposition to power and authority. After all, rights shall be inscribed in law, and lack of realisation and recognition of rights is contested through references to law and legal mechanisms of protection.

Nonetheless, 'how law matters depends on the complex, often changing dynamics of the context in which struggles occur. Legal relations, institutions, and norms tend to be double-edged, at once upholding the larger infrastructure of the status quo while providing limited opportunities for episodic challenges and transformations in that ruling order'[325]. Marshall demonstrates this through her study of 'Injustice frames, legality and the everyday construction of sexual harassment' wherein legal remedies dominate the injustice frame for sexual harassment, thereby 'deemphasizing collective solutions and instead encouraging women to pursue more individualistic strategies, such as confronting harassers, lodging complaints with employers, or filing lawsuits when other options fail'[326]. Furthermore, law may interact with other frames or schemas, as a result 'reinforcing the status quo and protecting the powerful, such as when women adopt management frames to trivialize the sexual behaviours of their employees and to interpret their interests as coinciding with protecting their employers'[327]. In

323 Filipe Carreira da Silva, "Outline of a Social Theory of Rights: A Neo-Pragmatist Approach," *European Journal of Social Theory* 16, no. 4 (2013): 467.

324 Ibid.

325 Michael McCann, "Law and Social Movements: Contemporary Perspectives," *Annual Review of Law and Social Science* 2 (2006): 19.

326 Anna-Maria Marshall, "Injustice Frames, Legality, and the Everyday Construction of Sexual Harassment," *Law and Social Inquiry* 28, no. 3 (Summer, 2003): 686.

327 Ibid.

addition to protecting the powerful, law, in this context, functions as 'a complex social force that both enhances and impedes social change on the ground'[328].

As has already been mentioned above, there is no one single way of understanding and studying law. The latter can be used to 'signify different types of phenomena', such as 'official legal institutions, like courts and administrative bureaucracies, legal officials or elites, such as judges, bureaucrats, or lawyers; and sometimes legal norms, rules, or discourses that structure practices in and beyond official legal institutions'[329]. Law plays a crucial role in our life and activity as citizens in the society. Moreover, 'legal constructs shape our very capacities to imagine social or political possibilities. Among the most important of liberal legal conventions constituting both national and transnational relations are what we call rights- those legal forms that designate the distribution of legitimate social entitlements and burdens among citizens'[330]. Legal consciousness is expressed in the ways people 'use the law, think about the law, interpret the law, conceive of their lives in legally inflected terms, and invoke legal concepts and rights'[331]. Perceiving themselves as rights-bearing members of the society as well as conceiving what a rights violation constitutes, people go to court for redress and make use of judicial mechanisms to address failure of the protection of their rights. In sum, 'legal consciousness is not a psychological state but an outcome of social processes through which meanings and identities are collectively constructed'[332].

Human rights are made and remade, constructed and re-constructed, produced and reproduced in a process of contestation, claims-making and continuous struggle and resistance whenever and wherever a rights violation occurs and is so perceived by individuals who regard themselves as rights bearers. The objective of a struggle for human rights is to bring about a social change the

---

328 Ibid.

329 Michael McCann, "Law and Social Movements: Contemporary Perspectives," *Annual Review of Law and Social Science* 2 (2006): 20–21.

330 Ibid., 21.

331 Margaret R. Somers and Christopher N. J. Roberts, "Toward a New Sociology of Rights: A Genealogy of "Buried Bodies" of Citizenship and Human Rights," *Annual Review of Law and Social Science* 4 (December, 2008): 407.

332 Sally E. Merry, "Getting Justice and Getting Even: Legal Consciousness among Working Class Americans" (University of Chicago Press, 1990): 247, quoted in Margaret R. Somers and Christopher N. J. Roberts, "Toward a New Sociology of Rights: A Genealogy of 'Buried Bodies' of Citizenship and Human Rights," *Annual Review of Law and Social Science* 4 (December, 2008): 407.

achievement of which requires the securing of what Alan Hunt terms 'local hegemony'[333]. The latter has it that 'on grounds of political contestation, ethical justification and legal recognition, some claim which at one time was controversial and contestable becomes self-evident and thus secure'[334]. Following Hunt's line of reasoning, 'such claims become secure when they achieve hegemonic status, that is, they become a component of good sense'[335]. Rights claims are made by actors – 'like-minded individuals who come together to pursue their common interests'[336]. The outlooks and behaviour of these actors 'range from culture and ideology to aspirations and principled beliefs, onto cause-effect knowledge of specific policy problems'[337].

3.5 'Personhood' in human rights theory

As political and social creations, rights possess 'the causal powers to constitute personhood and identity'[338]. As much as the concept of personhood is a significant notion in human rights study and talk, its abstractness presents a challenge from legal as well as sociological perspectives. Ohlin implies that personhood is not a self-standing concept but rather comprises three main components, and arguments surrounding the concept of personhood, should take note of those components[339]. In particular, questions to ask in this regard have to do with moral and legal considerations, that is, the person as a rational agent and the person as a legal subject. But the fact that, as Ohlin acknowledges, 'personhood' has been stretched to a breakpoint to include 'debates as diverse as the legal status of embryos and animals to the rights and responsibilities of corporations and nations'[340] makes consensus on the concept even more intricate. Furthermore,

---

333 Alan Hunt, "Rights and Social Movements: Counter-Hegemonic Strategies," *Journal of Law and Society* 17, no. 3 (1990): 323.

334 Ibid.

335 Ibid.

336 Ann Swidler, "Culture in Action: Symbols and Strategies," *American Sociological Review* 51, no. 2 (April, 1986): 276.

337 John Gerard Ruggie, "What Makes the World Hang Together? Neo-Utilitarianism and the Social Constructivist Challenge," *International Organization* 52, no. 4 (1998): 879.

338 Margaret R. Somers and Christopher N. J. Roberts, "Toward a New Sociology of Rights: A Genealogy of 'Buried Bodies' of Citizenship and Human Rights," *Annual Review of Law and Social Science* 4 (December, 2008): 407.

339 Jens David Ohlin, "Is the Concept of the Person Necessary for Human Rights?" *Columbia Law Review* 105 (2005): 209.

340 Ibid.

attempting to pin down the notion of personhood, one confronts biological, ethical and legal debates, each bearing an element of truth and conviction as to who the person is, how the person is different from the human being, whether animals are persons without a soul, whether children are full or partial human beings, how brain-dead patients should be regarded etcetera. Being a biological person is not enough would be a logical argument; if one is a person, one is not only a biological being, but also a rational agent and a legal subject that can make rights claims.

The focus on the concept of personhood in legal reasoning stands the toughest challenge not only for the understanding of the notion as a central point in making human rights claims but also Ohlin's suggestion later in the paper that the concept of personhood is based on emptiness[341]. One way of reading this paper would be to set forward the argument that Ohlin has presented cases from legal reasoning, cases which are exceptions and exceptionally hard to conclude based on one aspect only. On the other hand, Ohlin's proposition to look at the concept of personhood by looking at each of its separate components on their own merits is not an easy way out either[342]. The question that arises then is 'should the concept of personhood be used as the entirety of its components, namely, the person as a biological entity, rational agent and legal subject, or should the concept be viewed, argued and put forward taking each component alone and disintegrating the meanings of each and the specific cases in which they are used to make human rights claims?' Ohlin somehow swings between these mediations, which are interesting to follow, but challenging to agree with. Admittedly, the concept of personhood is a focal point in terms of both understanding human rights and making claims to them. Moreover, the word combination of 'human rights' itself pinpoints a human who has rights or a human with rights, meaning that living humans have rights. To put it a bit gloomily, a dead person cannot claim rights. This is one of the components of the concept of personhood which Ohlin goes at length to try and explain, persons as biological entities, biological human beings, whose bodies can still take oxygen[343].

Furthermore, the second component of the concept of personhood, the person being a rational agent is entertaining for both argumentation and academic purposes. Do only those biological persons have rights who are proven to be rational agents, that is, whose cognitive mechanisms are fully developed, or

341 Ibid.
342 Ibid.
343 Ibid.

do also those persons have rights or are able to claim rights who are proven to be biological entities but are yet to be recognized as rational agents? In Ohlin's paper this argument moves between adults, children, animals, brain-dead persons, persons with multiple personality disorder etcetera[344]. Each of the cases are interesting in their own right and deserve attention for the tension they create not only for legal cases but also for arguing for the concept of personhood as a central point in human rights theory. The rational agent component of the concept of personhood is equally significant in making human rights claims, since persons lacking rationality (depending on what we mean by being rational) won't be able to make rational choices and decisions. The third and not least important component of the concept of personhood is that of persons being legal subjects, that is to say, having their rights recognized within an established legal framework which covers them as biological entities and rational agents who fall under a particular jurisdiction and on whom they depend for protection.

Whether viewed in abstraction, or as the entirety of its components, the notion of personhood 'is a talisman that confers status, respect, and moral worth, and for this reason the concept is deeply ingrained in legal discourse in general and in human rights in particular'[345]. And although personhood is not a concept that 'wears its theoretical significance on its sleeve'[346], it does not cease to be essential in human right theory. All of the components of the cluster concept of personhood – persons as biological human beings, rational agents and legal subjects, can only be fully realized when the person comes into relationships with fellow human beings, rational agents and legal subjects. In the end, human rights themselves are relational; 'rights are relationships, not things; they are institutionally defined rules specifying what people can do in relation to one another. Rights refer to doing more than having, to social relationships that enable or constrain action'[347]. The rights to 'free speech, petition, and assembly are fundamentally associational rights'[348].

344 Ibid.

345 Ibid., 211.

346 Ibid., 247.

347 Iris Marion Young, "Justice and the Politics of Difference" (Princeton University Press, 1990): 25, quoted in Margaret R. Somers and Christopher N. J. Roberts, "Toward a New Sociology of Rights: A Genealogy of "Buried Bodies" of Citizenship and Human Rights," *Annual Review of Law and Social Science* 4 (December, 2008): 413.

348 Margaret R. Somers and Christopher N. J. Roberts, "Toward a New Sociology of Rights: A Genealogy of 'Buried Bodies' of Citizenship and Human Rights," *Annual Review of Law and Social Science* 4 (December, 2008): 413.

It was mentioned above that human rights are not a pre-given status, but are instead made and remade in a process of contestation. The making and remaking or construction and reconstruction of human rights take place within a certain social and political context, by individuals 'as rational agents with physical bodies, minds, continuity of consciousness, and a capacity for moral agency' capable of 'constructing social norms (such as human rights) for themselves'[349]. Furthermore, construction of human rights is a kind of local growth carried out by addressees themselves in which case 'they would carry an exceptional motivating power' since human rights constructed from below are 'locally sensitive', their validity 'is constructed as mundane, this-worldly, and contingent: as something achieved not given or revealed'[350]. It is for this reason that theological and interventionist arguments are rejected by social constructionists in that they lack local validity. Moreover, such arguments on human rights put local validity in peril. They follow an imperialist line of imposing an outsider's view on a local milieu where the outsider's perceptions of human rights may well stand in contradiction to those of the locals. As a result, human rights imposed at a level of generality are misunderstood, rejected and fail in local settings. One way of addressing this issue is specifying what is meant by human rights in different domestic settings. There exist numerous local settings and identifying what is meant by human rights in each of them is a Herculean task and one more realistically to be performed by local actors themselves.

Like the concept of personhood, human rights too, as a general notion, as an abstraction make little sense, rather, it is the lower-level components that they are made of that give them a concrete meaning, that is, human rights as democratic governance, social justice, economic equality, constitutional order, independent judiciary and accountable politicians. It is these lower-level components that make human rights, but it also depends which lower-level component of the notion of human rights plays what role in any given society. For instance, one society may perceive of human rights as democratic governance, in another society economic equality and social justice may shape their understanding of human rights, in more democratic societies where basic human rights are guaranteed and protected, the economic equality or social justice component of the concept of human rights may need to be further dissociated into sub-components

349 Benjamin Gregg, *Human Rights as Social Construction* (Cambridge University Press, 2011), 42.
350 Ibid., 3.

to reveal specificities of conceptions of human rights in that particular society. In other words:

> Normatively thin human rights can be generated out of thick local norms: thin can be derived from thick, that is, locally valid thick norms (whether civil, political, economic, social, or cultural) can become thin, or at least thinner. This thick-to-thin process is not likely to be linear. It is likely to be an interplay of goals immediately realizable and goals that remain aspirational, that is, realizable only progressively. Probably it would be an interplay of nonjusticiable claims that orient and direct political and social trends, on the one hand, and claims that *are* justiciable, on the other. Human rights so derived can motivate people insofar as people are more likely to embrace human rights because they are rooted in *local* cultural and political understandings[351].

If thinly formulated, human rights norms will be more likely to be accepted by a variety of cultural communities in the sense that there is a good chance that certain normatively thin human rights notions will find resonance with other cultures. A good example is the perception and experience of being subjected to torture. Victims of such ill-treatment will condemn the practice regardless of nationality, political or other affiliation and status. This is so owing to their sensitivity to pain and suffering that may happen to any other human being. If derived thinly from thick norms and socially constructed, human rights acquire local validity, valid meaning 'which, within a culture, marks an idea, belief, or practice in ways that members recognize and, to varying degrees, identify with'[352]. However, socially constructed thin human rights still need to be enforced to exist; enforcement takes place over time and 'is a matter of *local* recognition as well as broad embrace implying some degree of institutional support'[353]. This would 'render individuals merely passive recipients of rights' which would then become a matter of 'philanthropy and deprive their recipients of autonomy and equality'[354]. Therefore, the main guarantors of human rights do not necessarily (preferably) need to 'only be great powers possessed of significant economic and military might, or international organizations backed by coalitions of such powers'[355]. Rather, 'the moral-ennoblement of human beings is precisely that of humankind giving itself norms of social and political behaviour'[356].

351 Ibid., 67.
352 Ibid., 64.
353 Ibid., 93.
354 Ibid.
355 Ibid.
356 Ibid., 4

Human beings, based on historic, cultural differences, experience, level of socio-economic development and so on, construct for themselves, in their diverse communities 'a compelling code of behaviour – and, over time, compelling beyond the local venues where in each instance it begins'[357]. However, the social construction of human rights faces challenges as well in that it is carried out by 'a naturally evolved species of unparalleled cognitive capacity, emotional sensitivity, and psychological fragility'[358].

3.6 Constructing human rights from below

To start with, an entire community cannot construct human rights or other norms. Construction is a gradual process that begins with a certain group of individuals whom Gregg terms intermediaries[359]. Intermediaries possess the necessary education, skills and experience to frame human rights norms in a language comprehensible and acceptable to locals. Already in possession of human rights consciousness 'intermediaries may transfer human rights consciousness to locals, both those affected by a practice or condition and those unaffected'[360]. Furthermore, 'as intermediaries, framers likely have developed the "dual consciousness" that many locals may lack. Intermediaries are conscious of local grievances in all their particularity; they are conscious simultaneously of local and extralocal norms'[361]. Nevertheless, framers or the so-called 'potential self-authors'[362] do not stand on an equal footing. Construction of human rights 'depends critically on the participant's personality structure as well as on the structure of some of the social institutions he or she inhabits'[363]. If personality structure refers to 'the *internal* or psychological disposition of the individual insofar as it motivates his or her political behavior, social structure concerns the *external or formal and material arrangements* of political community'[364].

As much as social construction of human rights seems a preferable way forward, it does not present an unimpeded process where actors are completely free to exercise their agency along with their value systems to create the human rights

357 Ibid.
358 Ibid.
359 Ibid.
360 Ibid., 150.
361 Ibid.
362 Ibid., 92.
363 Ibid.
364 Ibid.

reality they aspire. Conflicting interests and values come into play, and various actors enter the human rights arena with competing value frames of their own. In a rather entertaining piece of writing, Goodale explicates value frames and moral action, the former being human rights (as a matter of example) and the latter activity aimed at upholding the former[365]. In Goodale's terms, 'value frames are modes of orientation that are grounded in values and ways of understanding self and the world that seem to form a connected whole'[366]. In addition, value frames hold two qualifications – first, they are plural and second, 'the integrity of value frames, their self-contained coherence, is more apparent than real'[367]. So, there exist plural/many value frames that are at odds with one another, that are situated in a social or ethical space and that are 'porous and imbricated with each other, forming a sort of loose assemblage that resists fine parsing and the demarcation of clear boundaries'[368].

The loose assemblage of value frames and resistance to the demarcation of clear boundaries means that value frames may both overlap and divert, as well as be resisted by competing value frames. Moreover, a value frame does not immediately trigger moral action. Through examples from Bolivia, China and the Israeli-Palestinian conflict Goodale aptly sustains the aforementioned claim[369]. In these examples, one can discern value frames such as human rights competing against other value frames that the state or the opposing side sets forth. In the Bolivian context at one time a peaceful transition of power collapsed once the ruling president initiated changes in the constitution to extend the terms he could run; in the Chinese context, criticism from external actors in respect of the Chinese government's violent crackdown on pro-democracy protests in Tiananmen Square prompted what later became famously known as 'the Asian-values', a debate that contributed a great amount of scholarship to the relativist stance of human rights norms. The value frame of human rights held by the pro-democracy protesters competed against and lost to 'Asian values' frame, the assumption that Western individualism and self-centredness were alien to the communitarian values prevailing in China. On the Israeli-Palestinian side, the 'Israelis approached the conflict from a position of a national security strength and a sense of historical-theological destiny, the Palestinians, by contrast, a stateless

---

365 Mark Goodale, "Human Values and Moral Exclusion," *Ethics & Global Politics* 9, no. 1 (2016).
366 Ibid., 3.
367 Ibid.
368 Ibid.
369 Ibid.

people living under conditions of occupation and violent microgovernance, viewed their actions as the result of resistance shaped by moral righteousness'[370].

In the aforementioned examples the plurality of value frames is evident. Plurality is a term that relates not only to value frames, however, but also to such terms as legal consciousness and civic consciousness. Consciousness 'embeds the study of ideas in social structure and social relations, drawing attention to the way similarly situated persons come to see the world in similar ways'[371]. Furthermore, consciousness suggests that 'subjectivity is not free floating and autonomous but is, instead, constituted, in a historically contingent manner, by the very objects of consciousness'[372]. Thus, the consciousness of the welfare poor would be different from the consciousness of other social groups[373]. Even amongst one another, the welfare poor have a varying perception of law and legal representatives[374]. In terms of action for change or redress of injustice, it would not be illogical to inquire whether these plural consciousnesses would drive individuals into collective action or whether subjective idiosyncrasies would prove more powerful. Following the protest school of thought, 'human rights articulate rightful claims made by or on behalf of the poor, the unprivileged, and the oppressed'[375]. This means that even if a human rights claim is made by an individual who is suffering from injustice, its positive solution or redress should in principle be beneficial to the entire social group or empower the particular social group to which the individual making the claim belongs, thereby extending the claim won for a certain right instead of confining it to one single individual, in which case the extension of the right would be terminated and the contest for the right prove self-centred. In other words, the possession or enjoyment of human rights shall not lead individuals to 'only use them for their own benefit. The loss of the sense of obligation to fight for the human rights of others is a betrayal of the human rights concept'[376]. Furthermore, a right once earned, is never possessed forever. It can always be lost again. Therefore, the fight for the realization of human rights is an ongoing process, 'a project always in the making (and reversible)'[377].

370 Ibid., 8.

371 Austin Sarat, "'. . .The Law is All Over': Power, Resistance and the Legal Consciousness of the Welfare Poor," *Yale Journal of Law & the Humanities* 2 (1990): 344.

372 Ibid.

373 Ibid.

374 Ibid.

375 Marie- Bénédicte Dembour, "What Are Human Rights? Four Schools of Thought," *Human Rights Quarterly* 32, no. 1 (2010): 3.

376 Ibid., 8.

377 Ibid.

The human rights project, to extend beyond universal norms, needs to be progressive, that is, 'translated into local cultures and become relevant to emancipatory legal practice'[378]. Translation involves resonance with local culture, framing issues in ways that are understandable to the local population and preferably, avoidance of abstractions and thickness. Emancipation, on the other hand, implies human rights becoming 'local, living, and counter-hegemonic'[379]. The states' ratification of international human rights instruments does not yet guarantee automatic and direct translation of those norms into practice or their internalization in domestic settings. Moreover, 'a state's promotion of human rights should not always be taken at face value as indication of a commitment to human rights norms'[380]. It is well documented in human rights literature that the state can rarely be trusted with internalization of human rights norms. Rather, it is those 'in the middle' – 'activists, movement leaders, academics, and those who speak for victims, including some victims themselves, who construct human rights cases, transform them in ways that will increase their appeal, and try to mobilize pressure behind the principles'[381].

Those in the middle – translators or mediators – operate between two extremes, that of power and vulnerability. The field within which they work is full of conflict and contradiction. Translators, thus, 'are able to manipulate others who have less knowledge than they do but still subject to exploitation by those who installed them'[382]. Furthermore, they possess a lot of information and knowledge, yet their loyalties may be questioned and they may be suspected of serving two masters. Their translation between the local and the global and vice versa 'takes place within fields of unequal power and is influenced by who is funding them; their ethnic, gender, or other social commitments; and institutional frameworks that create opportunities for wealth and power'[383]. Last but not least, translators

378 Boaventura de Sousa Santos, "The Rise of the Global Left: The World Social Forum and Beyond" (Zed Books, 2006): 134–135, quoted in Kate Nash, "Human Rights, Movements and Law: On Not Researching Legitimacy," *Sociology* 46, no. 5 (2012): 798.

379 Kate Nash, "Human Rights, Movements and Law: On Not Researching Legitimacy," *Sociology* 46, no. 5 (2012): 799.

380 Ranita Ray and Bandana Purkayastha, "Challenges in Localizing Global Human Rights," *Societies without Borders* 7, no. 1 (2012): 39.

381 Sally Engle Merry, "Introduction: States of Violence," In *The Practice of Human Rights: Tracking Law between the Global and the Local*, eds. Mark Goodale and Sally Engle Merry (Cambridge University Press, 2007), 41.

382 Sally Engle Merry, "Transnational Human Rights and Local Activism: Mapping the Middle," *American Anthropologist* 108, no. 1 (March, 2006): 40.

383 Ibid.

do not work in a political or institutional vacuum. Therefore, 'the repertoire of ideas and practices available to them' may be constrained[384].

Nonetheless, mediators recognize unequal and unjust conditions and act to restore order and justice, or retrieve the conditions that existed before the social conflict arose. Action could also be directed at improving the order and conditions, to make things better than they were before. The rights at stake in this case are not abstractly formulated principles which act as a mere driving force for moral action, but concrete claims for repair. 'Only in this way does one do justice to the original, emancipatory meaning of human rights: namely, as concretely-demanded basic conditions for establishing a just, or more just, society in political contexts'[385]. The demand for human rights arises out of internal conflicts, 'from within' and 'is directed at something "internal"'[386]. It is most of the time directed at the establishment that is trusted with just treatment of those who have put their faith and trust in it, but who have now come to realize that 'they are treated unjustly both as members of their culture and society and also simply as *human beings*'[387]. Furthermore, the demand for repair is not necessarily guided by abstract or philosophical ideas of what it means to be human, but 'in protesting people believe that there is at least *one* fundamental human – moral demand which no culture or society may reject: *the right to justification*, the right to be respected as moral person who is autonomous at least in the sense that he or she must not be treated in any manner for which adequate reasons cannot be provided'[388]. Adequacy of reasons is decided by moral persons in dialogue with others[389]. As Forst eloquently puts it: 'to speak of a *right* here – indeed of that most basic of all rights of every human being – is to say that it expresses a fundamental, absolutely binding subjective claim that cannot be denied intersubjectively'[390].

Construction of human rights should proceed at two levels- abstract and concrete. With regard to the former, human rights are held as moral constructs against any individual or state. On a concrete level, human rights are held as political constructs whereby 'legal, political, and social structures need to be

384 Ibid.
385 Rainer Forst, "The Basic Right to Justification: Towards a Constructivist Conception of Human Rights," *Constellations* 6, no. 1 (1999): 36.
386 Ibid., 40.
387 Ibid.
388 Ibid.
389 Ibid., 35–60.
390 Ibid., 40.

developed in which general rights are concretely justified, interpreted, institutionalized, and realized as basic rights in given historical and social contexts'[391]. Human rights are not made according to an ideal. Rather, their need arises in particular social and historical circumstances, out of conflict where citizens need protection most. It is their vulnerability at times of conflict that triggers the need for human rights protection. The process of human rights construction involves the holders of those rights, that is, the citizens as well as the state to which the claims are made. However, it is hardly the case that claims-making automatically translates into rights granting. Human rights construction involves conflicts and struggles as well as power play between various actors whose visions of just order may overlap or divert. Furthermore, the struggle engages not only the citizens and the state, but also the citizens vis-à-vis one another. As a result, citizens, as autonomous and moral persons, recognize that there is a problem with the social order and the way they are being treated as citizens. This recognition drives them to envision a human rights project that will restore the just order in terms of legal fairness, political equality, or social inclusion. Citizens, thus, form a political community, which 'is to be regarded as "sovereign" in the sense that its members regard it as a collective project of establishing just institutions founded on citizens' recognition of one another as persons with the right to justification'[392]. Recognition, to result in meaningful outcome, should work both ways, that is, citizens regarding one another as equal and the state recognizing citizens as rights-holders and participants in a social and political order. That is, 'rights are not "granted" vertically by a state, but instead are accepted and conferred horizontally in processes of justification, and thus are an expression of mutual recognition'[393].

For John Rawls, human rights are feasible not only in liberal but also in non-liberal (or what he terms well-ordered hierarchical) societies. Such societies possess their own conceptions of justice and 'their representatives in an appropriate original position would adopt the same principles as adopted by the representatives of liberal societies'[394]. Their own conceptions of justice condition the way 'each hierarchical society's interests are understood by its representatives'[395]. Rawls' constructivist view has it that conceptions such as justice and more

---

391 Ibid., 43.
392 Ibid., 48–49.
393 Ibid.
394 John Rawls, "The Law of Peoples," In *On Human Rights*, eds. Stephen Shute and Susan Hurley (Basic Books, 1993), 64.
395 Ibid.

general liberal ideas 'are constructed by way of a reasonable procedure in which rational parties adopt principles of justice for each kind of subject as it arises'[396]. At the start, a series of subjects are taken up by the constructivist doctrine; afterwards, claims for future generations are taken up, followed by principles for the law of peoples and then back to principles for special social questions[397]. The subject in question necessitates modifications of the constructivist procedure.

A constructivist liberal doctrine's 'authority rests on the principles and conceptions of practical reason, but always on these as suitably adjusted to apply to different subjects as they arise in sequence; and always assuming as well that these principles are endorsed on due reflection by the reasonable agents to whom the corresponding principles apply'[398]. Reasonableness and well-orderedness are key concepts in Rawls's theory of justice wherein societies need to be well-ordered and individuals possess sound reason. Provided the latter is the case, basic human rights will be possible to implement. Rawls's theory does not support theological or metaphysical understandings of rights, that is, 'rights do not depend on any particular comprehensive moral doctrine or philosophical conception of human nature'[399]. Moreover, human beings are not viewed as moral persons with equal worth or entitled to rights because of 'certain particular moral and intellectual powers'[400]. Was this the case, philosophical and moral theories would be brought forth and for relativist reasons those would be rejected by non-liberal and non-democratic societies and viewed as 'distinctive of the Western political tradition and prejudicial to other cultures'[401]. Instead, Rawls claims that 'human rights express a minimum standard of well-ordered political institutions for all peoples who belong, as members in good standing, to a just political society of peoples'[402]. Whether the society is liberal or hierarchical, systematic violation of rights poses a serious concern. The minimum standard requirement, in turn, should facilitate instalment of those rights. Those basic rights, for Rawls are: 'the right to life and security, to personal property, and the elements of the rule of law, as well as the right to a certain liberty of conscience and freedom of association, and the right to emigration'[403].

396 Ibid., 46.
397 Ibid.
398 Ibid.
399 Ibid., 68.
400 Ibid.
401 Ibid.
402 Ibid.
403 Ibid.

Rawls' theory is finely designed, but it is rather idealistic. Idealism is reflected in the way Rawls believes his theory should work: 'Perhaps there is no society anywhere in the world whose people, were they reasonably and rationally governed, and their numbers sensibly adjusted to their economy and resources, could not have a decent and worthwhile life'[404]. There are many societies whose people are not reasonably or rationally governed, societies where citizens do not have a decent and worthwhile life. Rawls himself acknowledges the underlying reasons as 'the nature of the public political culture and the religious and philosophical traditions that underlie its institutions'[405]. Again, referring to well-ordered societies, Rawls suggests that 'their political and cultural traditions, their human capital and knowledge as well as their capacity for political and economic organization'[406] are wealthy grounds for effective human rights guarantee and protection. The reverse is poorer societies with oppressive governments and corrupt elites, uneven distribution of resources, non-democratic governance etcetera. In sum, well-ordered or liberal societies are more likely to support human rights than those that are not well-ordered, are illiberal/non-democratic. This would make human rights beyond reach of countries outside the West.

3.7 Collective action for human rights

Collective action allows for mobilization and coming together of individuals motivated by perceived injustice or rights violations in order to put up claims for the perceived injustice and violations to be redressed and rectified. Extant resources, such as, 'relative or absolute frustrations, cultural identities, ideologies, networks, techniques of protest, popular demonstration and the control of information are capable of creating a collective form of mobilization'[407]. Collective action also pursues 'entry into political spaces and processes, thereby improving on their capacity to influence legal/political decisions which might be favourable to their interests'[408]. As such, collective action enables the participants to assemble in public spaces, voice grievances, put up claims and seek redress of their human rights violations and other perceived injustice. It plays an important role in

404 Ibid., 77.
405 Ibid.
406 Ibid.
407 Francois Dubet and Henri Lustiger Thaler, "Introduction: The Sociology of Collective Action Reconsidered," *Current Sociology* 52, no. 4 (2004): 559.
408 Ibid.

human rights struggles in that the participants/actors exercise their agency and power to press for change.

Human rights claims can be made through different forms of collective action such as protests, resistance, sit-ins and civil disobedience, which may or may not grow into social movements. Civil disobedience is a type of collective action that is carried out through opposing and protesting the law with the aim of bringing about political change. It is an act that is contrary to law and is considered unlawful but 'is defended as a mechanism for publicising issues that, because of the stifling effects of prevailing orthodoxies, receive insufficient attention in the public sphere'[409]. The goal of civil disobedience is to appeal to the wider community with regard to the urgency of a particular problem and convince the majority that a necessary action shall be taken[410]. Civilly disobeying actors aim at creating 'a public space in which people, as free and equal citizens, act and deliberate together'[411]. While citizens have a duty to comply with the law not to disrupt the democratic order, that duty implies a reciprocation of respect between the authority and the citizens; if the former fails to discharge its duty to respect the rights of its citizens and establish justice and equality in the society, the latter have the right to protest that authority, dispute its competence to rule and by resorting to disobedience rectify the injustice and inequality committed.

Stammers insists that social movement struggles have played an important role in 'the historical emergence and development of human rights'[412]. Those struggles, as a matter of fact, target 'extant relations and structures of power'[413]. As a result, human rights are to an extent made and remade in the process of these struggles. In contrast to views that once conquered, rights need to be institutionalized to secure their status, Stammers argues that institutionalization may lead to the opposite direction, that is, 'once institutionalized – human rights come to stand in a much more ambiguous relation to power'[414]. As much as social movements play a significant role in human rights construction, they shall be viewed against the background of the existing power relations, surrounding events and factors that extend well beyond the internal affairs of a

409 William Smith, "Civil Disobedience and the Public Sphere," *Journal of Political Philosophy* 19 (2011): 146.
410 Ibid., 145–166.
411 Candice Delmas, "Disobedience, Civil and Otherwise," *Criminal Law and Philosophy* 11, no. 1 (2017): 8.
412 Neil Stammers, *Human Rights and Social Movements* (Pluto Press, 2009), 2.
413 Ibid.
414 Ibid., 3.

particular state. Social movements or protests as well as other types of claims-making involve 'agency', that is the ability to take action and the 'power to change things'[415]. However, common people, that are deemed actors of change and architects of their rights, are 'aware but not omniscient, powerful but not omnipotent, creative but not unconstrained, free but not unlimited'[416]. Hence, social change is possible but also dependent upon 'potential capacity rather than ultimate achievement; dynamic but shifting concrete processes rather than any absolute, universal, external standard; historical possibilities as open options rather than necessary, inevitable, inexorable tendencies'[417]. Furthermore, it is essential to acknowledge that social progress is a 'product of (intended and unintended and even unrecognized) human collective actions, rather than a result of Divine Will, the good intentions of exceptional individuals, or the operation of automatic social mechanisms'[418].

Collective action, nevertheless, is not an uninterrupted unity of individuals who all agree upon a particular issue at all times. On the contrary, tendencies towards the rule of the few have been stated to be the case 'within even supposedly democratic associations'[419]. Altruism has been discussed at the start of this chapter and its role in human rights struggles emphasized as being essential in that claims are made on behalf of the poor, those whose voices have been silenced and those lacking the knowledge and the skills to do it for themselves. Such claims-making and/or activism, then, becomes 'other-centred'[420]. It extends feelings of empathy and justice to those outside of one's immediate milieu. Individual as well as collective actors are involved in movement activism. Action evolves around an 'I' or a 'we'. However, issues of interests, identity and recognition also form part of collective action and 'reliance on these categories effectively precludes the possibility of explaining solidarity with an 'other''[421]. One could make the case that wherever interests coincide, and there is no major identity conflict, collective actors shall seek recognition they are denied and extend

415 Ibid., 25.

416 Piotr Sztompka, "Agency and Progress: The Idea of Progress and Changing Theories of Change," in *Rethinking Progress*, eds. Jeffrey Alexander and Piotr Sztompka (London, Unwin Hyman, 1990): 250, quoted in Neil Stammers, *Human Rights and Social Movements* (Pluto Press, 2009), 30–31.

417 Ibid.

418 Ibid.

419 Neil Stammers, *Human Rights and Social Movements* (Pluto Press, 2009), 108.

420 Ibid., 186.

421 Ibid.

that rejection of denial to others by way of altruism and empathy. Furthermore, collective action for human rights 'is partly about building up a human rights culture built on understandings of threats posed by various forms of power'[422]. Subsequent action then aims at tackling those forms of power by creating social movements whose 'sociality and movement can go in any direction, positive or negative'[423].

Collective action takes place in the civil sphere which operates alongside non-civil spheres – state, economy, religion, family, and community[424]. These spheres pursue interests that contradict the civil sphere and 'the goods they produce and the powers they sustain are sectoral, not societal, particularistic not universalistic'[425]. The resultant hierarchies obstruct the creation of 'the wider solidarity that is the sine qua non of civil life'[426]. Collective action is aimed at the particular and the universal, that is, 'some particular injustice and the promises about the general good'[427]. Protests, movements and/or other types of collective action are never about eradicating a problem in relation to a particular social group. The target extends beyond that. The existence of the problem and the subsequent protests to find a solution attest that social solidarity needs to be reconstructed, that it is shrinking instead of extending and that it is in need of repair. For this process to succeed, collective actors need to 'convince people outside their groups by interweaving their particular struggles with universal civil themes'[428]. Civil society is not static; it evolves, it has flaws, successes and failures. Even when it records its greatest success, 'it cannot be fully achieved'[429]. Nor can it be 'completely suppressed despite tragedy and defeat'[430]. Civil society is defined as 'the realm of social activities', 'an aggregate of institutions whose members are engaged primarily in a complex of non-state activities – economic and cultural production, household life and voluntary association', activities that are 'sociable' and 'public spheres'[431].

---

422 Ibid., 238–239.
423 Ibid., 249.
424 Jeffrey C. Alexander, *The Civil Sphere* (Oxford University Press, 2006).
425 Ibid., 7.
426 Ibid.
427 Ibid.
428 Ibid.
429 Ibid., 9.
430 Ibid.
431 Ibid., 29–30.

In this sphere individuals come together to form a social bond and establish a 'fellow feeling'[432]. On a meaning level, however, 'the civility of the self always articulates itself in language about the incivility of the other'[433]. As much as collectivism is about the we-ness, the fellow-feeling, individualism positions one/self versus 'the other' and the language used in the public or the civil sphere signifies qualities that the self possesses and that do not characterize 'the other'. In democratically governed societies, 'the people who compose it are described as being capable of activism and autonomy rather than as being passive and dependent'[434]. Moreover, they are viewed as possessing rationality and reason rather than exhibiting irrationality and hysteria, calmness rather than excitability, control rather than passion, sanity and realism rather than insanity and fantasy[435]. Contrarily, passivity, dependence, irrationality, hysteria, excitability, passion, fantasy and/or madness are qualities that would justify restriction of civil society[436]. Such qualities are deemed unfit for a democratic actor, hence, 'these persons deserve to be repressed, not only for the sake of civil society, but for their own sakes as well'[437]. Not every associational grouping is civil. What matters and makes it one is what it is associated with as well as 'whether these other factors orient an association to engage with the broader solidarity groupings that exist outside itself'[438].

The civil sphere can penetrate other non-civil spheres just like the latter can penetrate into the civil sphere. If the civil sphere does not possess equal power, it will lead to fragmentation within, which will enable 'state power to function in a hegemonic way'[439]. Non-civil spheres, such as the economy and politics, pursue goals other than justice, solidarity, reciprocity and/or independence. The economic sphere, for instance, aims at wealth; 'it is organized around efficiency, not solidarity, and depends more upon hierarchy than equality to meet its goals'[440]. Polities, on the other hand, 'produce power, not reciprocity; they depend upon authority, not independence; they demand loyalty, not criticism; and they seek to exercise coercive if legitimate forms of social control'[441]. These spheres are in

432 Ibid., 45.
433 Ibid., 50.
434 Ibid., 57.
435 Ibid.
436 Ibid.
437 Ibid., 57.
438 Ibid., 98.
439 Ibid., 122.
440 Ibid., 203.
441 Ibid.

constant competition with the civil sphere, and when one is weakened, the other is able to penetrate and extend.

Myriad factors are involved in organizing/initiating, managing as well as successfully accomplishing an act of disagreement, be it a protest, a resistance, a civic action, a sit-in or a social movement. To start with, none of the latter is a solo act; it is a collective action that may involve like-minded supporters who share common interests or identify with the cause or who may just as well disagree with some aspects of the action but support the overall objective. Various theories of social movements have been put forward. Among them, the resource mobilization approach is the most well-known and widely written about. It 'emphasizes both societal support and constraint of social movement phenomena'[442]. Through the lenses of resource mobilization approach the 'variety of resources that must be mobilized, the linkages of social movements to other groups, the dependence of movements upon external support for success, and the tactics used by the authorities to control or incorporate movements' are examined[443]. Actors involved in collective action for social change do not operate in a vacuum, but are part of a structure that controls certain resources. Certainly, the amount controlled by various actors differs. For instance, 'mass constituents, adherents, bystander publics, and opponents are those individuals and groups controlling very limited resource pools'[444]. Time and labour are the most limited resource pool individuals can control, whereas 'elites are those who control larger resource pools'[445].

Resource mobilization can also be affected 'by authorities and the delegated agents of social control (e.g., police)'[446]. This group usually does not support collective action but is able to 'frustrate (normally termed social control) or to enable resource mobilization'[447]. Bystanders, adherents, and constituents may reconsider their participation based on police action and may even 'alter their own status and commitment'[448]. In some cases (although rare) social control agents may turn into adherents and constituents. The role identity plays in modern collective action has been the central issue that new social movement theory has focused

---

442 John D. McCarthy and Mayer N. Zald, "Resource Mobilization and Social Movements: A Partial Theory," *American Journal of Sociology* 82, no. 6 (1977): 1213.

443 Ibid.

444 Ibid., 1221.

445 Ibid.

446 Ibid., 1222.

447 Ibid.

448 Ibid.

on. According to Melucci, 'the social construction of collective identity is both a major prerequisite and a major accomplishment of the new social movements'[449]. On the other hand, 'much collective action is nested in networks of submerged groups that occasionally coalesce into self-referential forms of organization for struggle-but often on a temporary basis'[450]. Therefore, it is preferable to speak not of movements but of 'movement networks or movement areas to capture the transitory nature of much contemporary mobilization'[451].

Issues of the defensiveness or progressiveness of social movements as well as the extent to which these movements are emancipatory have been points of discussion wherein some view social movements as 'primarily defensive reactions to the colonizing intrusions of states and markets into the lifeworld of modern society'[452] and in this way, these social movements are not progressive towards transforming the society. Other scholars argue that, 'although movements are likely to emerge during qualitative breakthroughs in societal modernization (understood in Habermasian terms of increasing differentiation between and within the system and lifeworld), they may be proactive, reactive, or ambivalent with respect to these patterns'[453].

Questions concerning the political or cultural or other nature of social movements have not circumvented the debates. Whether characterized in one or the other way, the 'danger in these discussions is that such terminology can create and perpetuate unfortunate dichotomies that obscure more than they reveal about movements'[454]. Furthermore, in any social movement there usually are elements of cultural and political character. That is to say, 'all movements rest on cultural foundations and play some representational or symbolic

---

449 Alberto Melucci, "Getting Involved: Identity and Mobilization in Social Movements," *International Social Movement Research* 1 (1988): 329–348, quoted in Steven M. Buechler, "New Social Movement Theories," *The Sociological Quarterly* 36, no. 3 (1995): 446.

450 Ibid.

451 Ibid.

452 Jurgen Habermas, "The Theory of Communicative Action," (2 Volumes), (Boston: Beacon, 1984–1987), quoted in Steven M. Buechler, "New Social Movement Theories," *The Sociological Quarterly* 36, no. 3 (1995): 449.

453 Dieter Rucht, "Themes, Logics and Arenas of Social Movements: A Structural Approach," *International Social Movement Research* 1 (1988): 305–328, quoted in Steven M. Buechler, "New Social Movement Theories," *The Sociological Quarterly* 36, no. 3 (1995): 449.

454 Steven M. Buechler, "New Social Movement Theories," *The Sociological Quarterly* 36, no. 3 (1995): 451.

function-hence all movements are cultural in some basic way'[455]. In a similar vein, 'all movements take explicit or implicit political stances, and it can be argued that even those which opt out of any conventional contestation for power have taken a political stance of quietism- hence all movements are political in an equally basic way'[456]. If the emphasis is laid on the political dimension of the movements, there is the expectation that these movements shall be transformative in some way. Moreover, 'political movements are at least in part focused on influencing or altering state power, and such movements must thereby have some explicit strategy aimed at transforming power relations'[457].

Last but not least, in addition to the motivations for joining collective action, the strategies employed to achieve the set objectives, as well as the way relationships develop amongst the supporters alongside other factors, the role emotions play in collective action shall not be overlooked. Emotions are powerful sources that guide both the energy and the frustrations during protests and social movements. They 'do not merely accompany our deepest desires and satisfactions, they constitute them, permeating our ideas, identities, and interests'[458]. Emotions are 'the glue of solidarity- and what mobilizes conflict'[459]. Emotions are triggered through certain terms that are directed at the opponent or whoever is being resisted or protested against. Hence, 'a social movement organizer deploys different language and arouses different emotions in her listeners if she paints her opponents as inherently malevolent or well-meaning but ignorant'[460].

---

455 Doug McAdam, "Culture and Social Movements," in *New Social Movements: From ideology to identity*, eds. E. Larana, H. Johnston and J. R. Gusfield (Temple University Press, 2009), quoted in Steven M. Buechler, "New social movement theories," *The Sociological Quarterly* 36, no. 3 (1995): 451.

456 Ibid.

457 Steven M. Buechler, "New Social Movement Theories," *The Sociological Quarterly* 36, no. 3 (1995): 451.

458 James M. Jasper, "The Emotions of Protest: Affective and Reactive Emotions in and around Social Movements," *Sociological Forum* 13, no. 3 (September, 1998): 399.

459 Randall Collins, "Stratification, Emotional Energy, and the Transient Emotions," In *Research Agendas in the Sociology of Emotions*, ed. Theodore D. Kemper (Albany: Suny Press, 1990): 28, quoted in James M. Jasper, "The Emotions of Protest: Affective and Reactive Emotions in and around Social Movements," *Sociological Forum* 13, no. 3 (September, 1998): 399.

460 Marsha L. Vanderford, "Vilification and Social Movements: A Case Study of Pro-Life and Pro-Choice Rhetoric," *Quarterly Journal of Speech* 75 (1989): 166–182, quoted in James M. Jasper, "The Emotions of Protest: Affective and Reactive Emotions in and around Social Movements," *Sociological Forum* 13, no. 3 (September, 1998): 401.

While the role of ideology in movements is undoubtedly important, 'it is affects and emotional responses that political organizers appeal to, arouse, manipulate and sustain to recruit and retain members'[461]. It is, therefore, not surprising that some collective actions last longer than others or fail to mobilize bigger crowds altogether. It would be useful to illustrate this point through discussing some primarily affective and reactive responses that matter in terms of collective action. Hatred, hostility or loathing, primarily affective emotions 'are a powerful step in the creation of outrage and the fixing of blame'[462]. These emotions are aimed at a target that is to blame for the situation that has triggered outrage amongst the public. Furthermore, these affective emotions are capable of 'altering goals from practical results to punishment of opponents'[463]. Solidarity and loyalty are also primarily affective emotions, that is, 'positive feelings toward others that can lead to action on behalf of that group or category'[464].

Primarily reactive emotions are also involved in collective action. Amongst them anger, grief, loss, sorrow, compassion, sympathy or pity as well as joy and hope, and so on can be channelled in many directions and for different purposes. For instance, one may join a protest for a domestic abuse victim because 'one can imagine the plight of others and develop a desire to help them'[465]. Joy and hope, on the other hand, are positive reactions to the 'joys of empowerment, a sense of "flow" in protest and politics, or the anticipation of a better state of affairs in the future'[466]. Affects and responses, i.e. affective and reactive emotions outside the movement may be the stimuli for people to join a protest, identify with the cause or support a movement in one way or another. Moreover, affects and responses interact and both positive and negative emotions may prove decisive in respect of attracting supporters, losing them, mobilizing the movement further or stifling it. It is also noteworthy that affects and responses operate as much inside the movement as outside it. That is to say, anger can be channelled toward a state official regarding a certain decision, but it can also be channelled toward a movement member, thereby affecting the supporter's allegiance or defection[467].

---

461 James M. Jasper, "The Emotions of Protest: Affective and Reactive Emotions in and around Social Movements," *Sociological Forum* 13, no. 3 (September, 1998): 405.

462 Ibid., 406.

463 Ibid.

464 Ibid.

465 Ibid.

466 Ibid.

467 Ibid., 397–424.

3.8 Collective action frames

Movement actors play a key role in producing and maintaining meaning for constituents, antagonists, bystanders or observers[468]. Together with the media, local governments, and the state, movement actors are involved in "the politics of signification"[469]. Signification or meaning construction is conceptualized in social movement literature as 'framing'[470]. It signifies the process of defining the reality, packaging and representing issues to attract supporters. Framing comprises 'agency and contention at the level of reality construction'[471]. Agency is entailed 'in the sense that what is evolving is the work of social movement organizations or movement activists'[472]. Whereas contention denotes 'the generation of interpretive frames that not only differ from existing ones but may also challenge them'[473]. As a result of framing, 'collective action frames' are produced[474]. Primarily defined from the work of Goffman, frames are 'schemata of interpretation' enabling individuals 'to locate, perceive, identify, and label occurrences within their life space and the world at large'[475]. Collective action frames play a crucial role in the activities and campaigns of social movements in that they inspire, legitimate and guide the action that follows.

Moreover, framing aims at diagnosing the situation that is in need of change. Diagnosing proceeds with identifying 'the source(s) of causality, blame, and/or culpable agents'[476]. In other words, noncompliant actors seek to determine the responsible entity for a situation that is to be remedied. Oftentimes, however, agreement as to who is to blame for the situation gets tangled in controversies. This, in turn, may lead to tension and conflict among the actors of change jeopardising the direction or end result of collective action. Collective action

468 Robert D. Benford and David A. Snow, "Framing Processes and Social Movements: An Overview and Assessment," *Annual Review of Sociology* 26, no. 1 (2000): 611–639.

469 Ibid., 613.

470 Ibid., 611–639.

471 Ibid., 614.

472 Ibid.

473 Ibid.

474 Ibid.

475 Erving Goffman, "Frame Analysis: An Essay on the Organization of the Experience," (New York, Harper Colophon, 1974): 21, quoted in Robert D. Benford and David A. Snow, "Framing Processes and Social Movements: An Overview and Assessment," *Annual Review of Sociology* 26, no. 1 (2000): 615.

476 Robert D. Benford and David A. Snow, "Framing Processes and Social Movements: An Overview and Assessment," *Annual Review of Sociology* 26 (2000): 616.

frames, in addition to diagnosing the situation or the problem, need to be motivational, that is, provide a rationale for joining collective action for change. Motivational framing also includes 'the construction of appropriate vocabularies of motive'[477], that is, wording the problem in ways that attracts supporters and puts the struggle into a certain perspective.

Collective action frames are processes hardly bereft of conflict. The reality that is constructed as a result is not unquestionably imposed on and/or freely accepted by the targets. On the contrary, collective action frames have to counter other competing frames in the process of reality construction. The framing activity usually confronts three forms of challenges: 'counterframing by movement opponents, bystanders, and the media; frame disputes within movements; and the dialectic between frames and events'[478]. Counterframing implies 'attempts to rebut, undermine, or neutralize a person's or group's myths, versions of reality, or interpretive framework'[479]. Framing contests also make part of framing activity. Framing contests refer to 'attempts to ward off, contain, limit, or reverse potential damage to the movement's previous claims or attributes'[480]. Framing processes are not static, but dynamic and fluid and prone to be affected by the context in which they are situated. Thus, in the course of collective action, frames are continuously reviewed, altered, reproduced and remade.

As much as framing activity is aimed at change, its scope can also be limited by factors that cannot be easily contained, such, as for instance, the political situation, cultural constraints and the people that are intended to benefit from collective action frames. Collective action frames are a group activity built around like-minded people who agree that change is necessary and design and pursue a variety of strategies to resist power and domination. Resistance can take different forms, be it mass popular action, protests, civil disobedience or even armed struggle. The desired outcome is socio-political change, but whether it is achieved, 'depends on the balance of forces, the existence of a political subject prepared to take power and on contingent events'[481]. Also, since collective

477 Ibid., 617–618.

478 Ibid., 625.

479 Robert D. Benford, "Framing Activity, Meaning and Social Movement Participation: The Nuclear Disarmament Movement," PhD thesis (University of Texas, Austin, 1987): 75, quoted in Robert D. Benford and David A. Snow, "Framing Processes and Social Movements: An Overview and Assessment," *Annual Review of Sociology* 26, no. 1 (2000): 626.

480 Ibid.

481 Costas Douzinas and Conor Gearty, eds. *The Meanings of Rights: The Philosophy and Social Theory of Human Rights* (Cambridge University Press, 2014), 86.

action frames involve identity construction, internal rifts between activists and/or protest groups can influence the overall end result. Collective resistance is a joint action that thrives on the 'we' feeling of the resisting group. At the start 'we', a politically defined group seeks rights and when '"we" succeeds in obtaining rights it loses its "we-ness" and dissolves into individuals'[482]. However, the 'we-ness' needs to first be maintained throughout the resistance phase in order to conquer the claimed rights before dissolving into individuals.

Human rights define relationships, duties and responsibilities in addition to being entitlements for individuals. As much as 'human rights' is an overwhelmingly entertaining concept theoretically, the rigidity of theory needs to be tested in practice. It is in that pragmatic field that various actors interact by way of 'talking about, advocating for, criticizing, studying, legally enacting, vernacularizing, and so on, the idea of human rights in its different forms'[483]. Actors include 'all of the different individuals, institutions, states, international agencies, and so on, who practice human rights within any number of different social contexts'[484]. While human rights theory defines what human rights mean, what they stand for and what they should be like, it is in practice that the theory is tested and it is the practice that unveils the intricacy of diverse interactions, relationships, tensions among actors with regard to power and identity etcetera. After all, human rights do not exist in a vacuum; rather, 'human rights regimes coexist with other competing rule systems'[485]. The process of conquering rights does not imply automatic translation of abstractions into pure entitlements. It involves contestation, negotiation, disagreement, production and reproduction in respect of knowledge, meaning and experience. The existence of international human rights instruments – treaties, conventions, covenants etcetera, and the states' ratification of the latter, have proven to be of little use precisely for the fact that

482 Wendy Brown, "States of Injury: Power and Freedom in Late Modernity," (Princeton University Press, 1995): 98, quoted in Costas Douzinas and Conor Gearty, eds. *The Meanings of Rights: The Philosophy and Social Theory of Human Rights* (Cambridge University Press, 2014), 115.

483 Mark Goodale, "Introduction: Locating Rights, Envisioning Law between the Global and the Local," In *The Practice of Human Rights: Tracking Law between the Global and the Local*, eds. Mark Goodale and Sally Engle Merry (Cambridge University Press, 2007), 24.

484 Ibid.

485 Laura Nadel, "Introduction: Registers of Power," In *The Practice of Human Rights: Tracking Law between the Global and the Local*, eds. Mark Goodale and Sally Engle Merry (Cambridge University Press, 2007), 119.

international human rights regime is 'a fruitless endeavour unless achieved by indigenous actors comfortable in their own socio-legal contexts'[486].

3.9 Conclusion

In this chapter I have put together a sociological account of human rights which is the approach applied to my study of human rights perceptions and practices of non-state actors in Armenia, their role in holding the state accountable for its human rights violations and the ways in which these non-state actors interact with the state, one another and the citizenry at large. The aim is not to either confirm or deny the universality of human rights, but, rather to challenge it and examine the concepts, practices and experiences through which human rights have meaning at different levels and find out the 'dimensions through which universal rights, believed to be entailed by a common human nature, are enacted, debated, practiced, violated, envisioned, and experienced'[487]. For that purpose, I look at the main human rights actors and their claims-making through different forms of collective action – protests, acts of civil disobedience, demonstrations, rallies and local civic initiatives. Claims-making in relation to rights implies continuous struggle and negotiation with the state, struggle that takes place in the realm of practice.

Human rights actors, intermediaries or translators as they are also called are deemed as rational agents that translate universal human rights norms into domestic settings, frame issues in ways that are accessible to the local population and do so through schemata of interpretation that are concrete and thin. The field within which they operate contains tensions, disagreements and confrontations manifest in the ways these actors interact with the state, with one another and even in the ways they are perceived by the general public. It is these themes I aim to explore and explain in the following chapters in my study of the exercise of human rights in Armenia and the role and interactions of non-state actors in that process.

486 Faiz Ahmed, "Judicial Reform in Afghanistan: A Case Study in the New Criminal Procedure Code," *Hastings International and Comparative Law Review* 29, no. 1 (2005): 20, quoted in *The Practice of Human Rights: Tracking Law between the Global and the Local*, eds. Mark Goodale and Sally Engle Merry (Cambridge University Press, 2007), 127.

487 Mark Goodale, "Introduction: Locating Rights, Envisioning Law between the Global and the Local," In *The Practice of Human Rights: Tracking Law between the Global and the Local*, eds. Mark Goodale and Sally Engle Merry (Cambridge University Press, 2007), 133.

4 Methodology

4.1 Rationale for qualitative research

This thesis aims at exploring the role non-state actors play in improving the human rights situation in Armenia and pressurizing the Armenian state to comply with internationally recognized human rights standards. For the purposes of this particular research, non-state actors include both formal (NGOs) and informal (individual activists, lawyers, journalists and academics) civil society actors. Civil society in this regard is understood as the citizenry at large that is actively participating both in the social and political life in Armenia. Thus, civil society includes but is not limited to individual citizens, community organizations, Non-Governmental Organizations (NGOs), as well as Civil Society Organizations (CSOs) that are independent from the government. This research aims at revealing the ways these non-state actors interact with the state and its institutions, but also with one another and the civil society in general. Since human rights are based on the relationship between the state and the citizens, these two actors can both impact as well as hinder each other's activity with regard to human rights implementation. Their relationship is mutually constitutive, therefore, in order to get a full picture as to why human rights practice succeeds or fails in the Armenian context, as well as how the state and non-state actors interact with one another to shape the culture and politics of human rights in Armenia, it is paramount to carefully analyse the role played by each of these actors.

This research project focuses on the processes of meaning-making and interpretation in the course of public assemblies, rallies, demonstrations and/or protests in Armenia. It looks at the ways non-state actors 'engage in various actions to lead the general population to an alternative view' of human rights enjoyment and democratic governance in this particular case[488]. Individual non-state actors or activists as they are referred to throughout this research project are viewed as 'less constrained by social forces, albeit still embedded within, cultural forms, practices, and meaning'[489]. These individual actors 'have more agency by way of freedom, choice and autonomy' and 'can take preexisting cultural

488 Joshua D. Atkinson, *Journey into Social Activism: Qualitative Approaches* (Fordham University Press, 2017), 39.

489 Ibid.

meanings and use them to express their own thoughts and ideas'[490]. Hence, the key actors that lie at the core of this research project are viewed as 'creative, dynamic social *entities* striving and strategizing to manage their circumstances so as to construct a meaningful and satisfying life for themselves and those with whom they are closely bonded'[491]. This is a study of the perceptions and practices of key human rights actors (both formal and informal) in the Armenian context, their interactions with one another, the government and the civil society at large and the roles they play in pressing for change. The study takes account of the local context, the historical, socio-economic, cultural and political factors that may impact the human rights practices in Armenia, however, it recognizes that despite being embedded within a specific context, the key actors under study are capable of critically reflecting on that context and finding out ways to change it.

4.2 Sampling

Participants were selected from a variety of professional backgrounds dealing with issues of human rights, social justice, fair elections, fighting bribe and corruption, as well as media freedom and advocacy, amongst others. Bearing in mind the main research question this research study aims at addressing, the selection criteria had to be slightly broad since a focus solely on NGOs and activists interested in human rights would not prove fruitful. Human rights is quite a broad field, covering a wide range of rights, hence the choice for respondents who are active in the field of human rights in general, including women's rights, freedom of expression, right to a peaceful assembly and a peaceful protest, freedom from torture, inhuman, degrading treatment or punishment, LGBTIQ+ (Lesbian, Gay, Bisexual, Transgender/Transsexual, Intersex, Queer/Questioning) rights, to name a few. The objective of this research is to explore how local actors exercise and claim their human rights in Armenia by way of confronting the state and by means of using protests, demonstrations and rallies as sites for their activities. Despite their activity in various areas related to human rights, they are allegedly fighting for a common cause, i.e. strengthening the civil society, establishing democracy, improving Armenia's human rights record and holding the state accountable for failure to fulfil its duties as a rights provider.

For scientific research, a diverse sample of respondents is essential since each of these respondents engages in human rights advocacy and protection

---

490 Ibid.

491 Roger A. Straus, "The Theoretical Frame of Symbolic Interactions: A Contextualist, Social Science," *Symbolic Interaction* 4, no. 2 (1981): 266.

differently. The knowledge each of them produces respectively is different as well. For instance, activists may 'focus on telling compelling personal cases with simple story lines of suffering and responsibility supported by statistical documentation of the extent and frequency of the problem'[492]. These are intended 'to generate outrage and action'[493]. Academics, on the other hand, 'are likely to tell more complex stories', with abuses being 'typically understood in the context of systemic features of political and economic organization rather than individual villainy'[494]. While 'human rights activists frame their stories in universal terms, anthropologists and many local activists present more contextually specific accounts of social injustice and its possibilities for resolution'[495].

A third category of actors, 'legally oriented human rights organizations, shape their accounts as legal cases'[496]. Depending on the target audience, they may adopt different narratives. For example, 'in order to be persuasive to the general public, narratives need to be straightforward and emotionally engaging. To be persuasive to an academic audience, they require nuance and intricacy as well as a little jargon. Outrage and moral judgments must be muted, if they appear at all'[497]. Hence, 'these accounts differ in the more legalistic way evidence is considered, the more personal way narratives are constructed, the more universalistic framework for the violation, and the greater claim to truth and certainty'[498]. Lawyers and journalists, the other remaining categories of respondents that have formed part of this research, differ by way of their specialised approach to human rights. The former protect the rights of the abused in accordance with existing domestic laws and international human rights instruments. Their work follows a country's legal framework and international human rights instruments. Journalists, in turn, are helpful and crucial allies in bringing human rights abuses and violations to light. Their media coverage and publicity of abuses have often served as evidence against rights violating states and 'war crimes suspects from Rwanda and the former Yugoslavia, and most recently from Sierra Leone and Liberia'[499].

492 Sally Engle Merry, "Anthropology and Activism: Researching Human Rights across Porous Boundaries," *PoLAR* 28 (2005): 241.

493 Ibid.

494 Ibid.

495 Ibid.

496 Ibid.

497 Ibid.

498 Ibid.

499 Ibrahim Seaga Shaw, "Human Rights Journalism: A Critical Conceptual Framework," In *Human Rights Journalism*, ed. Ibrahim Seaga Shaw (London: Palgrave Macmillan, 2012), p. 26.

Participants were selected through purposeful sampling[500], that is, preference was attached to information-rich cases to aid the in-depth study of the research project in question. Selection of the participants proceeded according to the following criteria: aged 25 and above, University graduates, preferably individuals holding a degree in studies of human rights, democracy and related subjects, absent a degree in the said subjects, at least some sort of training or seminar participations in advocacy, awareness raising, democratization, elections monitoring and the like, individuals considering themselves activists or deemed as such by the media and the general public, possessing experience in protests, demonstrations or civic activities. In order to get diverse perspectives on the subject of study, participants from a variety of backgrounds were selected, such as journalists, lawyers, political scientists, political analysts, social, political activists, feminist and LGBTIQ+ activists, human rights defenders, politicians and a representative from the Office of the Ombudsman.

Additional criteria that played a role in the selection of the participants included their long-term experience in the field of human rights, in addition to them being covered in the media and having a large following on the social media, frequent activity in posting and engaging in discussions of social and political issues related to Armenia and last but not least, individuals cooperating with international organizations with regard to reports on country human rights performance as well as those that have in one way or another come into confrontation with law enforcement officials. Thus, I have sought individuals with knowledge of human rights, experience in human rights advocacy and campaigning and actively engaged in diverse social and political causes, such as, political prisoners, victims of domestic violence, discrimination against sexual minorities, and so on. Selection of NGOs followed a similar strategy. Preference was attached to those NGOs that deal with human rights advocacy and awareness raising, provide training in human rights, democracy and civil society related fields, have been active for at least 5–10 years, cooperate with international organizations, are frequently reported in the media and release reports on human rights issues in Armenia. An additional factor in selecting the NGOs has

---

500 Michael Patton, (1990). Qualitative evaluation and research methods (pp. 169–186). SAGE Publications, Inc.; Margarete Sandelowski, "Sample Size in Qualitative Research." *Research in Nursing and Health* 18, no. 2 (1995): 179–183; Janice M. Morse, (1991). "Strategies for sampling." In *Qualitative Nursing Research: A Contemporary Dialogue*, ed. Janice M. Morse (Sage Publications, 1990).

been provision of legal services/counselling to citizens whose rights may have been breached.

A year prior to fieldwork potential participants meeting the aforementioned criteria were filtered. NGOs were singled out using the website of 'Human Rights House Network' that has a list of member organizations working in the field of human rights and University of Minnesota Human Rights Library which has a Directory of NGOs based in Armenia. I created a file where I noted down all potential NGOs along with their date of foundation, mission, vision, donors, cooperation, activity, budget, staff and contact details. I focused on those NGOs whose mission statement had 'human rights', 'democracy', 'civil society' and 'rule of law' as key words. Additionally, I carefully examined their websites and news and publications section to determine their activity in the stated fields. Their annual reports were downloaded and separately saved to be examined in order to prepare the interview questions later on. I entered the names of the filtered NGOs in the Google Search Engine to find out the frequency of their coverage in the media, the frequency of publications of reports on human rights issues in Armenia as well as any other news in relation to their activity.

It was necessary to employ the best strategy to contact the selected individual participants. Since I have been living outside Armenia for the last few years and following the events from afar and am not an activist myself, I had mixed feelings about interviewing my potential respondents and was feeling slightly anxious about contacting them. Therefore, I decided to first thoroughly scan the field with its most known and active participants before opting for this or that activist, academic, political scientist, analyst and/or journalist and lawyer. The fact of having worked with one well-known and respected activist facilitated my search for more participants. I started my search on the social media since all activists are subscribed and actively upload and discuss issues of concern in Armenia. First and foremost, I carefully checked the friend list of my good acquaintance as she is connected with almost all activists in Armenia. Criteria for selection were the number of followers on social media, membership in social and political groups, type and frequency of posts as well as google search for their appearance in news items, TV debates and reports of Armenian NGOs and human rights monitoring bodies. Last but not least, their employment history and their actual employment status and function were also taken into account. Preference was given to those activists who have been involved in the civil sphere for a number of years, have taken part in more than one civic initiative or action as well as those who have become less active.

When selecting journalists, preference was given to those who are actively involved in the public sphere apart from performing their function as professional journalists. Most of them can be found on the social media along with their activity, content, the number of followers and the discussions that their content generates. These journalists are known for their visibility at various protests and demonstrations as well as their courage and bravery in illustrating cases of corruption, illegal activity, deaths in the army, etcetera. They have also often been targets of police interference into their professional activity and participation in protests, especially when covering the events. These journalists were selected from among my mutual friends on the social media after careful study of their activity, content and coverage of the events I was interested in researching. For example, one of the journalists I later accessed and interviewed shares several mutual friends with me on the social media and has made several films about social and political protests in Armenia, corruption cases as well as violations of human rights by police dressed in civil uniforms during demonstrations. She possesses the knowledge, the experience and the skills I needed for my research. Furthermore, she has got familiarity with and exposure to the subject matter under study.

Selection of lawyers was based on the requirement that they have the experience of handling cases of human rights violations, have submitted cases to the European Court of Human Rights and preferably have won at least one case in Strasbourg. The selected individual participants, activists in particular, helped me in this regard by recommending the lawyers that met the required criteria. I carried out additional search with regard to the recommended lawyers myself before opting for this or that one as a potential participant. Politicians were the one category that was quite a challenge for my fieldwork. Selecting potential respondents from among this group was a tough task. Preference was given to former politicians as well as to those that have studied abroad expecting them to be more willing to meet up with me. Furthermore, since my research aims at studying bottom-up struggle for human rights, interviewing politicians was desirable but not a priority.

Prior to contacting individual respondents, I created a file where I noted down each with their educational background, profession/employment and interests. I collected this information based on their Facebook and LinkedIn accounts. I also added a section where I inserted the date I contacted them and the medium via which I did it, that is, email or Facebook. Later on I would insert whether a request for an interview was confirmed or rejected.

4.3 Access

Access to selected participants was obtained via email and/or Facebook. I contacted the NGOs via email available on their websites. NGOs are formal civil society actors, therefore, I preferred to contact them via email to make it look more official and reduce the likelihood of rejection. Whereas informal civil society actors, that is, individual participants were contacted via Facebook. I share mutual friends with most of them and we happen to be in the same groups as well, such as 'Army in reality', 'Stop violence against women', 'Armenian civil society' and so on and that fact might contribute to them agreeing to meet up with me.

The email contained information regarding the subject of the research but caution was taken not to give out too much information about the research. Furthermore, reasons were given for the selection of particular participants: 'since you are active in promoting human rights in Armenia and therefore familiar with the issues and challenges that human rights activists, NGOs as well as the civil society are facing', it would be appreciated to meet up for a discussion. I also informed them in the email about the period I would spend in Armenia doing fieldwork requesting them to let me know whether they would be available for a meeting during that period. The email was prepared both in Armenian and in English. However, the Armenian version yielded faster responses. Over 80 potential respondents were contacted to ensure positive responses were obtained from at least 30 of them. Overall the responses that I received were more positive than I had initially expected. At least 50 respondents confirmed their willingness to participate in the research. The remaining 30 either did not respond, replied by mentioning their unavailability during the mentioned period or turned down the invitation for an interview.

In addition, once on site, I reviewed the list of participants and filtered it further, replacing some participants with others as recommended by some of my key informants and following a careful study of the history of the participants to determine whether they indeed met the required criteria. Newly added participants were contacted via telephone. I then introduced myself, briefly described what it was I was doing and named the contact that had recommended them. The latter helped me avoid rejection. During the entire fieldwork I had to review the list of my participants on a daily basis and as a result, new respondents were contacted and some of the initially selected ones were left out, since their activity in the field of human rights on the ground turned out to be different from what they demonstrated online. At the end of the fieldwork, 30 semi-structured interviews were completed with a variety of actors in the field of human rights in Armenia.

4.4 Data collection

Primary data for this research were collected through 30 semi-structured interviews. I had studied the field with its key actors for a year prior to conducting my fieldwork through reports in the media, by local and international NGOs and human rights organizations as well as live transmission of protests and demonstrations and last but not least, online interactions on the social media in order to familiarize myself with the main issues surrounding human rights protection and implementation in Armenia, successes or failures of protests and to find out for myself which actor played in which 'camp', what it was my (selected) participants agreed upon with one another and which aspects of the study in question they disagreed upon. Social and political protests and their outcomes were widely discussed on the social media throughout the active phase by not only the active part of the population, the focus of my research, but the citizenry at large, exposing me to various opinions on the subject matter as well as views the active part of the population held on each other. I noted down those aspects that were relevant to my research, such as, for example, the demarcation line between 'the civil' and 'the political', an oft-used call during protests, the irony some of my selected key informants employed when exchanging thoughts on 'activists', the pejoratives they used to address them as well as the accusatory exchanges I came across once the protests died down among others.

Examination of media articles, human rights reports by local and international NGOs and human rights organizations, observations of live transmissions of protests and online interactions on the social media helped me to design a subject guide where I listed all of the important topics I was interested in covering with the participants. I added a number of open-ended questions that I intended to use as icebreakers to start the conversations and get them going. Generally, I was interested in the participants' experiences of activism, protests, human rights violations, confrontations with law enforcement officials and so on. More specifically, I was interested in their individual stories about being active, what they thought of this or that protest or civic initiative in Armenia, how they had evolved as citizens through activism, what ideologies and principles they maintained and in which ways those had shaped their interactions with fellow citizens and law enforcement officials. I was also keen to find out why some of them had become more passive and wherever and whenever necessary quoted a line I had come across in the media about certain activists to discover their reactions and further comments on it.

As it turned out in the course of my research and the semi-structured interviews I conducted to collect the primary data, the flow of the conversations depended on individual participants, the stories they had to tell, the views they wished to share with me and the way they felt about me. Lawyers provided concise and professional answers, NGO representatives kept it formal adhering largely to their activities as organizations. I needed to probe to extend the scope of what I was being told, such as, for instance, asking them about the differences between what they were doing and what individual citizens were claiming in the street. I could even observe controlled irritation when I asked one NGO representative about a research project that had found out that environmental and humanitarian NGOs were trusted more than Human Rights NGOs. In some instances to make the conversations more relaxed I posed questions about cooperation between the NGOs and the activists or asked questions I had singled out based on their own reports on human rights in Armenia. The political scientists, the journalists and the activists provided more relaxed conversations with lengthier answers. In many of these cases questions arose out of their stories and I then probed further for more details and clarification.

The research is deemed to be low risk; therefore, verbal agreement was obtained prior to each interview. 29 out of 30 respondents agreed for the interviews to be audio recorded and their names to be public when quoting. The only interviewee who refused to be audio recorded justified his decision by 'I usually turn down invitations for such interviews, but I agreed to meet up with you because we have a mutual friend'. In this case I was perceived more as a journalist than a researcher and that feeling was also reflected in the way the interviewee was responding to my questions – often brief and making it sound like too obvious to require lengthy responses and explanations. The transcript of this particular interview was prepared in the form of notes. The remaining 29 interviews were audio recorded, transcribed and translated into English[501]. The length of the interviews is 1 hour 15 minutes on average. Despite having consented for their names to be made public, the full names of the participants won't be disclosed throughout this research. Most of my respondents know one another and some

501 It needs to be noted that not all interviews were translated into English due to it being time-consuming and some concepts not having direct equivalents in English; this problem was left until after data analysis was completed to check problematic concepts across the theoretical framework.

interviews are more critical than others. I am concerned that disclosing their full names will put strains on their relationships and further aggravate already existing tensions. Therefore, I will refer to them in terms of their professional or public activities, such as lawyers, journalists, NGO representatives, activists, political scientists and so on when quoting interview excerpts.

In addition to the aforementioned primary data, this research project has benefited from secondary sources as well which include public opinion polls and surveys regarding public perceptions on human rights, democracy, corruption and the rule of law in Armenia, data previously collected within other completed research projects such as the ones conducted by The Turpanjian Center for Policy Analysis (TCPA) in Armenia established by the AUA School of Political Science and International Affairs (PSIA). Information and data in relation to the status and violations of different human rights in Armenia were obtained from reports published by international organizations, such as Freedom House, Amnesty International, Human Rights Watch, US Department of State (The Bureau of Democracy, Human Rights and Labor Affairs), The European Court of Human Rights and EU Annual Reports on Human Rights and Democratization as well as domestic human rights NGOs. Media articles have proven quite helpful as secondary sources as well in that they have helped me to build the chronology of the events I have studied, to locate the key actors and obtain a more complete picture of my research.

4.5 Data analysis

As a result of exploring the role of non-state actors in pressurising the Armenian state to comply with internationally recognized human rights standards as well as the ways in which non-state actors interact with one another, the state and the civil society at large, 400 pages of transcripts were generated. As mentioned above, initially the interviews were transcribed into English in order to facilitate the analysis at a later stage. However, this task proved exhausting and the original language of the interviews, Armenian, was eventually elected for reasons of practicality as well as conceptualization. For instance, while the Armenian term 'iravagitakcutyun' most likely equals to 'rights consciousness' in English, 'civic consciousness' and 'legal consciousness' stand close in meaning. Also, 'social consciousness', 'national consciousness' and 'public consciousness' are but few of the terms that are important in the context of human rights perceptions within the Armenian society.

The above-mentioned tension concept-wise arose with regard to other terms as well. For instance, the Armenian 'viz dnel' which is not used in the literary language but is rather common in slang is not easy to find an equivalent for in the English language. It is surely possible to find words that come close, such as 'make effort', 'knock oneself out', 'go out of one's way' and so on but the intensity of meaning the word in Armenian transmits is not easy to equal in English. Rapley suggests that 'the "data" obtained are highly dependent on and emerge from the specific local interactional context which is produced in and through the talk (and concomitant identity work) of the interviewee *and interviewer* [emphasis original]. An awareness of this local context of data production is central to analysing interview data *whatever analytic stance* [emphasis original] is taken when analysing the data'[502]. Furthermore, I embarked on my fieldwork with theoretical and epistemological assumptions and both those assumptions and a detailed study of the local context determined the set of questions that were posed to my respondents and played an important role when analysing the data later on. It is the middle ground between the global and the local as well as the tension between the two that I have aimed to find out through analysing the collected data.

Thematic analysis has served as a tool to analyse the collected data and answer the research questions. In particular, I have been guided by Guest, MacQueen and Namey's (Applied thematic analysis, 2012) and Braun and Clarke's (Using thematic analysis in psychology, 2008) guide on thematic analysis. I have also made use of Ryan and Bernard's (2003) 'Techniques to identify themes'. Thematic analysis 'offers an accessible and theoretically flexible approach to analysing qualitative data'[503]. It proceeds with identifying, analysing, and reporting patterns (themes) within data through minimally organizing and describing the data set in detail[504]. However, besides a rich description, thematic analysis proceeds with interpreting various aspects of the research topic by showing the relationships between patterns (themes).

A 4-step guide to doing thematic analysis of the data includes (1) discovering themes and subthemes, (2) winnowing themes to a manageable few (i.e., deciding which themes are important in any project), (3) building hierarchies of themes or code books, and (4) linking themes into theoretical models[505].

---

502 Timothy Rapley, "The Art(fulness) of Open-Ended Interviewing: Some Considerations on Analysing Interviews," *Qualitative Research* 1, no. 3 (2001): 303.

503 Virginia Braun, and Victoria Clarke, "Using Thematic Analysis in Psychology," *Qualitative Research in Psychology* 3, no. 2 (2006): 77.

504 Ibid.

505 Gery Ryan and Russell Bernard, "Techniques to Identify Themes," *Field Methods* 15, no. 1 (2003): 85–109.

Furthermore, when doing thematic analysis one can adopt an essentialist or realist, a constructionist or a contextualist approach[506]. In the case of the former, the experiences, meanings and the reality of participants are reported. In the case of the constructionist approach the ways in which events, realities, meanings, experiences and so on are the effects of a range of discourses operating within society are examined. Whereas a contextualist approach 'acknowledges the ways individuals make meaning of their experiences, and, in turn, the ways the broader social context impinges on those meanings, while retaining focus on the material and other limits of "reality"'[507]. My analysis of the collected data has followed the contextualist approach; individuals are shaped by the social context in which they are situated. In the case of non-state actors resisting the political authority and power in Armenia, 'resistance' to authority as opposed to 'submission' to authority develops gradually as a result of exposure to injustice, repression, inequality that either directly affects the resisting actor or their close circles, i.e. family, friends, colleagues, acquaintances etcetera. Knowledge, education and experience were found to be important factors affecting motivations and decisions to join protests or civic action. Education enables gathering knowledge which is then invested into acquiring the experience. The reverse is also possible, i.e. educated individuals are more likely to take part in protests and use the experience they obtain during protests to acquire more knowledge by assessing gaps in their knowledge with regard to social movements, democratic governance etcetera.

Furthermore, the act of protest is not a one-man show, but depends on collective acts of resistance. As a matter of fact, knowledge and experience are obtained via interaction amongst individuals within the group. That interaction gives rise to civic consciousness as well as rights consciousness. I define the former as the awareness and perception of an individual citizen of themselves as a member of citizenry endowed with rights and responsibilities. Rights consciousness, in turn, I define as the awareness of rights and legal norms and do's and don'ts ascribed within a particular state and regulating the relationships amongst the individuals in a particular society.

Since this research project aims at answering a specific research question, the emphasis when sorting the data was laid on identifying patterns within the data in relation to interactions between non-state actors, the state and the civil society

506 Virginia Braun and Victoria Clarke, "Using Thematic Analysis in Psychology," *Qualitative Research in Psychology* 3, no. 2 (2006): 77–101.

507 Ibid., 81.

at large. In addition, the relationships between the themes also had to be identified. Themes have been identified at a latent (interpretative) level, that is to say, 'analysis has gone beyond the semantic content of the data. The underlying ideas, assumptions, conceptualizations and ideologies have been identified and theorised as shaping or informing the semantic content of the data'[508]. In other words, 'development of themes at a latent level involves interpretative work, and the analysis that is produced is not just description, but is already theorised'[509].

Phases of thematic analysis

Familiarisation with the data began already at the time of transcription. Both listening to the audio recordings as well as typing the information facilitated immersion in the data. After all audio recordings had been transcribed the data were repeatedly read to search for meanings, patterns and so on. The search to identify themes focused on: *repetitions* – 'topics that occur and reoccur'[510] or are 'recurring regularities'[511]. There are central themes that reoccur throughout the interviews with almost each participant. For instance, 'one has to conquer one's rights' has been reoccurring throughout the interview with one of the respondents.

Indigenous typologies or categories have also been searched for to identify themes, meaning 'local terms that may sound unfamiliar or are used in unfamiliar ways'[512]. 'Viz dnel' (slang) is used by local actors to denote one's efforts of achieving something, in this case, get to it that their rights be respected and conquered. Furthermore, transcripts were read and re-read in order to find metaphors and analogies, since some respondents represented their thoughts and experiences through those. Comparing Armenia's accession to the Council of Europe with 'a multi-unit block of flats' to demonstrate cosmetic changes but prevailing internal risks, the Constitution with 'a sword to attack and a shield with which to defend' accentuating the role of the Constitution as an important reference point for citizens of the Armenian state, as well as referring to political parties as 'customers/clients' are among the few metaphors that were extracted from transcripts. In addition, pro-Russian groups, seeking to distort the perception of human rights, use pejorative words (ethnic slurs) such as *'Gayrope'*

508 Ibid., 84.
509 Ibid.
510 Gery Ryan and Russell Bernard, "Techniques to Identify Themes," *Field Methods* 15, no. 1 (2003): 89.
511 Ibid.
512 Ibid.

('Europe' as it is called by the Russians who support Putin's policy. A widely used term in Russia aimed at constantly reminding the Russians that the Western world wants to destroy their powerful and flourishing nation spreading their filthy culture all over Eastern Europe, also 'a rude term ridiculing Europe's tolerance of gays or implying that Europe is all gays'), *'Pindos'* (used by the Russians to offend US citizens or people with Western way of thinking or people who think that democracy is good), *'Liberast'* ("liberal" + "pederast" (homosexual male)) to ridicule Western values and ways of thinking.

Similarly, the concept of 'gender' has been used pejoratively to spread hatred towards proponents of women's rights and women's rights NGOs. In order to insult one another people will often call each other 'genderast', 'genderik' etcetera. 'Gender' is wrongly perceived in the Armenian society except for the pro-European groups. The understanding is that adoption of 'gender equality' law will allow the LGBTIQ+ community to become more visible and since the LGBTIQ+ community is considered to be an immoral group with un-Armenian values, spreading pejorative words such as *'genderast'*, *'genderik'* pursues the aim of creating negative attitudes and intolerance towards them and their supporters. The '-ik' suffix in Armenian when added to nouns gives them diminutive-hypocoristic meaning. In the case of *'gender-**ik**'* it derogates the meaning of 'gender' reducing it to a mere Western propaganda for LGBTIQ+ rights aimed at the destruction of Armenian values.

The initial stage of theme identification produced a large set of text extracts from the transcripts. The next step included reducing the themes to several important ones through rereading the extracted texts. This phase was facilitated by looking at keywords in each of the selected themes that were commonly used by the respondents. The underlying logic was that commonly used keywords by a variety of respondents highlight the importance of the theme as well as the significance of the keyword for the reality as explained by the key players in the human rights context in Armenia. Below is the thematic analysis diagram that shows the role non-state actors play in the human rights arena in Armenia as well as the ways they interact with one another, the state and the civil society at large:

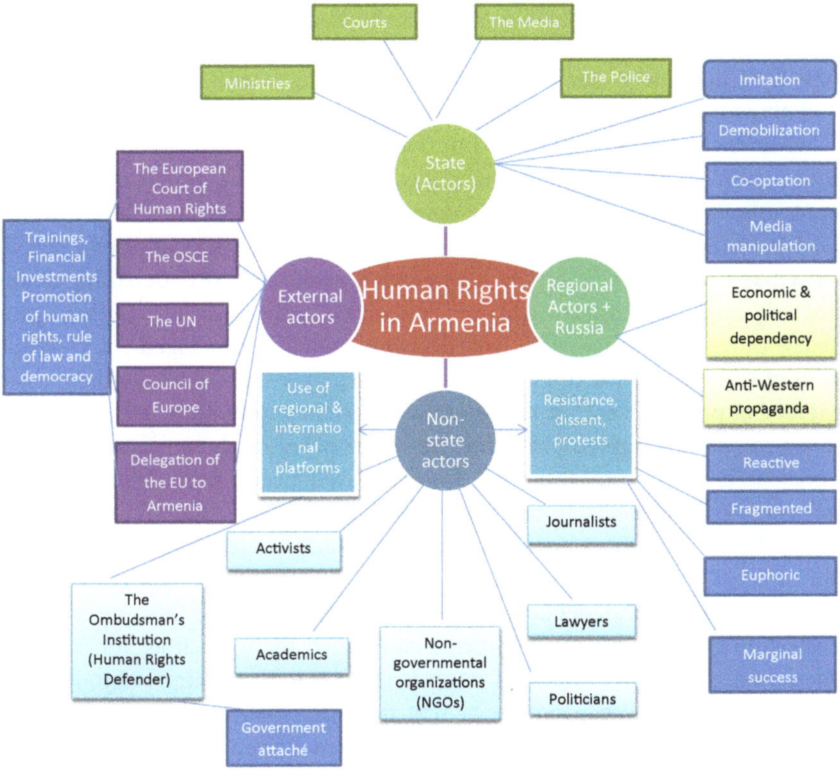

4.6 Limitations

Research is situated within a specific local context and collected data depend on and originate from that context[513]. The latter is a product of the talk between the interviewee and interviewer. Texts on interviews tend to put the interviewee in an active role side-lining the interviewer as an important agent in producing talk. However, the interviewer is just as important in the way he/she leads the conversation, interrupts it, keeps silent, thereby acting decisively upon the end product of the interview. Therefore, the interviewer and the presence of an audio recorder can affect the research in the sense of the responses provided and how

513 Timothy Rapley, "The Art(fulness) of Open-Ended Interviewing: Some Considerations on Analysing Interviews," *Qualitative Research* 1, no. 3 (2001): 303–323.

some respondents may feel about being recorded. Despite reassurances that they could refrain from answering questions they did not want to as well as refraining from the interview at any point, most participants in this research (except for one) opted to be recorded and did so willingly.

No financial reward was offered to them. I assume individual as well as collective motivations to participate ranged from curiosity, political empowerment, informing change, personal interest in the subject, etcetera. Nonetheless, it is hard to assess how lack of some form of reward may have affected research participants. As indicated by Clark 'research is not necessarily something that is passively consumed by those who are "researched" and is instead actively negotiated by those who engage, who make decisions about their engagement'[514]. While the motivations of some respondents might well have been ideology-driven and oriented at personal interest in the subject as well as making their voices heard, others might have agreed to be interviewed to promote the organizations they represent. It is my supposition that this may have placed a limit on the information I was able to obtain from these types of respondents. Namely, representatives of NGOs were more open about questions that had to do with their activity and projects, but rather circumventing when it came to discussing differences between them and independent activists and civic initiatives. At times a visible frustration was directed at me when I challenged them, such as, for instance, when asking them why the trust towards them is low as compared to humanitarian and charity organizations or that they are considered grant-eaters and what they think about it. Furthermore, questions related to political prisoners did not go down smoothly and despite my more than one attempt to get back to those questions later on, I confronted a 'solid wall' that could not be broken.

I believe interviews with NGOs have been produced with some limitations owing to their operating at an institutional level and being placed within limits themselves. Questions perceived as political would rather remain unanswered or talked around rather than having to give out something for which they might have to provide justification outside their institutions. Moreover, my being a PhD student may have limited my interaction with the NGOs. They are operating in Armenia and have to abide by the 'rules of the game' and balance their criticism of the government's actions in terms of human rights violations. I am placed outside of Armenia and am 'operating' in a foreign institution and from their perspective I may be perceived as 'foreign amongst their own' that shall

514 Tom Clark, "On 'Being Researched': Why Do People Engage with Qualitative Research?" *Qualitative Research* 10, no. 4 (2010): 400.

be treated with caution and distance. I believe my identity has been a limitation in my interaction with this group of respondents. Nevertheless, the question as to how heads of NGOs would behave or answer certain questions were the interviewer a foreign researcher or working for a foreign donor organization is not one that is easily answerable. Finally, I have used this limitation as data and through careful analysis of NGO talk have drawn some conclusions about the ways NGOs interact with activists and other state and non-state actors. The results are discussed in the findings section.

5 Soviet and post-Soviet human rights practices

5.1 Introduction

It was noted in previous chapters that rights exist in relation to the specific social, political and cultural contexts in which they are embedded. Furthermore, the approach to rights in this research project is dynamic, that is, how human rights norms come into being in different local settings and what factors – social, economic, cultural, political and environmental stand in the way of that process. It is those factors I address and illustrate in this chapter in addition to an overview of Soviet and post-Soviet human rights perceptions and practices and the role those have played in the Armenian context following independence.

Armenia was one of the republics that constituted the USSR (Union of Soviet Socialist Republics) from 1922–1991. As such, human rights were reflected in Soviet Constitutions and subject to them. Even though Armenia gained independence in 1991, the 70 year legacy of the Soviet Union cannot be erased at once. Following the break-up of the Soviet Union, Armenia has undergone different stages, including 3 presidents, switching to a parliamentary system of government with a 4th president, increase in the number of NGOs (Non-governmental organizations) as well as protest groups and, last but not least, improved relations with the European Union and other European institutions. This chapter aims at tracing the perception of human rights in the course of the above-mentioned periods starting with Soviet conceptions of human rights up to and including the ways key human rights actors in Armenia perceive and negotiate them with the Armenian state.

5.2 The Soviet Period

5.2.1 Human rights through different Soviet constitutions and leaders

The Soviet Union has historically displayed a different understanding of, and approach to human rights as compared to the US and the West. The Soviets have, as a matter of fact, prioritized the social, economic and cultural rights[515]. Their

---

515 Mark. B. Smith, "Social Rights in the Soviet Dictatorship: The Constitutional Right to Welfare from Stalin to Brezhnev," *Humanity: An International Journal of Human*

insistence on and prioritization of these rights bears political motifs – a socially and economically fulfilled citizen does not engage in civil and political disobedience. These differences in approach to human rights were reflected in the drafting process of the Universal Declaration which the Soviets abstained from but did not outright reject. Throughout the drafting process of human rights covenants and despite their participation, 'doubts remained about Soviet sincerity toward both the covenants and the Declaration'[516]. When it came to translating and disseminating the Declaration, the Soviets at first complained that their 'proposals had not been taken into consideration' and that 'the Declaration simply was a tool for capitalists, which the Soviet efforts had failed to shape'[517]. Moreover, they accused the Anglo-American bloc of using the declaration 'for purposes of reaction and aggression'[518] and of having cast aside Soviet proposals. In order to prevent any foreign influence at home, the Soviet Union adhered to the principle of non-interference as a norm of international law. Moreover, rights were used as a propaganda technique rather than as a tool to prevent atrocities and defend citizens from state encroachment.

Soviet Constitutions contained sections on rights, although the latter were provided selectively. The first *Soviet Constitution of 1918* had a section on fundamental rights, such as freedom of speech, association, assembly, press, conscience, unions and access to knowledge, as well as equality of civil rights and the right to asylum[519]. Yet, not all citizens could enjoy these rights. Only those who derived their income from their own labour could access the available rights. Access to rights was restricted to prevent slandering the Bolshevik Revolution (restriction of the freedom of speech), setting up counter-revolutionary organizations (restriction of the freedom of association), etcetera[520].

Rights, Humanitarianism and Development 3, no. 3 (2012): 385–406; Mildred Fairchild, "Social-Economic Classes in Soviet Russia," *American Sociological Review* 9, no. 3 (1944): 236–241; Dorena Caroli, "Bolshevism, Stalinism, and Social Welfare (1917–1936)," *International Review of Social History* 48, no. 1 (2003): 27–54.

516 Jennifer Amos, "Embracing and Contesting: The Soviet Union and the Universal Declaration of Human Rights, 1948–1958," In *Human Rights in the Twentieth Century*, ed. Stefan-Ludwig Hoffman (Cambridge University Press, 2010), 153.

517 Ibid., 155.

518 Ibid.

519 Thomas E. Towe, "Fundamental Rights in the Soviet Union: A Comparative Approach," *University of Pennsylvania Law Review* 115 (1967): 1251.

520 Ibid.

The *Stalin Constitution of 1936* contained 16 articles with regard to 'Fundamental Rights and Duties of Citizens'[521]. It granted rights conditionally. This meant that citizens depended on the state for material support and had duties toward it. Those duties 'were sacred and a matter of honor'[522]. Moreover, those engaged in labour could obtain the material means to exercise the provided rights. Hence, 'labor is the indispensable link between duties and rights; it is the key by which fulfilment of duty opens the door to rights'[523]. The Stalin Constitution provided an array of social and economic rights, namely, 'the right to employment, to leisure, to material security in old age and in the event of illness or incapacity to work, to education, up to and including higher education'[524]. It was prohibited to discriminate based on gender, race and/or nationality.

The post-Stalin period presented a different scenario – eliminate 'repressive Stalinist policies but maintain the Communist Party's authority'[525]. It was time for 'socialist legality' to be installed. Socialist legality implied 'adherence to procedural norms and rationalization' as well as '[t]he strict observance of law everywhere and in everything, mandatory for all state agencies, institutions, officials and citizens, provid[ing] a true guarantee for timely suppression of nefarious enemy attempts to harm our people and state'[526]. The new Constitution amended selective granting of rights. Under Article 135 'all citizens of the USSR aged 18 or older, regardless of racial or national membership, faith, educational level, residence, social origin, property status, and past activities'[527] could vote and be elected. In contrast to the 1918 Constitution of the USSR, which accorded freedoms and rights such as freedom of conscience, expression, assembly and

---

521 Ibid.

522 Benjamin Nathans, "Soviet Rights-Talk in the Post-Stalin Era," In *Human Rights in the Twentieth Century*, ed. Stefan-Ludwig Hoffman (Cambridge University Press, 2010), 171.

523 Ibid.

524 Ibid.

525 Jennifer Amos, "Embracing and Contesting: The Soviet Union and the Universal Declaration of Human Rights, 1948–1958," In *Human Rights in the Twentieth Century*, ed. Stefan-Ludwig Hoffman (Cambridge University Press, 2010), 156.

526 Ibid.; Russel E. Burford, "Getting the Bugs out of Socialist Legality: The Case of Joseph Brodsky and a Decade of Soviet Anti-Parasite Legislation," *The American Journal of Comparative Law* 22, no. 3 (1974): 465–508; George L. Kline, "Socialist Legality and Communist Ethics," *Natural Law Forum* 8 (1963): 21.

527 Benjamin Nathans, "Soviet Rights-Talk in the Post-Stalin Era," In *Human Rights in the Twentieth Century*, ed. Stefan-Ludwig Hoffman (Cambridge University Press, 2010), 171.

association only to toilers, the new Constitution 'guaranteed those rights and freedoms by law to citizens of the USSR'[528]. However, the state still used rights as a political tool. Even though 'citizens' were supposed to gain from freedoms, 'their exercise must "correspond to the interests of toilers and the strengthening of the socialist system" '[529].

Even though social mobilization took place following Stalin's death, the social process still remained well under control, 'guided by the Party with society following at a measured pace'[530]. Being a citizen of the Soviet Union was not yet a guarantee that one would be a rights-bearer/holder. Unlike liberal democratic systems where citizenship is interconnected with rights, in the Soviet practice 'the rights of citizenship could be divorced from citizenship itself; one could carry the title of citizen but lack all the rights and protections associated with it'[531]. Civic belonging appeared rather unstable and fragmented owing to rights being a political rather than a judicial matter. The Soviet society was a collectivist one, and individuals were expected to act in accordance with that collectivist spirit. In contrast to individuals as autonomous agents in the West, 'dissenting Stalinist subjects more often appear as selves in crisis, longing to overcome their painful separation from the collective body of the Soviet people'[532].

The post-Stalin era was notable for rights defenders, the other-thinkers whose 'attempts to persuade the Soviet government to obey its own laws, and eventually to obey international covenants signed by Moscow, garnered them considerable attention, especially from the contemporary western media'[533]. The most remarkable feature about this group was their focus on the rule of law in the Soviet Union[534]. They possessed good knowledge of both the local and the international law and 'insisted on practices formally protected by Soviet law – such as

528 Ibid.

529 Ibid.

530 Eugene D. Fryer, "Soviet Human Rights: Law and Politics in Perspective," *Law and Contemporary Problems* 43 (1979): 299.

531 Golfo Alexopoulos, "Soviet Citizenship, More or Less: Rights, Emotions, and States of Civic Belonging," *Kritika: Explorations in Russian and Eurasian History* 7, no. 3 (2006): 489.

532 Jochen Hellbeck, "Speaking Out: Languages of Affirmation and Dissent in Stalinist Russia," *Kritika: Explorations in Russian and Eurasian History* 1 no. 1 (2000): 96.

533 Benjamin Nathans, "The Dictatorship of Reason: Aleksandr Vol'pin and the Idea of Rights under 'Developed Socialism,'" *Slavic Review* 66, no. 4 (2007): 630.

534 Uta Gerlant, " 'The Law Is Our Only Language': Soviet Dissidents and Human Rights," In Rainer Huhle (Hg.), *Human Rights and History. A Challenge for Education* (Berlin, 2010), pp. 130–141.

freedom of assembly or transparency of judicial proceedings but frequently subject to the wrath of the regime'[535]. This strategy reinforced their case since they fought the regime with a weapon that was provided for in the Constitution but frequently withheld in practice. The Soviet law did not serve as a tool to regulate relations between citizens. Instead, its existence was a mere formality designed to 'regulate all aspects of economic and social life, including the circulation of thought, while leaving the critical questions of political power to be decided by informal, secret procedures beyond the scrutiny or control either of legislative or judicial bodies'[536].

Further to this point, within the context of the Soviet law, the state acted more like a mentor for the citizens, supervising every aspect of their social, economic and political life to make sure they did not go astray from the dominant ideology. Thus, the Soviet law functioned primarily 'to discipline, guide, train, and educate Soviet citizens to be dedicated members of a collectivized and mobilized social order'[537]. In the words of Harold Berman: 'In the Soviet concept there is an underlying assumption that the subject of law, legal man, is not a mature, independent adult, not the free-willing- and freewheeling-"reasonable prudent man" of our tradition, but an immature, dependent child or youth, whose law-consciousness must be guided, trained, and disciplined by official legal rules and processes'[538]. The teacher's role in the Soviet conception of law is intended to shape obedient citizens who observe their social duties as enshrined in Article 59 of the Soviet constitution: 'Citizens' exercise of their rights and freedoms is inseparable from the performance of their duties and obligations'[539]. In addition, Article 39 on rights and liberties states that 'the exercise of rights and liberties not be to the detriment of the interests of society or the state, or infringe the rights of other citizens'[540]. The Soviet law, however, underwent reforms following Stalin's death. According to Berman, changes in the Soviet law involved 6 tendencies – 'elimination of political terror, liberalization of procedures and substantive norms, systematization and rationalization of the legal system, decentralization

---

535 Benjamin Nathans, "The Dictatorship of Reason: Aleksandr Vol'pin and the Idea of Rights under 'Developed Socialism,'" *Slavic Review* 66, no. 4 (2007): 630.

536 Harold J. Berman, "The Dilemma of Soviet Law Reform," *Harvard Law Review* (1963): 930–931.

537 Ibid.

538 Harold Berman, "Human Rights in the Soviet Union," *Howard Law Journal* 11, no. 2 (1965): 333–341, quoted in Richard N. Dean, "Beyond Helsinki: The Soviet View of Human Rights in International Law," *Virginia Journal of International Law* 21 (1980): 64.

539 Richard N. Dean, "Beyond Helsinki: The Soviet View of Human Rights in International Law," *Virginia Journal of International Law* 21 (1980): 65.

540 Ibid.

and democratization of decision-making, introduction of popular participation in the administration of justice and threatening those who will not cooperate in building communism with harsh criminal and administrative penalties'[541].

The Soviet state approved only of one ideology, the one advocated by the Party. Any deviations from this norm were subjected to harsh punishments, often resulting in psychiatric confinement, internal exile, incarceration, and so on[542]. Even with the melting of the ice under Nikita Khrushchev (1955–1964), 'political prisoners remained confined in still inhumane, strictly run labor camps and prisons'[543]. Ideological deviance was selectively repressed. Khrushchev, like some of his predecessors, got caught between 'an autocratic regime and a program of rapid economic development'[544]. He 'soon confronted the classic problem which had perplexed Catherine and the two Alexanders. *How can one introduce reforms without jeopardizing the despotic basis of control? How can one revive initiative without stimulating insubordination?* [emphasis added]'[545]. The Khrushchev era provided more relaxation in the sense that repression was somewhat eased, citizens were able to debate but the latter would be curtailed every time it posed a threat to the communist project. The Khrushchev era was 'a time of contestation and change, but not in the familiar liberal-conservative mold'[546].

Brezhnev's years (1964–1982) bore signs of a social compromise, in the sense that his line of thinking edged towards ensuring a certain standard of living for the population and allowing 'a degree of private autonomy'. As a result, he hoped the population would not 'make excessive demands of the state such as

---

541 Harold J. Berman, "The Dilemma of Soviet Law Reform," *Harvard Law Review* (1963): 932.

542 Harvey Fireside, *Soviet Psychoprisons* (London: W.W. Norton & Company, 1979).

543 Peter H. Juviler, *Freedom's Ordeal: The Struggle for Human Rights and Democracy in Post-Soviet States* (University of Pennsylvania Press, 1998), 35–36; Robert Hornsby, "Political Protest and Dissent in the Khrushchev Era," PhD dissertation (University of Birmingham, 2009); Robert M. Cutler, "Soviet Dissent under Khrushchev: An Analytical Study," *Comparative Politics* 13, no. 1 (1980): 15–35; Stephen V. Bittner, *The Many Lives of Khrushchev's Thaw: Experience and Memory in Moscow's Arbat* (London: Cornell University Press, 2008).

544 Peter H. Juviler, *Freedom's Ordeal: The Struggle for Human Rights and Democracy in Post-Soviet States* (University of Pennsylvania Press, 1998), 36.

545 James H. Billington: *The Icon and the Axe: An Interpretive History of Russian Culture* (New York: Knopf, 1958), 551–52, quoted in Peter H. Juviler, *Freedom's Ordeal: The Struggle for Human Rights and Democracy in Post-Soviet States* (University of Pennsylvania Press, 1998), 36.

546 Miriam Dobson, "The Post-Stalin Era: de-Stalinization, Daily Life, and Dissent," *Kritika: Explorations in Russian and Eurasian History* 12, no. 4 (2011): 911.

calling for political involvement, self-governance' etcetera[547]. In other words, he made social compromises to gain political obedience. Brezhnev signed the International Covenant on Civil and Political Rights as well as the one on Social, Economic and Cultural Rights in 1966 and the Supreme Soviet ratified both seven years later[548]. He amended the Soviet Constitution in 1977[549]. In this version human rights were also featuring as part of Soviet foreign policy, especially with the United States, whose newly elected President Carter had criticized the Soviet rights record[550]. Human rights did appear, but only once and 'tellingly, it was in the section on the USSR's relations with foreign states, which were to be based on (among other things) "non-interference in internal affairs" and "respect for human rights and fundamental freedoms" '[551]. This Constitution was not an exception in terms of the interconnectedness of rights and duties. The State would provide the citizens with the material means to exercise their rights but the citizens in turn were expected to be loyal to the state, contribute to building communism and stay away from politics or activities that would challenge the state. The party and the state possessed effective means to fight against dissent and resistance of any kind[552].

The Soviet Constitution has undergone several amendments. The 1977 constitution again marked the significance of 'the goals of building Communism' and granted rights which could only be exercised if they did not 'harm the interests of society or the state'[553]. Rights granted by the Soviets bore asterisks, designed in a manner *as if* Soviet citizens had rights but also acting as deterrents at the same time, ensuring that the genie would not be let out of the bottle; political dissent and ideological deviance had to be contained internally, and

547 Richard Sakwa, *Soviet Politics: An Introduction* (Routledge, 1989), 84.

548 Benjamin Nathans, "Soviet Rights-Talk in the Post-Stalin Era," In *Human Rights in the Twentieth Century*, ed. Stefan-Ludwig Hoffman (Cambridge University Press, 2010).

549 Christopher Osakwe, "Soviet Human Rights Law under the USSR Constitution of 1977: Theories, Realities and Trends," *Tulane Law Review* 56 (1981): 249.

550 Benjamin Nathans, "Soviet Rights-Talk in the Post-Stalin Era," In *Human Rights in the Twentieth Century*, ed. Stefan-Ludwig Hoffman (Cambridge University Press, 2010).

551 Ibid., 183–184.

552 Stefan Troebst, "Sozialistisches Völkerrecht" und die sowjetische Menschenrech tsdoktrin. In: Norbert Frei/Annette Weinke (Hg.): Toward a New Moral World Order? Menschenrechtspolitik und Völkerrecht seit 1945, Göttingen: Wallstein 2013, S. 95 (= Jena Center Geschichte des 20. Jahrhunderts. Vorträge und Kolloquien, 15); David Kowalewski, "Religious Belief in the Brezhnev Era: Renaissance, Resistance and Realpolitik," *Journal for the Scientific Study of Religion* 19, no. 3 (1980): 280–292.

553 Peter H. Juviler, *Freedom's Ordeal: The Struggle for Human Rights and Democracy in Post-Soviet States* (University of Pennsylvania Press, 1998), 44–45.

any external spillover effects had to be blocked. The Communist Party was 'the leading and directing force of Soviet society and had the last word on the limits and meaning of rights'[554]. It was not only the public life of Soviet citizens that was under constant scrutiny, but their private lives as well. The Soviet state was present in the workplace. It intervened in literary creativity, intellectual thought and freedom of whatever type it was[555]. This stranglehold somewhat loosened under Khrushchev 'when the state reduced its policing of the private sphere and individuals began to create unregulated social spaces'[556].

5.2.2 Soviet versus Western/American perceptions of human rights

Human rights was not a welcome concept in Soviet circles at the start. With the Cold War shaping the foreign policies of both the Soviet Union and the Anglo-American bloc, as well as attempts at containing dissent at home while satisfying international audiences, the Soviet Union was playing a well-thought-out political game. Human rights were used as part of Soviet foreign policy. In response to accusations of abusive Soviet human rights practices or failures to secure human rights provisions for the home population, the Soviet Foreign Ministry 'highlighted the domestic successes in literacy, social security, scientific progress, workers' rights, freedom of the press, and other rights'[557]. Moreover, Soviet achievements were contrasted with 'American discrimination, English unemployment, French imperialism, Lebanese illiteracy, Mexican inequality, and issues in other countries'[558]. Human rights promotion internationally was not an issue, whereas 'similar discussions domestically were actively blocked by the Ministry'[559].

Differences in Soviet and Western conceptions of rights have got to do with the political philosophies that underlie both systems. As a Russian prosecutor told a private US human rights delegation to Moscow in 1989: 'We live on two different planets. An attempt to transplant U.S. legal institutions in the USSR would

---

554 Ibid.

555 Robert Horvath, "Breaking the Totalitarian Ice: The Initiative Group for the Defense of Human Rights in the USSR," *Human Rights Quarterly* 36, no. 1 (2014): 147–175.

556 Ibid., 150.

557 Jennifer Amos, "Embracing and Contesting: The Soviet Union and the Universal Declaration of Human Rights, 1948–1958," In *Human Rights in the Twentieth Century*, ed. Stefan-Ludwig Hoffman (Cambridge University Press, 2010), 155.

558 Ibid.

559 Ibid.

be like an agrarian project on Mars'[560]. Whereas the Western understanding of human rights is grounded in the natural law theory, according to which humans have rights by virtue of their humanity and possess rights from the moment they are born, the Soviet conceptions of human rights are grounded in Marxist and Leninist economic and political philosophy which 'reject the natural law theory of jurisprudence and substantially modify the positive law theory. There are no absolute laws derived from reason, nature or God upon which the legal system can be based'[561]. It is economics rather than fundamental laws that form the basis of the legal order.

Although in the post-Stalin period the notion of 'socialist legality' was introduced to curtail extra-legality and enforce greater observance of, and respect for the law, the notion was liberally misused in the higher Soviet ranks 'to implement party policy, whatever that policy may be'[562]. Examples are changes in policy in 1961 'to increase the punishment for embezzlement, theft and dishonesty in dealing with government property'[563]. When it came to the party, the concept, thus, had little practical content. The Communist Party had the final say in almost every aspect of social and, in particular, political life of the society. This placed them above the law, 'with their own code of behavior'[564]. Furthermore, 'the party had its procedures for censure and discipline of its members took precedence over court action'[565]. This extra-legality also provided the families of the party members with protection from criminal prosecution. What mattered was to know 'someone with connections and influence'[566].

State over individual prioritization is another telling difference that sets apart the Soviet system of government from that of the US. Whereas the Soviet Union system of government prioritises the state over the individual, in the US, for instance, government's powers are limited, and the individual is granted strong protections. In other words, 'The capitalist law is based upon the abstract "natural rights" of an individual; it places the individual in the center of the world, surrounds him with a cult and therefore establishes limits to the State

560 Peter H. Juviler, *Freedom's Ordeal: The Struggle for Human Rights and Democracy in Post-Soviet States* (University of Pennsylvania Press, 1998), 7.
561 Thomas E. Towe, "Fundamental Rights in the Soviet Union: A Comparative Approach," *University of Pennsylvania Law Review* 115 (1967): 1255.
562 Ibid., 1259.
563 Ibid.
564 Ibid., 1260.
565 Ibid.
566 Ibid.

... However, the proletarian State sets the limits not to itself but to its citizens. A collective body called the State, rather than the individual citizen, is at the center of the proletarian law. Emphasis is placed on collective action'[567], since 'only through the collective can the individual realize his rights and fully develop his natural potential'[568]. Furthermore, the collective is 'the unit of philosophical, political and *legal* primacy in the Soviet socialist system'[569].Therefore, any acts that run contrary to the collective should be repressed. In this case, collective is also understood as the socialist system, while dissent is considered individual action.

The biggest challenge to human rights in the Soviet Union has been presented by the judicial system. In contrast to the West, the three branches of the government were not separate in the Soviet Union. This has led to what Pribán terms *"telephone justice"*, in which 'courts could decide independently unless their deliberations were interrupted by a member of the Party élite members who exercised the power to influence the case'[570]. The guarantee of human rights in the Soviet Union was like a political deal struck on an economic base whereby 'the population was provided with some guarantee of its material existence but in return was required not to interfere in political affairs'[571]. Close oversight was exercised on the citizens' obedience to the established ideology by means of the secret police, the army and paramilitary organizations, the courts and prosecutors. Later though, as the army's role faded and the power declined, domination was executed through the 'judicial power and legal institutions. Instead of the party militia, it was courts and prosecutors who had become the real "iron fist" of the Party and working class'[572]. The Soviet perspective on human rights was tailored around duties of the individual towards the Soviet state. The state took care of the citizens with social welfare rights provisions, such as the right to

567 Thomas E. Towe, "Fundamental Rights in the Soviet Union: A Comparative Approach," *University of Pennsylvania Law Review* 115 (1967): 1264.

568 Richard N. Dean, "Beyond Helsinki: The Soviet View of Human Rights in International Law," *Virginia Journal of International Law* 21 (1980): 62.

569 Doriane Lambelet Coleman, "The Contradiction Between Soviet and American Human Rights Doctrine: Reconciliation Through Perestroika and Pragmatism," *Boston University International Law Journal* 7 (1989): 72.

570 Jiří Přibáň, "Political Dissent, Human Rights and Legal Transformations: Communist and Post-Communist Experiences," *East European Politics and Societies* 19, no. 4 (2005): 558.

571 Ibid., 559.

572 Ibid., 562.

employment, the right to housing, access to free health care, etcetera. However, these rights carried certain impediments. The right to employment, for example, implied the legal duty to work, the right to housing made the employee dependent on the employer to provide housing, and access to free health care existed side by side with corrupt doctors and health care executives[573].

Western and Soviet conceptions of human rights differ in terms of 'semantics'[574]. The Americans', as well as most Westerners' use of 'the single term "human rights" is fraught with a cultural, ideological and political significance that is, ultimately, very different from the significance attached to the term by Soviets and socialists generally'[575]. Hence, when one criticizes the other for their human rights violations, the rights each target are different. In the case of Americans and/or Westerners accusing the Soviets of rights violations, the latter are freedom of speech, association, religion, emigration, and the press[576]. The Soviets, on the other hand, focus on 'concepts such as the absolute right to work, the right to shelter, the right to medical care and the right to education'[577]. The Soviet Union only recognises conventional law and customary law as binding[578]. It rejects general principles since non-interference in its domestic affairs has always been paramount. The Soviet Union, thus, has 'a highly positivistic approach to international as well as domestic lawmaking'[579]. This means that the Soviet Union only recognizes as binding those human rights norms which are enshrined in Soviet law.

Last but not least, for Soviet citizens rights are not protections against government oppression but, rather, '"opportunities" guaranteed by the state'[580]. Soviet human rights theory as well as traditional international law coincide in terms of the significance they attach to the primacy, centrality, and sovereignty

---

573 Jiří Přibáň, "Political Dissent, Human Rights and Legal Transformations: Communist and Post-Communist Experiences," *East European Politics and Societies* 19, no. 4 (2005): 553–572.

574 Doriane Lambelet Coleman, "The Contradiction Between Soviet and American Human Rights Doctrine: Reconciliation Through Perestroika and Pragmatism," *Boston University International Law Journal* 7 (1989): 61.

575 Ibid., 61–62.

576 Ibid.

577 Ibid.

578 John T. Evrard, "Human Rights in the Soviet Union: The Policy of Dissimulation," *DePaul Law Review* 29 (1979): 819.

579 Ibid., 823.

580 Richard N. Dean, "Beyond Helsinki: The Soviet View of Human Rights in International Law," *Virginia Journal of International Law* 21 (1980): 69.

of the state[581]. This is because the state has the duty to protect and it is a primary actor in international law[582]. Soviet human rights theory, thus, 'reflects legal conservativism, as well as ideological conviction'[583]. Ironically, some civil and political rights were guaranteed in the Soviet Constitution; however, their enjoyment had to be channelled at 'reinforcing the status quo through their civic behavior'[584]. Any citizen deviating from the established norm and expected mode of behaviour faced 'long imprisonment or even death; hence, the vast majority of people remained silent and assembled only in approved places under official auspices'[585].

5.2.3 The rise of dissent and the Helsinki Final Act

Prior to the 1970s, human rights did not have much resonance in the Soviet Union and did not feature in East-West relations. Despite its approval of the 1948 Universal Declaration of Human Rights and signing of the two Covenants, 'these documents were neither well-known to people living under Communist rule nor taken seriously by the Communist authorities'[586]. The 1970s marked the period when human rights ideas became prevalent in the Communist bloc. The Initiative Group for the Defense of Human Rights was the first Soviet human rights NGO that stood up for human rights[587]. Although the NGO provoked a crackdown with '11 of its 15 founding members serving terms of imprisonment, punitive psychiatry, or internal exile, it stood defiantly for at least six years, from 1969 to 1975, as the public face of the Soviet rights-defense movement'[588]. It made a great contribution to shaping 'both the ideology and the persona of the Soviet rights-defender (pravozashchitnik)'[589].

Activists in the Soviet Union thought of and considered themselves "other-thinkers' *(inakomyslyashchii)*, denoting being of a different mind or heterodox'[590].

---

581 Ibid., 55–96.

582 Ibid.

583 Ibid., 79.

584 Robert Sharlet, "Party and Public Ideals in Conflict: Constitutionalism and Civil Rights in the USSR," *Cornell International Law Journal* 23 (1990): 342–343.

585 Ibid.

586 Daniel C. Thomas, "Human Rights Ideas, the Demise of Communism, and the End of the Cold War," *Journal of Cold War Studies* 7, no. 2 (2005): 117.

587 Robert Horvath, "Breaking the Totalitarian Ice: The Initiative Group for the Defense of Human Rights in the USSR," *Human Rights Quarterly* 36, no. 1 (2014): 147–175.

588 Ibid., 149.

589 Ibid.

590 Richard Sakwa, *Soviet Politics: An Introduction* (Routledge, 1989), 320.

However, despite being ideologically equipped, 'other-thinkers' lacked the social-economic base to resist the universal employer, that is, the Soviet state[591]. Their demands could 'only be cast in the language of intellectual and social demands', thus being 'primarily cerebral'[592]. Nonetheless, dissidents that were involved in monitoring the Soviet compliance with international human rights norms kept pressuring the Soviet state to implement the provisions enshrined in the Helsinki Final Act (1975)[593]. Their advocacy took place at both local and international levels. Furthermore, human rights norms were reflected in documents that the Soviet Union and its allies had signed and finally, there was increasing pressure to implement reforms and a political will to execute those changes on the part of the new leadership headed by Gorbachev[594].

The rise of dissent proved significant for the Soviet government's attention to its human rights commitments. In addition, negotiations for the Helsinki Final Act were under way. However, before it was signed, both sides, the EC (European Community) as well as Moscow had to go through tough negotiations. Free flow of ideas and information, of great significance to the EC, was not welcome by Moscow since 'they viewed it as a threat to Communist hegemony, and the EC determined, as one British diplomat put it, to "squeeze the Russian lemon very hard to demonstrate to public opinion how little juice there is in *détente a la russe*"'[595]. Unsurprisingly, Moscow was strongly committed to Principles 3 and 6, the inviolability of frontiers and non-intervention in internal affairs. Moscow was pursuing certain motives in regard to both principles. Principle 3 was favoured 'to secure the status of the GDR (German Democratic Republic, or East Germany), prevent German reunification, and perhaps achieve Western recognition of the Soviet Union's annexation of the Baltic states'[596]. Principle 6, on the other hand, was a means to secure 'a non-intervention formula that would ensure their prerogative over that which they considered to be internal affairs – especially ideology, culture, and human rights'[597].

591 Ibid.

592 Ibid.

593 Ernst Wawra, "The Helsinki Final Act and the Civil and Human Rights Movement in the Soviet Union," In Rainer Huhle (Hg.), *Human Rights and History. A Challenge for Education* (Berlin, 2010), 142–154.

594 Daniel C. Thomas, "Human Rights Ideas, the Demise of Communism, and the End of the Cold War," *Journal of Cold War Studies* 7, no. 2 (2005): 110–141.

595 Daniel C. Thomas, *The Helsinki Effect: International Norms, Human Rights, and the Demise of Communism* (Princeton University Press, 2001), 60.

596 Ibid., 72.

597 Ibid.

The Helsinki Final Act of August 1, 1975, achieved in the Conference on Security and Cooperation in Europe, does not impose legal obligations on states, but is rather left to their good will[598]. Moreover, if states do not observe its provisions, they are not considered to have violated any obligation under international law[599]. The Act is rather a moral guide to states to respect human rights and focuses on 'greater international security and closer relations between states with special recognition of the inviolability of participants' frontiers as they existed at the end of World War II'[600]. The key basic principles adopted therein were "non-intervention in internal affairs" (principle 6) and 'respect for human rights and fundamental freedoms, including the freedom of thought, conscience, religion or belief (principle 7)'[601]. Furthermore, Basket VII lays out human rights principles which are based upon 'agreement among the states to "respect" freedom of thought, conscience and religion or belief, and to "promote and encourage" the exercise of civil, political, economic, social, and cultural rights and freedoms'[602]. It is widely accepted that the Helsinki Final Act, along with its commitment to respect human rights, played a big role in the break-up of Communism and the end of the Cold War[603].

Human rights ideas and norms had greater effect 'on the Soviet political system with Gorbachev's ascendance to power in 1985'[604]. Gorbachev had the political will to transform the Soviet political system and democratize the Soviet society. His desire to bring about changes coupled with activist movements proved crucial in the late 1980s. When he came to power, Michael Gorbachev intended to execute his liberal ideas to open the Soviet Union to the outside world, revitalize the economy and grant more freedoms to citizens, including, amongst others, freedom of information and the media, and freedom to

598 Richard Schifter, "Human Rights and the Helsinki Final Act: From USSR to Contemporary Russia," *Journal of Global Policy and Governance* 1, no. 2 (2013): 197–202.

599 John T. Evrard, "Human Rights in the Soviet Union: The Policy of Dissimulation," *DePaul Law Review* 29 (1979): 819.

600 Ibid., 830–831.

601 Daniel C. Thomas, *The Helsinki Effect: International Norms, Human Rights, and the Demise of Communism* (Princeton University Press, 2001), 4.

602 John T. Evrard, "Human Rights in the Soviet Union: The Policy of Dissimulation," *DePaul Law Review* 29 (1979): 830–831.

603 Daniel C. Thomas, *The Helsinki Effect: International Norms, Human Rights, and the Demise of Communism* (Princeton University Press, 2001), 4.

604 Daniel C. Thomas, "Human Rights Ideas, the Demise of Communism, and the End of the Cold War," *Journal of Cold War Studies* 7, no. 2 (2005): 139.

criticize, something which had been brutally repressed for decades before him. Gorbachev attempted to replace the old thinking with a new one, where law and rights would be supreme[605]. A law graduate from Moscow University, he adopted '"socialist pluralism" that is, "pluralism" as freedom for diverse views with no CPSU monopoly on truth, but "socialist" in the sense of the CPSU's political monopoly'[606]. Gorbachev was more open to incorporate human rights and freedoms into the Soviet system and 'spurred by a shuddering economy to open Soviet society, he freed political prisoners and granted considerable liberty to religion, the press, and dissident political groups'[607].

The embrace of human rights by the Soviet society, as well as their provision and implementation by the Soviet government, was a slow and gradual process that would go through several leaderships, constitutional amendments, historic moments, terror, dissent, etcetera before eventually giving in to the pressure from internal and external factors. The incremental change, before it would establish itself, had to endure the Stalinist terror; the melting of the ice under Khrushchev, the rise of dissident movements under Brezhnev and at last, 'the emergence of a nascent civil society'[608]. Thus, the Helsinki Final Act was not the only factor that contributed to the collapse of the Soviet Union. True, it did mobilize non-state actors against the Soviet state and pile pressure on it to comply with the provisions of the Helsinki Final Act, but other factors also played a part in the break-up of the Soviet Union. The ultimate collapse of the USSR was 'due to decay of central institutions, over-extension, and revolt of the periphery'[609]. Moreover, increased acceptance of human rights expanded the civil society. Dissent had a 'corrosive effect on the legitimacy and self-confidence of the party-state' and in turn, 'Western governments insisted on linking diplomatic relations to implementation of human rights norms which convinced a growing number of Communist elites of the necessity of political (rather than purely economic) reform'[610].

---

605 Peter H. Juviler, *Freedom's Ordeal: The Struggle for Human Rights and Democracy in Post-Soviet States* (University of Pennsylvania Press, 1998).

606 Ibid., 53.

607 Ibid., 65.

608 Ibid., 34.

609 David Rowley, "Interpretations of the End of the Soviet Union," *Kritika: Explorations in Russian and Eurasian History* 2, no. 2 (2001): 396.

610 Daniel C. Thomas, *The Helsinki Effect: International Norms, Human Rights, and the Demise of Communism* (Princeton University Press, 2001), 221.

5.3 Armenia as an independent state

Armenia has existed as an independent state since 1991 and following the break-up of the Soviet Union has changed 3 presidents (currently the 4th is presiding after switching to a parliamentary system of government). The human rights situation, it must be said, has not proceeded in the same manner and evenly. On the contrary, as much as the tendencies to violate human rights and encroach on citizens' fundamental freedoms have been more or less the norm under all 3 presidents, there are subtleties each has employed to consolidate their grip on power. Those range from repressions against the media, jailing political dissidents, restricting freedom of assembly to manipulative means such as implanting agitators amongst activist circles, government propaganda against human rights concepts considered un-Armenian and so on. The human rights field in Armenia has for a long time comprised non-governmental organizations (NGOs) as formal civil society actors and a counterweight to government's human rights violations. However, since 2007 new informal actors have emerged. Locally termed 'civic initiatives', these activist groups act on their own initiative, are issue-oriented, independent of donor funding and have come into being both as a result of the rise in what I name 'plural consciousnesses' amongst the Armenian public as well as themselves have made essential contributions to the understanding of [active] 'citizenship' in Armenia. This section addresses the social, economic, cultural and political factors that impact the human rights implementation and state-society relations in Armenia. It is the latter that begs more attention and detail, however, since after all, human rights are negotiated, fought for and demanded by citizens vis-à-vis the state. The main actors, both formal and informal, and the ways in which they interact with one another, the state and the public at large, are also discussed here. It is concluded that human rights are not static but, rather, they are bound to evolve over time as the society undergoes social, economic, cultural and political changes.

5.3.1 Post-independence hardships

It is commonly known that following the collapse of the Soviet Union the newly formed independent states embarked on a path of state building. However, it would by no means be easy to put behind 70 years of historical legacy. History turned out to be 'the dowry borne by leaders and citizens of these new states' as they left 'the Soviet family to set up housekeeping on their own'[611]. The Baltic States started state-building relatively easily following their break-up from

611 Simon Payaslian, *The Political Economy of Human Rights in Armenia: Authoritarianism and Democracy in a Former Soviet Republic* (London: I.B. Tauris, 2011), 2.

the Soviet domination. For these states the process meant going back to their roots, back to democratic values whereas for Armenia with absent democratic traditions, the process turned out to be rather tough and problematic. For a long time since independence the citizens of Armenia have suffered from a state of lawlessness, an environment of impunity and law existing merely on paper and failing in practice.

Moreover, the issue of 'stateness' has also played a role in the slow and arduous process to transition, but the trajectory and experience of the Baltic republics differ from Moldova and Armenia for instance. In the case of the Baltic republics 'where nationalist governments came to power and the "stateness" problem was not severe, democracy was the outcome'[612]. Conversely, in both Moldova and Armenia, 'where there was a severe "stateness" problem reflected in the outbreak of armed conflict, having a nationalist government did not ensure a democratic outcome'[613]. Unlike Moldova though, Armenia had the issue of the primarily ethnic Armenian enclave of Nagorno-Karabakh in Azerbaijan, an issue 'at the top of the agenda in both countries since 1987'[614]. In 1990 the popular front and its allies won a majority in Armenia and 'the conflict over Nagorno-Karabakh and especially the economic difficulties this created stifled the development of liberal forces, with the popular front movement spawning a party that used electoral manipulation and force to maintain power'[615]. This led to further consolidation of power and authoritarianism using the conflict and economic conditions as justifications and means to legitimize power.

The authoritarian power in Armenia was 'further reinforced by a statist political culture and a highly oligarchic system at the expense of political, civil, social, and economic rights'[616]. Elections have been far from democratic and transparent. Rather, they provided 'merely the veneer of legitimacy for political leaders whose exercise of authority is motivated by power, money, and in general by interests removed from the citizenry'[617]. Payaslian argues that 'traditional societies, especially those characterized by economic and physical insecurities, stress economic and physical security and the imperative of 'social conformity

612 Graeme Gill, "Nationalism and the Transition to Democracy: The Post-Soviet Experience," *DEMOKRATIZATSIYA: WASHINGTON-* 14, no. 4 (2006): 621.

613 Ibid.

614 Ibid., 622.

615 Ibid.

616 Simon Payaslian, *The Political Economy of Human Rights in Armenia: Authoritarianism and Democracy in a Former Soviet Republic* (London: I.B. Tauris, 2011), vii.

617 Ibid., 5–6.

rather than individualistic striving, support deference to authority, and high levels of national pride and a nationalistic outlook"[618]. This statement does characterize the situation in Armenia to a large extent. The elites that came to power following the independence in 1991 have relied on two main sources, 'the Nagorno-Karabakh conflict, which bolsters nationalist feelings and the diaspora, which is an important source of revenues and international pressure'[619]. Since then nationalist sentiments have prevailed and 'not only because of necessity but also preceding from the fact that continuation of the conflict assured personal power'[620].

The break-up of the Soviet Union has not put the 15 newly independent states on the same path of development. The latter comprised 'three distinct models: the Baltic model, when Estonia, Latvia and Lithuania joined the Euro-Atlantic security structures; the Belarusian model, when the country opted for an authoritarian rule with a possible transition from the communist totalitarianism to an open society; and the Russian model, when under the slogans of democracy and market economy a new type of regime was established in Russia and a number of post-Soviet countries'[621]. This new type of regime has been termed 'kakistocracy' which merges 'the state structures and the oligarchic elements as a result of the systematic plunder of national assets and establishment of a rule of lawlessness and illegal usurpation of power under the slogans of democracy and market economy'[622].

The formation of independent states has brought with it the 'oligarchs' who 'appropriated major enterprises and other economically significant assets'[623]. Consequently, a handful of powerful 'oligarchs' obtained economic as well as political interests while the rest of the population was left in need and poverty. This post-Soviet economic situation did not occur outside political quarters. Under the pretence of transition, political leadership 'took active part in the

618 Ibid., 8.

619 Maria Raquel Freire, and Licínia Simão, "The Armenian Road to Democracy – Dimensions of a Tortuous Process. CEPS Working Document No. 267, May 2007." (2007): 4–5.

620 Ali Abasov & Haroutiun Khachatrian, *Karabakh conflict. Variants of settlement: Concepts and realities*, 3rd ed. (Baku-Yerevan: Areat/Noyan Tapan, 2006), p. 22, quoted in Freire, Maria Raquel, and Licínia Simão, "The Armenian Road to Democracy - Dimensions of a Tortuous Process. CEPS Working Document No. 267, May 2007." (2007): 4–5.

621 Vahram Abadjian, "Kakistocracy or the True Story of What Happened in the Post-Soviet Area," *Journal of Eurasian Studies* 1, no. 2 (2010): 153.

622 Ibid.

623 Ibid., 156.

shameful appropriation of popular assets'[624]. This led to 'usurpation of power through unfair and falsified elections; growing polarization of the society, impoverishment of the bulk of population and enrichment of a handful of nouveaux riches; selling out to the foreign capital the economic and other assets based on clan interests; thriving corruption and the rule of lawlessness'[625]. The oligarchs that arose in the process gained power not only through usurpation of economic power but through their entry into the National Assembly as well. The latter 'provided them with greater political clout, opportunities to strengthen their political ties with the regime through demonstrations of loyal voting and, quite conveniently, also immunity from prosecution'[626]. These oligarchs have recorded many absences from National Assembly sessions, thereby displaying that 'their entry into the National Assembly is more for securing economic power and to be part of the ruling clique than as a result of their interest in playing a role in drafting legislation'[627].

It is noteworthy however, that not all post-Soviet republics share the above-mentioned characteristics. For example, Armenia, Belarus, Kazakhstan, Kyrgyzstan, Tajikistan and Uzbekistan 'have found themselves in the sphere of Russian influence not only from the security but also from political and economic viewpoints'[628]. And the developments in these countries 'represent a mirror reflection of what has happened in Russia – the founding mother of kakistocracy'[629]. Moreover, societies of the former Soviet bloc have low levels of trust in political institutions, a trait inherited from the Soviet times. A culture of mutual suspicion has been created 'as a result of the Stalinist legacy, the networks of spies that permeated the entire system, and the imposition of foreign rule'[630]. For example, a survey conducted in Armenia in 2004 revealed that '64 % of Armenians agree that people like them have little or no influence over

---

624 Ibid.

625 Vahram Abadjian, "Kakistocracy or the True Story of What Happened in the Post-Soviet Area," *Journal of Eurasian Studies* 1, no. 2 (2010): 157.

626 Armine Ishkanian, *Democracy Building and Civil Society in Post-Soviet Armenia* (Routledge, 2008), 124.

627 Ibid.

628 Vahram Abadjian, "Kakistocracy or the True Story of What Happened in the Post-Soviet Area," *Journal of Eurasian Studies* 1, no. 2 (2010): 158.

629 Ibid., 159.

630 Simon Payaslian, *The Political Economy of Human Rights in Armenia: Authoritarianism and Democracy in a Former Soviet Republic* (London: I.B. Tauris, 2011), 9.

the way things are run in Armenia, while 36 % think there is no way to influence government officials'[631].

In addition to traits inherited from Soviet times, Armenian culture – a blend of collectivism and parochialism – has played a role in the understanding of state-society relations. Collectivist cultures attach a preference to 'repression of dissident voices and nonconformist behaviour'; 'the structure of government preserves durable authoritarian stability interrupted only by sudden bursts of turbulence'[632]. A parochial culture, in turn, 'embodies ethnocentrism and fear and hatred toward other (sub)groups; a highly centralized elite in command of the state arrogates to itself the power to decide on vital issues of power and patronage, while delegating decisions on routine matters to functionaries and loyal groups'[633]. Furthermore, a parochial culture supports a structure of government 'consisting of an oligarchic circle of elites, where conflicts between elites and with opposition groups are often 'resolved by intrigue or low levels of violence (e.g. assassination),' and where a high level of cynicism regarding politics also reflects a low level of trust toward political leadership'[634].

Church and family have been important means of survival for Armenians throughout centuries of domination under different empires. The family plays a principal role in 'political socialization and resocialization in Armenia'[635]. On the one hand it 'serves as a safety net', on the other, 'it creates a culture of governance based on kinship rather than the rule of law and a culture of suspicion toward outgroups, with deleterious consequences for the development of civil society and civic order'[636]. As much as 'the statist and authoritarian political culture has become an extension of the rigidly patriarchal rule in the family'[637], the Armenian Apostolic Church has not been separate from the state and has since long been viewed as a political institution following the same line of thought as the authorities. Unlike the Catholic Church in Poland against the Communist rule and/or 'the involvement of Catholic priests in the liberation theology movement against

---

631 Lusine Hakobyan et al., "Armenian Civil Society: From Transition to Consolidation," *Analytical Country Report. CIVICUS Civil Society Index. Yerevan, Armenia: Counterpart International.* http://program.counterpart.org/Armenia (2010), p. 25.

632 Simon Payaslian, *The Political Economy of Human Rights in Armenia: Authoritarianism and Democracy in a Former Soviet Republic* (London: I.B. Tauris, 2011), 10.

633 Ibid.

634 Ibid.

635 Ibid., 35.

636 Ibid.

637 Ibid.

dictatorial regimes in Latin America,' the Armenian Church both in the Soviet as well as the post-Soviet period has refrained from getting involved in 'the pressing human rights issues of the day'[638]. Moreover, it has supported the government in its stance towards gender equality, sexual minorities, political prisoners, etcetera.

5.3.2 Human rights under Presidents Levon Ter-Petrosyan, Robert Kocharyan and Serzh Sargsyan

Following independence, attempts were made by the Armenian political leadership to bring the country closer to Western values, establish democracy and human rights as well as amend the constitution. However, these efforts were a mere veneer for the elite 'to legitimate its exercise of power through a post-Soviet political culture that, at least in appearances, would emulate democracy'[639]. The political culture in Armenia has mainly revolved around personalities and their close circles 'rather than an authority structure whereby formal rules and procedures govern processes of legislation and implementation of rules through democratically oriented institutions'[640]. Closed in nature, the Armenian political system has been controlled by a 'clan-based elite' that has maintained authority over discourse and democracy[641]. While similar trends have been observed in other post-Soviet states, the political and economic power in Armenia has been shaped by the frozen conflict in Nagorno-Karabakh. Both the first as well as the second president of independent Armenia, Levon Ter-Petrosyan and Robert Kocharyan, have been connected to Nagorno-Karabakh. Levon Ter-Petrosyan (1991–1998) 'emerged with the first opposition movement to the Communist Party of Soviet Armenia, after Nagorno-Karabakh asked Moscow to be integrated within Armenia, fully supported by important groups of the diaspora in Moscow'[642]. Kocharyan (1998–2008), on the other hand, 'was President of Nagorno-Karabakh and has also been elected President of Armenia with support from the most influential parties in Armenia, namely the Republican Party, the nationalist party Dashnaktsutiun, veteran diaspora-based Ramkavar-Azatakan

638 Ibid., 38.

639 Ibid., 13.

640 Ibid.

641 Richard Giragosian, "From Partisan Confrontation to Political Stalemate: The Struggle for Stability in Armenia," In *Spotlight on Armenia*, ed. Adam Hug (London: Foreign Policy Centre, 2011).

642 Maria Raquel Freire, and Licínia Simão, "The Armenian Road to Democracy – Dimensions of a Tortuous Process. CEPS Working Document No. 267, May 2007." (2007): 5.

and Orinats Erkir'[643]. Both presidencies 'established a preference for emotional militancy over rational democracy'[644]. Moreover, 'moderate political leaders were discredited amid the rhetoric of Armenian nationalism'[645].

Robert Kocharyan's presidency was tainted by human rights violations and repressions against the media. More specifically though, the ten years of his ruling Armenia were marked by two dramatic events; storming of the National Assembly by five gunmen in 1999, shooting dead 8 people, including the Prime Minister Vazgen Sargsyan and Speaker Karen Demirchyan[646]. The other date infamously engraved in the memories of the Armenian public is March 1, 2008, referring to 'the brutal response to opposition demonstrations on March 1st 2008 brought about by the perception of electoral fraud in the February 19th 2008 Presidential elections, which resulted in a 52.8 % first round victory for then- Prime Minister Sargsyan, narrowly avoiding a second round run-off'[647]. Following 10 days of mass protests in Yerevan's Freedom Square, 'the police attacked the several hundred demonstrators who had remained in the Square overnight with batons and tasers, early in the morning of March 1st'[648]. As a result, 10 people were killed, 8 civilians and 2 policemen and at 10 p.m. 'the outgoing President Kocharyan called a 20 day state of emergency during which public demonstrations were banned, media broadcasts were censored to prevent them straying from the government line and a number of websites were temporarily blocked'[649]. Kocharyan was succeeded by Serzh Sargsyan (2008–2018), whose legitimacy as a president has been questioned throughout his ten years in office. His term has also been marked by human rights violations and electoral fraud, however, unlike Kocharyan, his approach to media in particular has evolved in a different way. The excerpt below sums up Kocharyan's presidency quite well:

> At the time of Kocharyan's presidency, Armenia was much more authoritarian; there was an apparent leader which was Kocharyan. The latter was very aggressive in his relationship with the society and the opposition. He was uncompromising, and anyone opposing him risked being sent to prison. Furthermore, Kocharyan was not trying 'to buy'

---

643 Ibid.

644 Richard Giragosian, "From Partisan Confrontation to Political Stalemate: The Struggle for Stability in Armenia," in *Spotlight on Armenia*, ed. Adam Hug (London: Foreign Policy Centre, 2011), 17–18.

645 Ibid.

646 Adam Hug ed., *Spotlight on Armenia* (London: Foreign Policy Centre, 2011).

647 Ibid., 9.

648 Ibid.

649 Ibid.

> his opponents; the division between the opposition and the ruling regime was clear-cut, the opposition did not negotiate with the government nor have any dialogue, etcetera. There were repressions against the opposition, civil society institutions and individuals, political parties, NGOs and so on. He was very repressive and that is why there were a lot of prisoners; that is why, the West's reaction was very strict. Kocharyan was saying democracy is a stupid thing.
>
> (Activist, 25 September 2015)

Serzh Sargsyan's presidency has seen a rise in civic activism and initiatives. In fact, the latter became more pronounced during his term in office. While Sargsyan's strategy was to allow protests to take place, his tolerance bore a threshold beyond which civic resistance and protests got suppressed.

> When Serzh Sargsyan came to power his very first speech in 2008, prior to March 1, when he organized a meeting in the Republic Square 'dear brothers and sisters, together we shall build a democratic and sovereign Armenia, human rights are supreme values' and within the period 2008–2015 if you read Sargsyan's speeches you can easily put them beside Nelson Mandela's speeches. The style of the authorities has changed; if previously we had a clear-cut authoritarian regime with a clear-cut authoritarian leader who aroused a negativity amongst the public, there was a lot of negativity against Kocharyan and it is the case until now, it created hatred, it was a clear target, the opposition, the civil society, the opposition press etc. etc. united under him.
>
> (Activist, 25 September 2015)

In contrast to Kocharyan who persecuted opposition media, such as A1+, Aravot, etcetera, Serzh Sargsyan allowed them to go on air. In fact, he allowed anything as long as they were not demands for his resignation. Sargsyan established imitation democracy with one dominant party. Under imitation democracy, the regime remains semi-authoritarian, but creates an imitation as if it supports democracy[650]. One of the notable events that took place during Sargsyan's term in office came in 2011 when 'Armenia decided to join a new Russian-sponsored free-trade zone, whose other signatories include Belarus, Kazakhstan, Kyrgyzstan, Tajikistan and Moldova'[651]. The said free-trade zone was supposed 'to be transformed into the Eurasian Economic Union (called EURASEC by Moscow) in 2015, an entity President Putin has sponsored as a countervailing organization to the European Union'[652].

---

650 Ivan Krastev and Stephen Holmes, "Imitation and Its Discontents," *Journal of Democracy* 29, no. 3 (2018): 117–128.

651 M. Wesley Shoemaker, *Russia and The Commonwealth of Independent States 2014* (Rowman & Littlefield, 2014), 213.

652 Ibid.

Interestingly, until 2013, Armenia seemed intentioned to elect the EU's Eastern Partnership program instead. However, despite the concluded talks with EU representatives, President Sargsyan was invited to Moscow in September 2013[653]. Following the meeting with President Putin, Serzh Sargsyan 'announced that Armenia would join the current Customs Union and was ready to take part in the establishment of a Eurasian economic union'[654]. This move demonstrated once again how dependent Armenia is on Russia, not only economically but politically as well[655]. The reality is aggravated by Russia being viewed as the main security guarantor for Armenia and holding the security card to put pressure on the authorities whenever it feels Armenia may slide out of its zone of influence.

Throughout their terms in office both Kocharyan and Sargsyan have stratified the Armenian society where economic and political power have been concentrated at the hands of a small elite, while the rest of the society has been left struggling for livelihood[656]. Furthermore, that elite has been able to survive through corruption and has strongly hindered democratic processes by way of 'political pressure and coercion to sharply restrict access to positions of political power and economic influence'[657]. Consequently, corruption, selective application of the law, and impunity for powerful officials and those related to them, have been common problems in post-Soviet Armenia[658]. There have been many instances when 'law enforcement bodies either refused to prosecute high-profile cases involving individuals linked to the government or were lenient towards such perpetrators'[659]. As a result, a culture of lawlessness has been created where

653 Ibid.

654 Ibid., see also 'Armenia Joins Eurasian Union', *Radio Liberty*, 3 January 2015, accessed 21 August 2018, https://www.azatutyun.am/a/26774782.html.

655 'Stuck with each other- Armenia and Russia', *The Economist*, 20 March 2015, accessed 21 August 2018, https://www.economist.com/europe/2015/03/20/stuck-with-each-other.

656 Nora Dudwick, "Political Transformations in Postcommunist Armenia: Images and Realities," In *Conflict, Cleavage and Change in Central Asia and the Caucasus*, Vol. 4, eds. Karen Dawisha and Bruce Parrott (Cambridge University Press, 1997).

657 Ibid., 70.

658 United States Department of State, *Bureau of Democracy, Human Rights and Labor, Country Reports on Human Rights Practices for 2015*, ARMENIA. 2., accessed 7 June 2016, https://photos.state.gov/libraries/armenia/231771/PDFs/hr2015.pdf.

659 Ibid., 10.

'powerful people are above the law and ordinary citizens are not protected by the law'[660].

As mentioned above, corruption is amongst the problems that have been prevalent in Armenia since independence. It is of systemic character and has permeated all institutions and layers of the society. Over the years there have been 'numerous reports of systemic government corruption in urban maintenance, construction, public administration, the judiciary, state procurement and auctions, health care, taxation, law enforcement bodies, and military personnel'[661]. In addition, 'embezzlement of state funds, involvement of government officials in questionable business activities, and tax privileges for government-linked companies' have been reported[662]. Nearly all the elections since 1995 have been flawed; there have been many instances of 'intimidating voters, bribing the population before the elections, stealing ballot boxes, stuffing boxes, counting anomalies by local elections commissions, and so on'[663]. Accepting pre-election bribe did not always mean people voted for the candidate on whose behalf bribe was distributed. Often bribe was accepted but the vote went to another candidate. Voters became victims of poverty and 'relied on patron-client relations as they lacked trust in state authorities and in the actual practice of social and political rights'[664].

Furthermore, voting for this or that party was often coerced, 'by bosses or other power-holders'; voters 'tolerated such treatment due to insecurity, lack of rights' protection, fear for future days, in order not to lose jobs, private or state welfare, or good relations with intermediaries'[665]. Reciprocal relations with the patron and intermediaries were a means to improve their lives, since 'universal state policies designed and implemented by anonymous or corrupt state authorities' could not be trusted[666]. A survey conducted by USAID in 2008 with regard

---

660 Danish Immigration Service, *Armenia: State Actors, Political Situation, Vulnerable Groups and Citizenship*, September 2016, 3/2016, available at: http://www.refworld.org/docid/583c4aec4.html (accessed 21 August 2018).

661 United States Department of State, *Bureau of Democracy, Human Rights and Labor, Country Reports on Human Rights Practices for 2015*, ARMENIA. 2., accessed 7 June 2016, https://photos.state.gov/libraries/armenia/231771/PDFs/hr2015.pdf.

662 Ibid.

663 Vahe Sahakyan and Arthur Atanesyan, "Democratization in Armenia: Some Trends of Political Culture and Behavior," *Demokratizatsiya* 14, no. 3 (2006): 350.

664 Milena Baghdasaryan, "The Practice of Political Rights and Patron-Client Relations: A Case Study of a Party in Armenia," *Citizenship Studies* 21, no. 8 (2017): 1046.

665 Ibid., 1048.

666 Ibid.

to corruption perceptions of Armenians revealed 63 % considering corruption to be a serious problem, 23 % thinking it is a somewhat serious problem for Armenia while 51 % agreeing with the statement that corruption is a fact of life in Armenia[667].

Since the power structures are interconnected, and independence of either the judiciary or the police exists only on paper, 'any change in the incumbent leadership-party configuration of power also constitutes a radical, nearly revolutionary, change'[668]. The leadership as well as politics in Armenia have been more about personalities than institutions with the leader being the 'ultimate authority in government and society, the singular power beyond the scope and reach of the constitution, the law, and the juridical agencies'[669]. The judiciary was deemed the most corrupt institution according to 'about 40 percent of those surveyed in 2010, followed by state civil service bureaucracies (31 percent), and the police (20 percent)'[670]. Courts fare badly in the public eye as well. The Constitutional Court is considered corrupt or very corrupt by 51.9 %, the Court of Cassation by 64.2 %, the courts of appeal by 66.4 % and the courts of first instance by 69.4 %[671]. Armenia's political culture has largely been an inheritance from Soviet times, an authoritarian rule where concepts such as human rights and democracy have not been met with public confidence and politics, its leaders and institutions have been distrusted[672]. The latter has led to 'cynicism and exacerbated existing cultural propensities of fatalism'[673] in the population.

5.3.3 Domestic and international human rights framework

If one studies the RA Constitution, one will come across the rights and freedoms that make up democracy. Chapter 1 of the Constitution lays out Fundamentals of the Constitutional Order[674]. 'The Republic of Armenia is a sovereign, democratic,

---

667 Lusine Hakobyan et al., "Armenian Civil Society: From Transition to Consolidation," *Analytical Country Report. CIVICUS Civil Society Index. Yerevan, Armenia: Counterpart International.* http://program.counterpart.org/Armenia (2010), p. 43.

668 Simon Payaslian, *The Political Economy of Human Rights in Armenia: Authoritarianism and Democracy in a Former Soviet Republic* (London: I.B. Tauris, 2011), 13.

669 Ibid., 13–14.

670 Ibid., 126.

671 Ibid.

672 Ibid.

673 Ibid., 155.

674 Amendments to the Constitution of the Republic of Armenia, 2015, accessed 21 August 2018, http://www.parliament.am/parliament.php?id=constitution&lang=eng#1.

social state governed by the rule of law' according to Article 1. Article 2 states that 'In the Republic of Armenia, the power belongs to the people'. Article 3 addresses 'The Human Being, His or Her Dignity, Basic Rights and Freedoms', while the remaining articles cover such essential principles as separation and balance of powers (Article 4), legal norms (Article 5), and so on.

Basic rights and freedoms of the human being and the citizen are enshrined in Chapter 2 of the RA Constitution[675]. In fact, a number of the rights and freedoms provided for in this chapter bear similarities with international human rights instruments, such as the Universal Declaration and the European Convention on Human Rights (ECHR). Article 24 of the RA Constitution provides for the right to life in line with Article 3 of the Universal Declaration of Human Rights[676] and Article 2 of the European Convention on Human Rights[677]. Article 26 of the RA Constitution prohibits torture, inhuman or degrading treatment or punishment in line with Article 5 of the UDHR and Article 3 of the ECHR (European Convention on Human Rights). Article 42 of the RA constitution guarantees freedom of expression of opinion in line with Article 19 of the UDHR and Article 10 of the ECHR. Article 63 of the RA Constitution guarantees the right to a fair trial in line with Article 10 of the UDHR and Article 6 of the ECHR and so on and so forth.

Armenia is also a member of a number of international organizations and has signed and ratified international human rights treaties and conventions; since 30 January 1992 it has been a member of the Organization for Security and Cooperation in Europe (OSCE), of the Council of Europe since 2001[678]. Amongst the major human rights instruments ratified by the Republic of Armenia are the Framework Convention for the Protection of National Minorities (1998), the Convention for the Protection of Human Rights and Fundamental Freedoms in

675 Ibid.

676 UN General Assembly, *Universal Declaration of Human Rights*, 10 December 1948, 217 A (III), available at: http//www.refworld.org/docid/3ae6b3712c.html (accessed 21 August 2018).

677 Council of Europe, *European Convention for the Protection of Human Rights and Fundamental Freedoms, as amended by Protocols Nos. 11 and 14*, 4 November 1950, ETS 5, available at: http://www.refworld.org/docid/3ae6b3b04.html (accessed 21 August 2018).

678 Human Rights Council, *Report of the Special Rapporteur on the Situation of Human Rights Defenders*, Margaret Sekaggya, 23 December 2010, Addendum, Mission to Armenia, available at: http://www2.ohchr.org/english/bodies/hrcouncil/docs/16session/A-HRC-16-44-Add2.pdf (accessed 21 August 2018).

2002, the European Convention for the Prevention of Torture and Inhuman or Degrading Treatment or Punishment (2002) and the European Social Charter (2004). Furthermore, Armenia has established relations with the European Union. Those relations are governed by the EU-Armenia Partnership and Cooperation Agreement, signed in 1996 and entered into force in 1999[679]. In 2004 Armenia became part of the European Neighbourhood Policy.

Armenia is a party to the ECHR and is bound to the jurisdiction of the European Court of Human Rights, meaning that 'citizens who exhaust domestic legal remedies can appeal cases involving alleged government violations of the European Convention on Human Rights to the EC[t]HR'[680]. In 2017, 356 applications were submitted to the Court from Armenia, of which 109 were declared admissible, 44 were communicated, that is, questions were posed to the government, and decisions were delivered with regard to 12 applications[681]. Since 2004 the European Court has delivered a number of judgments against the Republic of Armenia. It has predominantly found the State in violation of Article 3 (Prohibition of torture), Article 11 (Freedom of assembly and association), Article 6 (Right to a fair trial) and Article 1 of Protocol No. 1 (Protection of property)[682].

While the government 'has generally complied with ECHR awards of monetary compensation, it has usually not reopened cases on which the ECHR ruled, and courts have not followed the applicable ECHR precedent'[683]. Between the period of 2007–2018 the European Court has delivered 93 decisions against the Republic of Armenia. As a result of those decisions, the government has had to comply with ECHR awards of monetary compensation, totalling 1.150.000.290 Euros[684].

---

679 Ibid.

680 United States Department of State, *Bureau of Democracy, Human Rights and Labor, Country Reports on Human Rights Practices for 2015*, ARMENIA. 2., accessed 7 June 2016, https://photos.state.gov/libraries/armenia/231771/PDFs/hr2015.pdf.

681 Naira Bulghadaryan, 'Hayastanic Evradataran nerkayacvats dimumneri tive krknaki pakasel e,' [There Has Been Double Decrease in the Number of Applications Submitted to the European Court from Armenia] *Radio Liberty*, 26 January 2018, accessed 21 August 2018, https://www.azatutyun.am/a/29000023.html.

682 *Judgments and Decisions in Respect of Armenia*, accessed 21 August 2018, http://agent.echr.am/en/judgments/judgmentsanddecisionsinrespectofarmenia.html.

683 United States Department of State, *Bureau of Democracy, Human Rights and Labor, Country Reports on Human Rights Practices for 2015*, ARMENIA. 2., accessed 7 June 2016, https://photos.state.gov/libraries/armenia/231771/PDFs/hr2015.pdf.

684 Araks Mamulyan and Gagik Aghbalyan, '1 mln evroyic avel Hayastane vtcharel e Mardu iravunqneri konvencian khakhtelu hamar (infografika),' [Armenia Has Paid

Domestically, the office of the Human Rights Defender of the Republic of Armenia, founded in 2004, is aimed at protecting 'human rights and freedoms by state and local self-government bodies and officials, and in cases defined by the Law on Human Rights Defender – by organizations as well'[685]. The Ombudsman 'contributes to the restoration of violated rights and freedoms and improves the normative legal acts related to the rights and freedoms (Article 191)'[686]. Despite the law formally providing the opportunity for the Ombudsman to be independent, 'he is still appointed by the ruling system – the National Assembly – and is dependent on the political will in the ruling elite'[687]. Moreover, if the criticism of the authorities crosses the tolerable threshold, the system will 'indirectly induce the resignation' of the Ombudsman[688]. Such has been the case of all former Ombudsmen, who have 'either resigned or not been re-elected after raising criticism of the system'[689].

Last but not least, Armenia is a state party to major UN human rights treaties, including the International Covenant on Civil and Political Rights and its two Optional Protocols, concerning the right to individual petition and the abolition of the death penalty, the International Covenant on Economic, Social and Cultural Rights, the International Convention on the Elimination of All Forms of Racial Discrimination, the Convention on the Elimination of All Forms of Discrimination against Women and its Optional Protocol, the Convention against Torture and Other Cruel, Inhuman or Degrading Treatment or Punishment and its Optional Protocol, the Convention on the Rights of the Child and its two Optional Protocols, on the involvement of children in armed conflict and on the sale of children, child prostitution and child pornography. In addition, it has signed the Optional Protocol to the International Covenant on Economic, Social and Cultural Rights, the Convention on the Protection of the Rights of

---

More than 1 mln Euros for Violations of the European Convention on Human Rights] *Hetq*, 26 July 2018, accessed 21 August 2018, http://hetq.am/arm/news/91662/1-mln-evroyic-avel-hayastany-vtcharel-e-mardu-iravunqneri-konvencian-khakhtelu-hamar-infografika.html.

685 *Human Rights Defender of the Republic of Armenia*, accessed 21 August 2018, http://www.ombuds.am/en/defender/history.html.

686 Ibid.

687 Danish Immigration Service, *Armenia: State Actors, Political Situation, Vulnerable Groups and Citizenship*, September 2016, 3/2016, available at: http://www.refworld.org/docid/583c4aec4.html (accessed 21 August 2018).

688 Ibid.

689 Ibid.

All Migrant Workers, the Convention on the Rights of Persons with Disabilities and its Optional Protocol, and the International Convention for the Protection of All Persons from Enforced Disappearance. Armenia is also a party to the Geneva Conventions of 12 August 1949, and to the Additional Protocols I and II. Armenia signed the Rome Statute of the International Criminal Court[690].

Since joining the Council of Europe in 2001, the Armenian authorities 'have proved extremely skilful at appearing to adopt European standards in all aspects of government, while every time doing the bare minimum to avoid the obloquy of suspension or, worse, expulsion from the Council of Europe'[691]. Despite fulfilling all the requirements in theory to be a member of the human rights family and bring the domestic laws into compliance with internationally recognized human rights standards, in practice the Armenian government's human rights record since independence has left much to be desired. Since democratic, constitutional political culture and institutions are not in place, the Armenian state 'has opted for imitative behaviour, "importing" the symbols of democratization (e.g. elections, a constitution) but without the substance of democracy'[692]. In order to preserve power, the ruling elite has exerted pressure on the judiciary, the media, the human rights defenders, and the NGOs amongst others. The Court of Cassation's 'control over judicial decisions remained an overarching problem affecting judicial independence'[693]. Judges have been subjected to political pressure 'from every level of the executive, including law enforcement agencies, as well as from the judicial hierarchy'[694].

---

690 Human Rights Council, *Report of the Special Rapporteur on the Situation of Human Rights Defenders*, Margaret Sekaggya, 23 December 2010, Addendum, Mission to Armenia, available at: http://www2.ohchr.org/english/bodies/hrcouncil/docs/16session/A-HRC-16-44-Add2.pdf (accessed 21 August 2018).

691 Elisabeth Robson, "Media Freedom in Armenia: One Step Forward, Two Steps Back," In *Spotlight on Armenia*, ed. Adam Hug (London: Foreign Policy Centre, 2011), 21.

692 Simon Payaslian, *The Political Economy of Human Rights in Armenia: Authoritarianism and Democracy in a Former Soviet Republic* (London: I.B. Tauris, 2011), 285.

693 Helsinki Citizens' Assembly Vanadzor Office, *Situation of Human Rights Defenders in Armenia in 2013 Report*, 29 September 2014, accessed 21 August 2018, http://hcav.am/en/publications/situation-of-human-rights-defenders-in-armenia-in-2013-report/; United States Department of State, *Bureau of Democracy, Human Rights and Labor, Country Reports on Human Rights Practices for 2015*, ARMENIA. 2., accessed 7 June 2016, https://photos.state.gov/libraries/armenia/231771/PDFs/hr2015.pdf.

694 United States Department of State, *Bureau of Democracy, Human Rights and Labor, Country Reports on Human Rights Practices for 2015*, ARMENIA. 2., accessed 7 June 2016, https://photos.state.gov/libraries/armenia/231771/PDFs/hr2015.pdf.

Human rights defenders- journalists, activists, lawyers, NGOs, etcetera have been attacked and threatened on more than one occasion, yet, 'no criminal cases were instituted on the majority of the attacks and threats against human rights defenders recorded in 2011–2012'[695]. Moreover, the Committee to Protect Freedom of Expression recorded '10 cases of physical violence against journalists in 2013, of which 3 were related to elections and 3 occurred during actions of protest', '57 cases of intimidation and obstruction of journalists, of which 12 occurred during elections and 6 took place during actions of protest'[696]. In 2014 the Committee to Protect Freedom of Speech (CPFS) 'registered 9 instances of physical violence against journalists, 44 instances of various types of pressure brought to bear on media outlets and their staff and 13 instances of violations of the right to receive and impart information'[697]. In 2015 'on several occasions police used violence against reporters who were covering citizens' protests. Journalists were beaten and detained, their equipment was damaged, and memory cards were erased'[698].

Also in 2015, a constitutional referendum was intended to allow the citizens to vote for proposed amendments to the constitution as well as to switch from a semi-presidential system to a parliamentary system of government. Electoral violations, including use of administrative resources, multiple voting, ballot-box stuffing, and intimidation of commission members and observers by officials were reported by local and international observers, members of civil society, and journalists[699]. The string of human rights violations continued in the summer of 2016, when on July 17, 'the armed group Sasna Tsrer stormed and occupied a police compound in Yerevan, taking police hostages'[700]. A two-week standoff

695 Helsinki Citizens' Assembly Vanadzor Office, *Situation of Human Rights Defenders in Armenia in 2013 Report*, 29 September 2014, accessed 21 August 2018, http://archive.hcav.am/wp-content/uploads/2014/09/HRD-Eng-Final2.pdf.

696 Annual Report -2013, Committee to Protect Freedom of Expression, http://khosq.am/en/reports/annual-report-2013/, cited in Helsinki Citizens' Assembly Vanadzor Office, *Situation of Human Rights Defenders in Armenia in 2013 Report*, 29 September 2014, accessed 21 August 2018, http://archive.hcav.am/wp-content/uploads/2014/09/HRD-Eng-Final2.pdf.

697 Helsinki Committee of Armenia, *Human Rights in Armenia*, 2014, accessed 21 August 2018, http://armhels.com/wp-content/uploads/2015/02/Ditord-69-Eng.pdf.

698 United States Department of State, *Bureau of Democracy, Human Rights and Labor, Country Reports on Human Rights Practices for 2015*, ARMENIA. 2., accessed 7 June 2016, https://photos.state.gov/libraries/armenia/231771/PDFs/hr2015.pdf.

699 Ibid.

700 United States Department of State, *Bureau of Democracy, Human Rights and Labor, Country Reports on Human Rights Practices for 2016*, ARMENIA. 2., accessed 10 June 2017, https://www.state.gov/documents/organization/265604.pdf.

followed, during which 'numerous protests and demonstrations in support of Sasna Tsrer took place in Yerevan and other parts of the country'[701]. Illegal detentions, disproportionate and excessive force were used toward peaceful demonstrators, journalists were abused and other serious human rights abuses took place, in particular on the night of July 29, when police charged crowds supporting Sasna Tsrer's political demands[702]. The year was mostly notable for such human rights problems as 'law enforcement impunity; officials' use of government resources to maintain the political dominance of the ruling Republican Party of Armenia (RPA) combined with the use of economic and political power by the country's elite to enrich supporters and corrupt the law enforcement and judicial systems; and limited judicial independence'[703].

In 2017, 26 years into its independence, the Armenian state had made little progress towards improving the human rights situation. A US Department of State Human Rights Report detailed the most significant human rights issues, such as, 'harsh and life threatening prison conditions; arbitrary arrest and detention; lack of judicial independence; failure to provide fair trials; violence against journalists; interference in freedom of the media, using government legal authority to penalize critical content; physical interference by security forces with freedom of assembly; restrictions on political participation; systemic government corruption; failure to protect lesbian, gay, bisexual, transgender, and intersex (LGBTI) persons from violence; and worst forms of child labor, which the government made minimal efforts to eliminate'[704].

The government's attitude towards NGOs has not been favourable either. The latter are not deemed potential partners, 'nor are they perceived by society as representative'[705]. Furthermore, 'human rights defenders have been time and again labelled as foreign agents, spies, cronies and the "fifth column" '[706]. NGOs have been accused of 'collusion with foreigners and of importing foreign values'

701 Ibid.
702 Ibid.
703 Ibid.
704 United States Department of State, *Bureau of Democracy, Human Rights and Labor, Country Reports on Human Rights Practices for 2017*, ARMENIA. 2., accessed 22 August 2018, https://www.state.gov/documents/organization/277381.pdf.
705 Human Rights Council, *Report of the Special Rapporteur on the Situation of Human Rights Defenders*, Margaret Sekaggya, 23 December 2010, P. 13, Addendum, Mission to Armenia, available at: http://www2.ohchr.org/english/bodies/hrcouncil/docs/16session/A-HRC-16-44-Add2.pdf (accessed 21 August 2018).
706 Ibid.

as a way of 'delegitimizing their activities'[707]. Human rights defenders, working on civil and political issues, are more at peril than those involved in social and economic issues. Civil and political issues place human rights defenders vis-à-vis the authorities who are often criticized for vested interests, such as corruption for instance[708].

5.3.4 Formal and informal human rights actors

Post-Soviet civil societies have suffered from 'high levels of anomie, apathy and cynicism'[709]. The memory and experience of repression of opposing thought and action coupled with economic deprivation led to weak civil societies in most post-socialist states, including Armenia. In the latter context, civil society has mostly been associated with NGOs. Secondly, the collapse of the Soviet Union did not lead to changes anticipated by most people. In spite of 'the belief that the end of the communist rule, the emergence of new democratic and market institutions, and the right at long last to speak freely, associate openly with others, and travel to the West would change their lives for the better, many postcommunist citizens feel that they have been let down, even cheated by the new system that quickly replaced the old one'[710]. However, as 'new demographic cohorts replace the older generations, those people who dislike and avoid voluntary organizations will eventually die off and be replaced by younger generations that might be more sympathetic to such activities'[711].

Armenian civil society has gone through different stages, 'witnessing dramatic mass mobilization in the late 1980s, an equally dramatic public withdrawal in mid-1990s, paralleled with an artificial growth of NGO sector, and, recently,

707 Armine Ishkanian, *Democracy Building and Civil Society in Post-Soviet Armenia* (Routledge, 2008), 49.

708 Human Rights Council, *Report of the Special Rapporteur on the Situation of Human Rights Defenders*, Margaret Sekaggya, 23 December 2010, P. 13, Addendum, Mission to Armenia, available at: http://www2.ohchr.org/english/bodies/hrcouncil/docs/16session/A-HRC-16-44-Add2.pdf (accessed 21 August 2018).

709 Armine Ishkanian et al., *Civil Society, Development and Environmental Activism in Armenia*, 2013, P. 5, accessed 12 April 2015, http://eprints.lse.ac.uk/54755/1/Ishkanian_Civil_Society_Development_Enviromental_Activism_America_2013.pdf.

710 Marc M. Howard, "The Weakness of Postcommunist Civil Society," *Journal of Democracy* 13, no. 1 (2002): 163.

711 Ibid., 166.

a rise of spontaneous activism'[712]. Civil society has not been an influential actor within the Armenian context. Most funding has been allocated by foreign donors, whereas the business and government sectors have 'viewed investments in civil society as a waste of resources and time'[713]. Doubts have been cast over the impact of civil society, with 54 % thinking it has either limited or no impact in addressing social issues[714]. According to the Civil Society Index (CSI) survey data, the most trusted types of Civil Society Organizations are the church (78 %), followed by humanitarian organizations (59 %); women's organizations (49 %); environmental organizations (47.7 %); political parties (19.1 %) and labour unions (18.7 %)[715].

The weakness of post-communist civil societies owes to certain features inherited from the Soviet times. To start with, repression of any independent activity perceived as threatening the state or the military resulted in mistrust in organizations by the general public. This negative experience has kept post-communist citizens away from joining organizations[716]. The history of civil society in Armenia can be viewed from two perspectives; based on the modern, Western definition of civil society as an agent of democratization, in which case civil society in Armenia is a recent phenomenon, having gained importance in the late 1980s[717]. Based on the notion of civil society as an associational life outside of the state, it has a long history in Armenia[718]. Throughout centuries the Armenians have had strong ties with the church and family[719].

---

712 Yevgenya Jenny Paturyan and Valentina Gevorgyan, "Armenian NGOs and Civic Activists: Seeing Eye to Eye?" *Póznan, Poland.* http://tcpa.aua.am/files/2016/08/Armenian-NGOs-and-Civic-Activists-Seeing-Eye-to-Eye.pdf (2016): 1.

713 Lusine Hakobyan et al., "Armenian Civil Society: From Transition to Consolidation," *Analytical Country Report. CIVICUS Civil Society Index. Yerevan, Armenia: Counterpart International.* http://program.counterpart.org/Armenia (2010), PP. 18–19.

714 Lusine Hakobyan et al., "CIVICUS Civil Society Index Rapid Assessment: Armenia Country Report," (2014), P. 40, accessed 22 August 2018, https://www.civicus.org/images/Civicus-Report_August-2014_FFinal.pdf.

715 Lusine Hakobyan et al., "Armenian Civil Society: From Transition to Consolidation," *Analytical Country Report. CIVICUS Civil Society Index. Yerevan, Armenia: Counterpart International.* http://program.counterpart.org/Armenia (2010), p. 40.

716 Marc M. Howard, "The Weakness of Postcommunist Civil Society," *Journal of Democracy* 13, no. 1 (2002): 157–169.

717 Lusine Hakobyan et al., "Armenian Civil Society: From Transition to Consolidation," *Analytical Country Report. CIVICUS Civil Society Index. Yerevan, Armenia: Counterpart International.* http://program.counterpart.org/Armenia (2010).

718 Ibid.

719 Ibid.

The NGO sector, a formal and professionalized civil society institution, is engaged in the following categories – humanitarian aid, gender, children, youth, minorities, sustainable development in education, health, agriculture, science and technology, community development, human rights, civil society, and democracy, environmental, including biodiversity issues, culture, art, and sports as well as provisions of legal services, accountancy and management services, social services for disabled and elderly people, and research and analytical services[720]. The Armenian CS sector suffers from fragmentation and competition, rendering it ineffective in terms of bigger impact on society. Since the sector is largely reliant on external donors and foreign funding, often several NGOs tackling women's rights or domestic violence or other human rights causes for instance, have to compete for funding from the same donor. This leads to each working in their niche instead of 'banding together', 'sharing resources' and 'thus having a greater impact on society'[721].

Following the 1988 earthquake and the Karabakh conflict NGOs provided humanitarian assistance to the refugees. During that period most NGOs fulfilled humanitarian or environmental functions. In order to assist Armenia in its path to democratization foreign funding was invested and more NGOs were created, this time not only for humanitarian or environmental purposes but for objectives such as human rights, women's rights, LGBTIQ+ (Lesbian, Gay, Bisexual, Transgender/Transsexual, Intersex, Queer/Questioning) rights, press freedom to name but a few. It is noteworthy that, 'in the 1990s, creating or joining NGOs became an economic survival strategy for countries as far apart as Albania and Zambia, thanks to the influx of donor aid'[722]. Beginning in the early 2000s Armenia joined a number of international organizations as well as became a party to international human rights instruments. Some of these also had committees overseeing the implementation of the corresponding treaty, covenant or convention. Moreover, international organizations were willing to fund projects directed at improving the human rights situation in Armenia, democratizing state institutions and strengthening the civil society. Consequently, more funding contributed to the increase in the number of NGOs in Armenia, focusing on themes that were prioritized by funding organizations. This meant

---

720 Asian Development Bank, *Civil Society Briefs (ARMENIA)*, 2011, accessed 27 July 2015, https://www.adb.org/sites/default/files/publication/29304/csb-arm.pdf.

721 Ibid., 2.

722 Armine Ishkanian, *Democracy Building and Civil Society in Post-Soviet Armenia* (Routledge, 2008), 31.

rapid multiplication of NGOs, more competition for resources and low trust towards the NGOs amongst the general public.

Among the several thousand pro forma NGOs, there is a small group of advocacy-oriented ones characterized by 'project implementation, international funding, intra-organisational competition (resulting in internal tensions), latent critical behaviour towards government, ability to introduce issues (but lose momentum to follow-up) and, importantly, a questionable access to (and formation of) public opinion'[723]. The institutional civil society in Armenia remains 'largely fragmented and representative of diverse groups maintaining their existence per different missions'[724]. Some NGOs, 'for reasons of economic dependency, are compelled to address issues that are deemed important by donors, to constantly keep up with the shifting demands of these donors and to address issues in the paradigms suggested by donors'[725]. This has distorted the view the local population has on NGOs, thinking of the latter as 'grant seekers who shift priorities and address issues promoted by donors instead of addressing issues that are considered important locally'[726]. For this reason, NGOs have been accused of 'grant eating (*grantakerutyun*)'[727]. The government has countered the NGOs by 'accusing them of collusion with foreigners and of importing foreign values to undermine their activities'[728]. It has also created 'government-funded 'front' organizations or GONGOs (government-organized NGOs)'[729]. 'Grbanayin' or pocket NGOs are particular groups directly or indirectly sponsored or supported by Armenian government officials and political parties[730]. The name means exactly what it says; these groups are in the pocket of the authorities and promote the ruling regime's agenda. In their speeches they praise the government efforts and receive more media coverage than independent NGOs[731]. This is not

723 Valentina Gevorgyan, "The Next Step in the Development of Armenian Civil Society," (2017): 10, accessed 28 July 2018, http://www.osf.am/wp-content/uploads/2017/11/The-Next-Step-in-the-Development-of-Armenian-Civil-Society-paper.pdf.

724 Ibid.

725 Armine Ishkanian, *Democracy Building and Civil Society in Post-Soviet Armenia* (Routledge, 2008), 83.

726 Ibid.

727 Ibid.

728 Ibid.

729 Ibid., 49.

730 Ibid.

731 Ibid.

surprising since the media in Armenia is state controlled and allows for little tolerance for opposing or alternative views.

Against this background, civic activism has been accorded a positive outlook in that with each triumph, albeit marginal, 'civil society becomes more self-reliant and demanding'[732]. Civic activism, a novel component of Armenian civil society, has been particularly appealing to the younger generation. It has channelled concerted efforts towards a variety of causes. A 2014 survey revealed that '51 % (39 % of total) consider civic activism useful (for their family, friends, colleagues, neighbours, and people in general), while 49 % (38 % of the total) consider it not useful or not useful at all'[733]. While the difference between those considering civic activism useful and those who don't presents a narrow margin, the figures will certainly have increased since 2014 due to the increase in the number of protests, as well as new issues being at stake.

The emergence and further growth of civic initiatives can be explained by three main factors. First, the generation born in 1991 and beyond never had the Soviet experience and holds a different world-view with regard to state-citizen relationships. They prefer to actively participate in solving issues of public concern rather than passively accept what the state has to offer. Also, 'the introduction and spread of social media, including Facebook and YouTube, as well as the greater availability and affordability of broadband technology allowing for uploading videos and Live Streaming, has given the civic activists an opportunity to organise and mobilise much more effectively and rapidly'[734]. However, beginning from 2007 civic initiatives have emerged and increased in numbers in 2010–2011[735].

Civic initiatives are represented by 'volunteer based, non-partisan groups usually consisting of between twenty to a couple hundred (in rare instances) individuals, who come together to collectively raise awareness of and to address a particular issue'[736]. These groups are mostly based in Yerevan, involving 'the

---

732 Lusine Hakobyan et al., "CIVICUS Civil Society Index Rapid Assessment: Armenia Country Report," (2014), P. 7, accessed 22 August 2018, https://www.civicus.org/images/Civicus-Report_August-2014_FFinal.pdf.

733 Ibid., 27.

734 Armine Ishkanian et al., *Civil Society, Development and Environmental Activism in Armenia*, 2013, P. 28, accessed 12 April 2015, http://eprints.lse.ac.uk/54755/1/Ishkanian_Civil_Society_Development_Enviromental_Activism_America_2013.pdf.

735 Ibid.

736 Ibid., 10.

active participation of Yerevan-based activists'[737]. The average age of participants ranges between 20–45, 'with the most active participants being in their mid-20s-mid-30s'[738]. There is no formal leadership in civic initiatives, the structure is horizontal and decision-making involves consensus with discussions taking place in person or in closed Facebook groups[739]. Civic initiatives are 'issue-oriented horizontally structured groups of individual activists united around a common, often very specific, cause (a prevention of construction in a public park, preservation of an architecturally valuable building, protests against a new mine and so on)'[740].

NGOs, the 'old' sector, and civic initiatives, the 'new' elements of the Armenian civil society, coexist amid both cooperation and tensions[741]. 'Old' supposedly refers to the older generation comprising NGOs that were established soon after Armenia gained independence and in the years following it. Most of those NGOs have been headed by the same person since the start. 'New' on the other hand, refers to civic activism or rather, civic initiatives, comprising the younger generation, born in the years following independence, with different ideas, vision and mentality. They are seemingly more flexible and innovative/creative. Moreover, they act on their own initiative, without external funds and unlike NGOs, are free from the confines of their jobs. Interaction between NGOs and civic initiatives ranges from 'close cooperation to being barely visible and involved on the margins'[742]. For example, sometimes NGOs prefer to remain out of the spotlight and provide logistics, awareness raising, court litigation, etcetera[743]. Sometimes NGOs do not take part in civic initiatives at all or are barely involved.

NGOs and civic initiatives differ in their modus operandi as well. Whereas the former 'choose to maintain a smooth operation mostly manifested in lack of open criticism towards government', civic initiatives 'tend to be more radical'[744].

737 Ibid., 23.

738 Ibid.

739 Ibid.

740 Lusine Hakobyan et al., "CIVICUS Civil Society Index Rapid Assessment: Armenia Country Report," (2014), P. 13, accessed 22 August 2018, https://www.civicus.org/images/Civicus-Report_August-2014_FFinal.pdf.

741 Yevgenya Jenny Paturyan and Valentina Gevorgyan, "Armenian NGOs and Civic Activists: Seeing Eye to Eye?" *Póznan, Poland.* http://tcpa.aua.am/files/2016/08/Armenian-NGOs-and-Civic-Activists-Seeing-Eye-to-Eye.pdf (2016).

742 Ibid., 12.

743 Ibid.

744 Ibid., 11.

More importantly, informal civic actors' 'personal attachment to issues makes their participation effective'[745]. Many join causes because the issue resonates with their personal experience. Their voluntary involvement distinguishes them from formal actors, that is, NGOs whose mandatory involvement and advocacy are not a matter of choice but part of their employment[746]. Civic groups are independent of donor funding, therefore more need-driven and responsive to public problems necessitating urgent solutions[747]. However, they suffer from strategic shortcomings, long-term coordination and stability[748]. Their campaigns are small scale and short-term. Furthermore, civic initiatives differ from formal NGOs in certain aspects, such as 'organisational structures and forms of decision-making, strategies and repertoires of action, rejection of foreign funding and lack of reliance on foreign donors'[749]. Nonetheless, the two cooperate in some ways as well, for instance, NGO employees 'often join civic initiatives in their personal capacity, and NGOs subsequently provide advice and support to help scale-up and widen impact'[750]. Being an NGO employee has the advantage of 'greater freedom in participating in civic initiatives without the fear of being penalised for activism'[751].

It has already been noted that the social media as well as livestreaming on YouTube and Facebook have facilitated mobilization. Moreover, online media outlets along with social networks are important alternative sources of information, allowing for diverse political opinions[752]. Since 2015 important political events have increasingly been livestreamed[753]. The same is not true about the Armenian broadcast and print media that have met with low levels of trust amongst the public like the civil society, the NGOs and political institutions.

---

745 Ibid.

746 Ibid.

747 Lusine Hakobyan et al., "CIVICUS Civil Society Index Rapid Assessment: Armenia Country Report," (2014), accessed 22 August 2018, https://www.civicus.org/images/Civicus-Report_August-2014_FFinal.pdf.

748 Ibid., 13.

749 Armine Ishkanian et al., *Civil Society, Development and Environmental Activism in Armenia*, 2013, P. 11, accessed 12 April 2015, http://eprints.lse.ac.uk/54755/1/Ishkanian_Civil_Society_Development_Enviromental_Activism_America_2013.pdf.

750 Ibid., 23.

751 Ibid.

752 United States Department of State, *Bureau of Democracy, Human Rights and Labor, Country Reports on Human Rights Practices for 2015*, ARMENIA. 2., accessed 7 June 2016, https://photos.state.gov/libraries/armenia/231771/PDFs/hr2015.pdf.

753 Ibid.

Since independence, it has held many of the characteristics inherited from the Soviet era, 'such as a casual disregard for objective information, an intolerance of opposing views, a tendency to hammer away at one-sided messages, and an inability to grasp the need to engage the public'[754].

As much as the social media has facilitated raising grievances, exposing human rights violations and so forth, it has not come without drawbacks: 'there is a tendency of transferring the real struggle from offline to online platforms'[755]. Furthermore, social media may come under government surveillance and not all of the information posted online is trustworthy. There are examples of fake news and exaggerated media content, especially during protests to misinform and mislead. The quality of reporting plays a role as well in that 'the rapid pace of work and lack of restrictions for starting online publications compromise the quality of journalistic work because of unchecked sources and misleading reporting'[756]. And last but not least, civic resistance in Armenia locally resonates with the global trends directed at the lack of democracy and social justice[757].

5.3.5 2018: A change for the better?

As discussed above, there have been civic unrests, protests and demonstrations especially in the periods leading to elections. Those have been accompanied by police intervention, usually through exertion of force to prevent demonstrators from gathering again. As a result, some have selected 'the voice option', others 'the exit option'[758]. The latter involves 'withdrawal from participation in the political process because of alienation and apathy but also, as in the case of Armenia, the physical exit from society (i.e. emigration)'[759]. Throughout the 10 years of presidency of Serzh Sargsyan 372.800 people have left Armenia and never returned,

---

754 Marina Kurkchiyan, "The Armenian Media in Context: Soviet Heritage, the Politics of Transition, Democracy, and the Rule of Law," *Demokratizatsiya* 14, no. 2 (2006): 272.

755 Lusine Hakobyan et al., "CIVICUS Civil Society Index Rapid Assessment: Armenia Country Report," (2014), P. 7, accessed 22 August 2018, https://www.civicus.org/images/Civicus-Report_August-2014_FFinal.pdf.

756 Tatevik Sargsyan, "Online Media in Armenia: A Taste of Free Expression," *Southeast European and Black Sea Studies* 14, no. 2 (2014): 293–294.

757 Armine Ishkanian et al., *Civil Society, Development and Environmental Activism in Armenia*, 2013, accessed 12 April 2015, http://eprints.lse.ac.uk/54755/1/Ishkanian_Civil_Society_Development_Enviromental_Activism_America_2013.pdf.

758 Simon Payaslian, *The Political Economy of Human Rights in Armenia: Authoritarianism and Democracy in a Former Soviet Republic* (London: I.B. Tauris, 2011), 219.

759 Ibid., 220.

that is, more than 37.000 citizens per year[760]. Emigration has affected Armenia not only demographically, but has resulted in 'the loss of significant human and material resources (e.g. brain drain)[761] and in general apathy and hopelessness, further impeding economic development and growth'[762]. The availability of 'the exit option' and its frequent use run the risk of stifling the 'voice option'[763].

This is further aggravated by certain weaknesses of civic activism. The majority of civic initiatives, both completed and ongoing, have been 'reactions to government decisions or events, rather than pro-active goals of changing the Armenian reality'[764]. Despite the raised issues being inherently political, 'many activists position themselves as "outside of politics," such as the opposition to the government-proposed pension reform'[765]. Rejecting politics implies rejecting 'political players, such as the opposition political parties, who could be valuable allies in many cases'[766].

The events of the spring of 2018, however, took an unexpected and unprecedented turn. Armenia switched to a parliamentary system of government following a 2015 referendum. While the then President Serzh Sargsyan had 'dispelled concerns that he was planning to cling to power' through the switch,

760 ANI Armenian Research Center, 12 November 2018 'Serzh Sargsyani nakhagahutyan amen or Hayastanic heracel ev chi veradardzel 102 mard,' [On Each Day of Serzh Sargsyan's Presidency 102 People Have Left Armenia and not Returned] accessed 15 January 2019, https://www.aniarc.am/2018/11/12/102-persons-each-day-serzh-sargsyan-in-numbers/.

761 ANI Armenian Research Center, 28 June 2017 'Artagaght. Hayastani bnakchutyune 2017-i hunvar-mart amisnerin nvazel e 4.600- ov,' [Migration. Armenia's Population Has Decreased by 4.600 during January-March 2017] accessed 22 August 2018, http://www.aniarc.am/2017/06/28/migration-2017-january-march/.

762 Simon Payaslian, *The Political Economy of Human Rights in Armenia: Authoritarianism and Democracy in a Former Soviet Republic* (London: I.B. Tauris, 2011), 221.

763 Albert O. Hirschman, *Exit, Voice, and Loyalty: Responses to Decline in Firms, Organizations and States* (Harvard University Press, 1970); Joseph M. Colomer, "Exit, Voice, and Hostility in Cuba," *International Migration Review* 34, no. 2 (2000): 423–442; Joy Langston, "Breaking Out Is Hard to Do: Exit, Voice, and Loyalty in Mexico's One-Party Hegemonic Regime," *Latin American Politics and Society* 44, no. 3 (2002): 61–88; Steven Pfaff and Hyojoung Kim, "Exit-Voice Dynamics in Collective Action: An Analysis of Emigration and Protest in the East German Revolution," *American Journal of Sociology* 109, no. 2 (2003): 401–444.

764 Yevgenya Jenny Paturyan, "Armenian Civil Society: It's not All about NGOs," *Civic Education and Democratisation in the Eastern Partnership Countries* (2015): 3.

765 Ibid.

766 Ibid.

stating in 2014: 'I officially declare that I, Serzh Sargsyan, will never again nominate my candidacy for the presidency of the Republic of Armenia', pledging that if Armenia voted for a parliamentary system, 'then I will not seek the post of prime minister either'[767], he later 'walked back on that promise'[768]. While the switch to a parliamentary system was not a bad move in and of itself, it took place amid fears that the ruling party would consolidate its power. Against this background, Nikol Pashinyan, a long-time political dissident announced 'plans to organise mass protests if the outgoing president declared his candidacy'[769]. Whereas Pashinyan's alliance partners were against the idea, many parts of civil society supported his plan.

On March 24, the 'We will change' civil initiative held a march named 'Reject Serzh' in Yerevan[770]. The march was aimed at protesting against the possibility of Sargsyan becoming the next prime minister of Armenia[771]. Pashinyan started what later turned into mass protests from 'passing through seven cities: Vanadzor, Spitak, Dilijan, Sevan, Hrazdan, Abovyan, Yerevan'[772]. Under the ImQayle (#MyStep) hashtag, Pashinyan started his walk on March 31 in Gyumri and intended to arrive in Yerevan's Liberty Square on April 13 in time for their first major anti-government protest[773]. The Armenian National Assembly, dominated by Serzh Sargsyan's Party, was to elect a new prime minister on April 17. A new president was sworn in on April 9. On March 2, Armen Sarkissian, former ambassador of Armenia to the United Kingdom was elected President of Armenia, a largely ceremonial position after constitutional changes that would enter into full force with the election of the new prime minister[774].

---

767 Zia Weise, "Armenia's Disputed Move toward True Democracy: Critics Worry a Parliamentary Shift Is Designed to Help President Serzh Sargsyan Maintain His Grip on Power," *POLITICO*, 4 June 2018, accessed 22 August 2018, https://www.politico.eu/article/armenia-true-democracy-disputed-move-eu-agreement-turkey/.

768 Ibid.

769 Ibid.

770 'Serzh Sargsyan: From President to Prime Minister?' *CIVILNET*, 28 March 2018, accessed 22 August 2018, https://www.civilnet.am/news/2018/03/28/Serzh-Sargsyan-From-President-to-Prime-Minister/332448.

771 Ibid.

772 'Protest Against Serzh Sargsyan's Prime-Ministership,' *CIVILNET*, 10 April 2018, accessed 22 August 2018, https://www.civilnet.am/news/2018/04/10/Protest-Against-Serzh-Sargsyan%E2%80%99s-Prime-Ministership/333140.

773 Ibid.

774 Ibid.

The ruling Republican Party 'decided to set forth Serzh Sargsyan's candidacy as the first person in government because it is extremely important to move towards the new governance system smoothly, efficiently, and with minimized risks'[775]. Nikol Pashinyan, who was in Gyumri at the time, stated in response 'our action plans include blocking roads, blockading buildings and generating the kind of civic activity that would enable us to go to the National Assembly and halt the work of the deceitful state and deceitful regime created by Serzh Sargsyan'[776]. A former newspaper journalist, Pashinyan became an opposition activist as a young man, and entered parliament in 2017[777]. He said he took inspiration from the peaceful transition of power under Vaclav Havel in Czechoslovakia and Nelson Mandela in South Africa[778]. Pashinyan himself was forced to spend a year in hiding following the infamous events of 1 March 2008.

On April 13, protesters gathered in the central intersections connecting Yerevan's "France Square" and remained there throughout the night, closing traffic in the busy city junction[779]. Serzh Sargsyan was elected prime minister on April 17. On Sunday, April 22, 'a day after he saw the new president, Pashinyan came face-to-face with Sargsyan before live TV cameras at Yerevan's Marriott Hotel after securing a meeting with the premier'[780]. The meeting did not last long and after 'only a few minutes, the prime minister rose from his seat and walked out, muttering about blackmail after his opponent had said he was there to demand Sargsyan's resignation'[781]. Later that morning Pashinyan was grabbed by security forces at the latest protest rally in Yerevan and detained for over 24 hours before being released on Monday, hours before the prime minister's

775 Ibid.

776 Ibid.

777 Amie Ferris-Rotman, "Armenia's Charismatic Opposition Leader Whips up Pressure after Talks Break Off," *The Washington Post*, 25 April 2018, accessed 22 August 2018, https://www.washingtonpost.com/world/europe/armenias-charismatic-opposition-leader-whips-up-pressure-after-talks-break-off/2018/04/25/e158f47a-488d-11e8-8082-105a446d19b8_story.html?utm_term=.5e1a34025e9d.

778 Ibid.

779 "Demonstrations in Yerevan: Chronicle of April 14," *CIVILNET*, 14 April 2018, accessed 22 August 2018, https://www.civilnet.am/news/2018/04/14/Demonstrations-in-Yerevan-Chronicle-of-April-14/333656.

780 Alasdair Sandford, "How 11 Days of Protests Brought Down Armenia's Leader Serzh Sargsyan," *euronews*, 23 April 2018, accessed 22 August 2018, http://www.euronews.com/2018/04/23/how-11-days-of-protests-brought-down-armenia-s-leader-serzh-sargsyan.

781 Ibid.

resignation[782]. Pashinyan's detention did not stifle the protests. On the contrary, it brought an even bigger number of people onto the streets and 'facing a renewed wave of thousands of demonstrators, including deserting soldiers, Sargsyan resigned, after issuing a stark mea culpa on Monday'[783]. "I was wrong", "Nikol was right" "The street movement is against my tenure. I am fulfilling your demand"[784] said he in a statement on the government's website. The news of Sargsyan's resignation sparked joyful celebrations on the streets of the capital city Yerevan.

On May 1, the ruling party, which holds 58 out of 105 seats in Parliament, voted down Pashinyan's bid to become interim prime minister[785]. Pashinyan went to Yerevan's central Republic Square, where an estimated 250,000 people had gathered, and called for a nationwide strike at 8:15 the next morning[786]. The Parliament met again on Tuesday to elect a prime minister, and this time Pashinyan's bid was successful. He became the 15th prime minister of the Republic of Armenia[787]. Pashinyan has vowed 'to break the cozy system of oligarchic monopolies and invigorate an economy that has left a third of the country in poverty'[788]. These are promising signs in the Armenian reality, and it remains to be seen what changes the new prime minister will introduce to improve the human condition in Armenia.

---

782 Ibid.

783 Andrew Roth, "Shock as Armenia's Prime Minister Steps Down after 11 Days of Protests," *The Guardian*, 23 April 2018, accessed 22 August 2018, https://www.theguardian.com/world/2018/apr/23/serzh-sargsyan-resigns-as-armenias-prime-minister-after-protests.

784 Ibid.

785 Neil MacFarquhar, "He Was a Protester a Month Ago. Now, Nikol Pashinyan Leads Armenia," *The New York Times*, 8 May 2018, accessed 22 August 2018, https://www.nytimes.com/2018/05/08/world/europe/armenia-nikol-pashinyan-prime-minister.html.

786 Ibid.

787 Vahe Sarukhanyan, "Nikol Pashinyane 15-rd andzn e vore zbaxecnum e HH varchapeti pashtone," [Nikol Pashinyan Is the 15th Person that Is Occupying the Position of the RA Prime Minister] *Hetq*, 8 May 2018, accessed 22 August 2018, http://hetq.am/arm/news/88609/nikol-pashinyany-15-rd-andzn-e-ory-zbaxecnum-e-hh-varchapeti-pashtony.html.

788 Neil MacFarquhar, "He Was a Protester a Month Ago. Now, Nikol Pashinyan Leads Armenia," *The New York Times*, 8 May 2018, accessed 22 August 2018, https://www.nytimes.com/2018/05/08/world/europe/armenia-nikol-pashinyan-prime-minister.html.

5.4 Concluding remarks

Armenia is one of 15 post-Soviet states that embarked on a difficult path both economically and politically following the break-up of the USSR. The Soviet residue persisted for years to come ranging from violations of human rights and fundamental freedoms, repressions against the media, imprisonment of political dissidents, restrictions of the freedom of assembly to manipulative means such as implanting agitators amongst activist circles, government propaganda against human rights concepts considered un-Armenian and so on. Though Armenia joined the Council of Europe in 2001, the authorities have merely provided the façade of importing European standards as to different aspects of government. This façade has thus far helped Armenia not to be suspended or expelled from the Council of Europe. Furthermore, Armenia has signed and ratified most of the international human rights instruments, but lacking democratic, constitutional political culture and institutions, the Armenian state has imitated democracy, that is, it has imported the symbols of democratization (e.g. elections, a constitution) but without the substance of democracy.

Non-governmental organizations – the formal civil society actors, have for years attempted to counter the government's human rights violations and hold it accountable for the committed abuses. However, they have not been treated with much trust by the general public, explained to an extent by the government's attempts to portray them in a negative light and label them as promoters of the Western agenda, detached from local values. Signs of gradual change for the better were discerned in 2007 following the emergence of new informal actors, locally known as 'civic initiatives'. The latter succeeded in recording marginal success in the social and environmental sectors in particular, but failed to bring about political change.

The events of the spring of 2018 attempted to achieve what previous protests had failed. Headed by long-time political dissident Nikol Pashinyan mass protests took place throughout Armenia. The turn they took was unexpected and unprecedented. The details, outcome as well as the significance of these protests will be discussed in the following chapter. Furthermore, previous protests, along with their similarities and differences will be illustrated to demonstrate the role of non-state actors in claiming human rights by using protests as platforms for their claims-making, voicing of grievances and civic activities at large. The human rights perceptions and practices of both formal and informal civil society actors as well as the modus of interactions between them, the state and the citizenry at large will be discussed to demonstrate the incremental rise in rights and legal consciousness, the shift between self-centred and other-centred claims and last but not least, the different ways in which human rights ideas are encouraged, resisted and appropriated in Armenia.

6 Research findings: Roles, perceptions and practices of key human rights actors in Armenia

6.1 Introduction

It is noteworthy that activism in Armenia is divided into pro-government and anti-government discourse and it is hard to find a middle ground. Most activists belong to a circle and know each other quite well. They usually hold opinions on one another, based on political preferences, performance during protests and activists they associate with. There exists visible fragmentation in terms of issues different circles of activists campaign or advocate for and it rarely happens that the same activist takes an interest in all protests, the reasons being existence or lack of professional knowledge, skills, experience, or potential to contribute to a successful solution. As a matter of observation, new individuals who enter the public or civil sphere are accepted with suspicion as to their real intentions and motives in 'joining the club'. There is the risk that they may be linked to this or that political force. Since the civil sphere in Armenia has become politicized and 'activists' are not viewed as citizens fighting for the public good but for private gain, newcomers are not immediately trusted.

The interview process throughout my research in situ was not always smooth and moments of frustration and power asymmetry were manifest. Provided that I was dealing with interview subjects from various backgrounds, with differing knowledge, skills and experience as well as achievements in their respective fields of expertise in addition to factors such as age, sex and political views, each interview was different in the sense of reactions to certain questions, the way my interviewees perceived themselves and me throughout the interviews as well as the way they viewed my research and its contribution to the improvement of human rights in Armenia. Heads of NGOs (with exceptions) manifested a more authoritative behaviour, often dictating the interviews and attempting to deviate from questions related to their relationships with other NGOs as well as the government. It is noteworthy that when I contacted the NGOs, the only members of staff I could meet were the heads. In fact, the latter made the decision as to who I could meet for the interview and it was them in all the cases. Some of my questions seemed to frustrate the heads of the NGOs, especially questions having to do with public trust towards them, the differences between their activity and that of the individual activists as well as cooperation with other Armenian NGOs. Some of their responses indicated that similar questions would not be elaborated on further. However, they willingly responded to questions related to their activity, their relationship with the citizens and the civil society in general, the projects they have implemented as well as what rights violations they have addressed. Questions about protests and demonstrations, outcomes, police behaviour and the like did not pose problems to this category of respondents.

Interestingly, the activists who are mostly representatives of the younger generation freely talked about their struggles, experiences, disappointment, etcetera. Moreover, most of them are very well educated young people who have travelled abroad and who both appreciated that an Armenian studying abroad is researching the issue of human rights and were happy to be part of this research and help in whatever way they could. The same is true about the journalists that I interviewed. A term that has been in frequent use in Armenia is 'investigative journalist', that is, a journalist who does not merely illustrate issues of concern in the Armenian society, but also actively researches the matter in question before any materials are published. More publicly active journalists have been targeted by police during protests, involving damage to their cameras, memory sticks as well as verbal abuse, etcetera. This category of interview subjects was quite approachable and accessible. Some of the respondents were remaining within the scope of their professions and refraining from touching upon subjects that they thought would be best explained by others, such as activists, political analysts or academics.

6.2 Pros and cons of researching human rights practitioners

The gap between human rights theory and practice is well known. As much as theories are produced to be applied in practice, the reality comes to the fore once human rights practitioners start sharing their stories of struggle. They are situated at the core of issues that arise on the ground, and often it may seem as if academia and practice are disengaged. Human rights practitioners carry the burden of localizing human rights, adapting them to domestic settings, empowering and educating ordinary people to stand up for their rights. In this regard they are more familiar with what human rights issues the local population is facing as well as what is required to try and solve those issues. In other words, human rights practitioners perform the role of mediators between the theory of human rights and practice in domestic settings.

Researching human rights practitioners is an important way to find out what is going on locally, what the relationships between the state and themselves are, what success or failure stories there are and what lessons these practitioners have learnt from their struggles and campaigns. However, not being one of them, or rather, not being a member of a circle where nearly everyone knows one another, be they an activist, a member of an NGO, a political analyst, a political scientist, an academic, a journalist, a lawyer, etcetera, can present challenges such as issues of trust, withholding information, talking around the subject and so on. Being outside of a circle can also be advantageous for the researcher since interview subjects may open up more easily to 'an outsider', they may feel more at ease to talk about certain questions and they may have the 'expert' feeling of knowing the subject matter more deeply, all of this contributing to their self-worth when interacting with the researcher.

In the case of this particular research, I felt both accepted and rejected at the same time. Having lived outside Armenia for the last few years, exactly at the time when protests became more frequent, I have watched the events unfold at a distance. And while I am familiar with the more or less successful civic initiatives that have been organized in Armenia in relation to issues of social, economic, political or environmental nature, not having been part of it placed me in a difficult position when interacting with some of my respondents. On a few occasions I was indirectly reminded of the fact that I have not been a participant of this or that civic action, initiative or protest and that I am situated in a comfortable zone in Germany where the rule of law is incomparable to that in Armenia. At times I ended up being at the receiving end of the disappointments and frustrations experienced by some of my respondents. Some questions were returned to me with 'now I ask you…', 'what do you think of that?' etcetera.

Interestingly, Europe implies negative connotations amongst some layers of the Armenian population; they feel mistrust towards European organizations operating in Armenia and are convinced that they shall be the ones to bring about a change and rely only on themselves as full-fledged citizens of the Republic of Armenia. That feeling was reflected in the responses of some of my respondents who introduced themselves to me as the ones going to provide me with 'unconventional responses' as opposed to the pro-European ones they assumed I would already have received. Furthermore, the activist (active citizenry) circle in Armenia has been suffering from mistrust towards newcomers. The scene is fragmented, and there is the concern that a newcomer may be playing from the opposing camp. Therefore, some level of trust needed to first be established before their views were made known. Having previously had the experience of co-opted activists and encountered disillusionment, some of the activists I interviewed are now passive, that is, they may join the protests but do not participate in the decision-making processes. Therefore, to overcome the barrier of the Armenian studying in Europe versus the Armenians fighting for a better Armenia, I had to be sensitive to the way I phrased some of the questions and when necessary, mention facts and statements from reports and responses of other interviewees seeking their agreement or disaccord.

Being outside the circle of those one researches has advantages too. In the case of this research its academic objective placed me in a neutral position as a researcher with no hidden agenda. The fact that I was trying to build up knowledge to contribute to the perceptions and experiences of human rights actors in Armenia being an Armenian myself lowered the risk of being taken as a pro-government tool in my interactions with most of my respondents. The scientific value of this research was appreciated by the majority of my respondents and trust was established soon after the first exchanges took place. Both they and I had to give away something of ourselves to achieve the reciprocity that turned out to be essential as the interviews went on. As some of the interviews turned into discussions and/or debates around heated human rights issues such as their nature, interpretation, applicability and practice, I shared my theoretical knowledge with my respondents while they shared their practical experiences and skills with me. As a result, most of them placed me on a par with themselves, that is, working for a better Armenia regardless of the geographical location.

The upcoming chapter presents and discusses the main findings of this research project, illustrating how the key human rights actors' interpretations and strategies unfold in the Armenian setting and demonstrating the ways in which human rights ideas are appropriated, encouraged and resisted in Armenia. Through studies of key human rights actors, the main findings reveal their perceptions and practices in claiming, exercising, as well as negotiating about human rights in the Armenian context. Claims-making, pressing for redress and change as well as interactions between state and non-state actors and the citizenry at large take place at public assemblies, protests and demonstrations which serve as platforms for their speech and actions. The following chapter, thus, presents the ways in which key human rights actors in Armenia encourage, resist, appropriate and translate human rights ideas in 'The Street'.

6.3 Formal non-state actors

6.3.1 Soviet residues and malaise

Armenia as well as other post-Soviet republics have not had 'the pre-World War II tradition of civic development which took place in some Central and East European countries'[789]. Similarly, a human rights movement 'even a mini-movement of human rights, of support'[790] has not been seen in Armenia. There has been radical dissent, 'inextricably linked to irredentism'[791]. As Nora Dudwick puts it[792]:

> It arose among a small group of people born toward the end of the Stalin era into working-class or lower-middle-class families, most of whom had roots in Turkish Armenia. They instrumentalized human rights issues to serve "Hai Dat" (literally, "the Armenian Cause," or Armenian irredenta). Their activities received little support either in Armenia or in the diaspora. For despite the fiercely anti-Turkish and irredentist sentiments of many diaspora Armenians, the majority hesitated to challenge the Soviet Union, which they saw as the only guarantor of Armenia's physical survival, and which allowed Armenia at least formal "national" and cultural self-expression.

In 1977 a small group of Armenian dissidents founded the Armenian Helsinki Watch Group aimed at monitoring civil rights violations and the "anti-nationality policies" of Moscow and Yerevan[793]. By 1978 the organization had ceased to exist. In the 1980s an ecology 'initiative group' was formed to address concerns over chemical and nuclear pollution[794]. However, soon the initiative also became a platform for discussing political and social issues. In September 1987 and February 1988, 'Karabagh activists used ecology rallies to announce demonstrations in support of the Armenians in Karabagh, which soon displaced ecology as the unifying symbol of the movement'[795]. Nationalism became the unifying ideology and 'the rallying point in 1988, when Armenians demonstrated to support the Armenian majority living in Nagorno-Karabagh, where the oblast soviet had unanimously voted to request that Armenia and Azerbaijan approve of the region's unification with Armenia'[796]. In February 1988 the struggle evolved between the nationalists and the reformists. The former were pressing for the unification of Nagorno-Karabagh, while the latter viewed 'democratization as a prerequisite to a peaceful, democratic resolution'[797]. This contention between

789 Nora Dudwick, "Political Transformations in Postcommunist Armenia: Images and Realities," In *Conflict, Cleavage and Change in Central Asia and the Caucasus*, Vol. 4, eds. Karen Dawisha and Bruce Parrott (Cambridge University Press, 1997), 76.

790 Interview with a political scientist, 8 September 2015.

791 Nora Dudwick, "Political Transformations in Postcommunist Armenia: Images and Realities," In *Conflict, Cleavage and Change in Central Asia and the Caucasus*, Vol. 4, eds. Karen Dawisha and Bruce Parrott (Cambridge University Press, 1997), 76.

792 Ibid.

793 Ibid., 76–77.

794 Ibid., 77.

795 Ibid.

796 Ibid., 77–78.

797 Ibid., 78.

the nationalists and the reformists (or liberals as they are called nowadays in Armenia) still exists. As a well-known political scientist in Armenia remarked:

> Well they created, it did not come out of the blue, they created it, their associated life started in 1901, in France and elsewhere, in the very struggle of women, how much they suffered, they did this and that, yes there must be a pamphlet... pamphlet, they got educated, we are lagging very much behind, we are lagging with centuries, we never had either a state or a civic state, up to date it is constantly mentioned nationalist, and with the war hanging, the presence of war, as long as we have war and external debt, we won't be able to stand on our feet, we cannot, we cannot...
>
> (7 September 2015)

The post-Soviet inertia has settled not only in Armenia, but in other former Soviet republics as well. Furthermore, the evolutionary philosophical thought presented by Hobbes, Locke, Rousseau, Hegel and others in Europe, that is, the debate over political thought, has been absent in Armenia. Such ideas were not possible to discuss since there was no civic state to start with. Armenian philosophy of law and jurisprudence 'developed in the environment of feudalism but amid various political and religious difficulties. Rather than a unilinear progression, the process involved phases of advancement and decline, recovery and reverses'[798].

Similarly, the educational system still carries remnants from the Soviet system; a human rights culture, a political school of thought is absent. Debates revolve around the personalities of idea holders rather than ideas *per se*. In other words, any criticism of social and/or political issues takes place at a personal rather than an ideological level. Neither school nor university education teaches critical and/or analytical thinking, questioning the authority, challenging the teachers, lecturers, and the rector etcetera. As a political scientist noted:

> ...an idea, to argue over an idea and not over each other's person(ality), well it is a culture, where should it come from? Is the university like that? Can you question your rector or teacher?
>
> (7 September 2015)

The Soviet residue in education coupled with increased poverty has meant that 'human rights' are based on top of the pyramid which in turn means that until poverty is reduced and the educational system reformed, the majority of Armenian citizens won't prioritize human rights as basic human needs. In the words of a prominent feminist activist:

798 Simon Payaslian, *The Political Economy of Human Rights in Armenia: Authoritarianism and Democracy in a Former Soviet Republic* (London: I.B. Tauris, 2011), 47.

> When the person is poor, when he cannot earn his daily bread, no matter how much you speak to him about human rights, he will not comprehend you, will not listen to you, as long as he is hungry to put it roughly, that is why you shall also improve the economy in general and education in a similar way, that is to say, children shall not only be taught addition, subtraction and Armenian for them to go and all the time study like zombies without knowing why, but for us to make them citizens and humans, that is why education is also very important.
>
> (27 August 2015)

The generation that lived through Soviet times and values still teaches in schools and universities, transferring those values onto the younger generation. Back in 2005 Lilit Umroyan and Lucig Danielyan concluded in their baseline study on Human Rights Education in Armenia that 'the quality of teaching in general is poor, especially connected with the fact that a majority of the faculty members at the universities and institutes are old Soviet lecturers with conservative approaches to education, who do not allow young scholars with good education and fresh ideas to enter the system and try to reform it'[799]. Ten years later, in 2015 when I conducted my own research, the situation on the ground was different. There are still representatives of the Soviet generation teaching in higher educational institutions in Armenia, however, 'today's youth who were born in the times of independence, they did not have what existed during the times of the Soviet Union, they are more free, today the youth have access, that is to say, they have a window into Europe, into the US, into other countries'[800].

Access to foreign countries, study and travel opportunities bear both advantages and disadvantages. On the upside, it allows young Armenian citizens to expose themselves to foreign cultures, which may in turn help reflect back on their own culture, reinterpret it and act for change. Exposure to alterity enables them to critically reflect outside the conditions within which they have been socialized, as well as sufficiently distance themselves from habits to re-examine them[801]. Furthermore, once exposed to alternatives, otherness and ways of thinking and doing different from what they are accustomed to, agents draw comparisons, reflecting on two different realities and drawing inferences regarding their society's 'historically fashioned social inheritance, that is, its

---

799 Lilit Umroyan and Lucig Danielyan, "Human Rights Education in Armenia – A Base Line Study," In *Armenia: A Human Rights Perspective for Peace and Democracy. Human Rights Education and Minorities*, eds. Anja Mihr et al. (Universität Potsdam, 2005), 96.

800 Interview with a human rights lawyer, 25 August 2015.

801 Rob Stones, "Rights, Social Theory, and Political Philosophy, a Framework for Case Study Research," In *Rights: Sociological Perspectives*, ed. Lydia Morris (Routledge, 2006).

historically situated ideals, customs, beliefs, institutions, and practices'[802]. On the other hand, exposure to alterity bears downsides:

> The new generation that is more or less educated and detached from that Soviet past, relatively educated, does not have those skills, they don't get them, they get them abroad but migration is an issue here; people go and acquire skills abroad and do not return or return for a short period and go back again, that is, even if knowledge is gathered, skills are acquired, they are not applied in Armenia, they are not utilized since there is migration, that is, the domestic university does not deliver, foreign universities do, but those getting them do not stay in Armenia. For that reason we have this situation to a large extent.
>
> (Activist, 25 September 2015)

Young people who get education abroad find it difficult to return to Armenia and face the 'reality' at home. The rule of law and equality of opportunity are pull factors that have kept a number of foreign educated young Armenians abroad:

> ...of course they go back. And second, those people are all in international bodies. Those who studied through Chevening are involved in international organizations. The NGOs, I have not seen that a young person goes to study abroad, returns and keeps their promises. They in reality go the way that boosts their career, that is to say, they go abroad and continue it there, they find a job there etc. That is because Armenia is closed. I opened the list of people who have studied in London through Luys Foundation; they have gone there through Luys and stayed there. They continue to study.
>
> (Human rights lawyer, 25 August 2015)

6.3.2 NGOs, related issues and [mis]perceptions

For a long time since the collapse of the Soviet Union, civil society in Armenia has largely comprised NGOs that have survived on foreign grants. For this reason, amongst others, the competition between NGOs has been based more on getting funding than ideology, setting them apart from foreign NGOs, such as the ones in Europe for example. Moreover, state and politics in the Armenian context in turn have played an essential role both in the way the formal (NGO) civil society sector has developed as well as how public perceptions have shaped towards them. Armenian NGOs do not get funding from the state; their activity remains confined to an institutional level instead of spilling over since they are 'viewed not as one of us, but oh well, they are busy, perhaps they get money, they are busy...'[803]. In the eyes of the majority of the Armenian public NGOs provide

---

802 Ibid., 140–141.

803 Interview with a political and social activist, 25 August 2015.

employment opportunities having little or no impact upon the social or political life of the society. To make matters worse, the media picture the NGOs in a negative light, qualifying them as 'foreign agents', living on foreign money and posing a threat to Armenian values.

In the early years post-independence, NGOs in Armenia were of humanitarian and/or charity nature. They were founded in response to the situation present in Armenia at that time, such as the Karabakh conflict for example. Along with the hardships following the 1988 earthquake, humanitarian NGOs provided help to the refugees and displaced people. However, from 2000 onwards new NGOs were founded aimed at civil society projects, human rights, democratization, etcetera. Moreover, Armenia became a member of international organizations, as well as a party to major human rights instruments. More donors were willing to fund human rights, civil society and democratization projects in Armenia. To an extent, civil society became a popular term, and one can come across the term in the vision/mission statements on NGO websites. This is not entirely a shortcoming of the NGOs themselves. They operate on foreign funding, therefore, have to abide by the requirements and expectations of the donors, otherwise, their survival will be threatened:

> Organizations in Armenia cannot survive without those grants, for different reasons because there is no state funding, even if there is it is not available to many organizations which do not belong directly or do not obey, go and check there is a foundation, there was a lot of thing in the media as well, where that money had gone, how many organizations and how and when those were founded; later it turned out that those organizations were founded by state officials. In Armenia it will take a long long long long time for that sector to develop...
>
> (NGO representative, 26 August 2015)

The dependency of NGOs on foreign funding doesn't allow them to pursue their own agendas in Armenia. Rather, NGOs tend to switch agendas based on the issues prioritized by the donors. If the donors emphasize environmental issues, NGOs switch their focus onto those agendas, if during a particular period the donors prioritize LGBTIQ+ (Lesbian, Gay, Bisexual, Transgender/Transsexual, Intersex, Queer/Questioning) issues, NGOs prepare their project proposals accordingly. This turns them into bystanders rather than direct actors of change. There are NGOs that stand out, such as women's organizations for instance that 'directly organize activities, they enter into conflicting situations'[804] but human rights NGOs take a more implicit stance towards controversial topics or debates.

---

804 Interview with a feminist activist, 27 August 2015.

Differentiation should be made between the Armenian NGOs. The ones founded following the break-up of the Soviet Union were intended to provide for employment. Scientists and/or professionals remained jobless once the Soviet Union ceased to exist, and once foreign grants started flowing in, they were used to create workplaces. Recently founded NGOs follow a particular ideology, are aimed at solving particular issues and are more democratic. Some of them have been founded by friends, are jointly managed and there is no director-employee hierarchy. There is also the third type – specialized organizations that operate according to international models, Transparency International being one example. The work of committed NGOs is, however, overshadowed by the existence of a big number of GONGOs (government-organized NGOs) that appear on grant lists but whose activity has not been heard of.

> NGO activity ranges from legal assistance, defending applicants' interests in courts, taking part in trials to 'hold the judicial system in our hands', i.e. to ensure transparency, to see what attitude the judge has, whether he is partial or impartial, in case of something going wrong all of it is publicized; media representatives go and cover the trials, they organize actions; publicizing helps to attract attention.
>
> (Feminist activist, 27 August 2015)

International organizations do not always help the way NGOs are perceived, not only by the general public but by one another as well. There is the general perception amongst the Armenian NGOs that international organizations such as the Organization for Security and Cooperation in Europe (OSCE), the EU and the UN apply double standards by advocating values while at the same time acting against them. A notable case is the OSCE mission to Armenia (office operations discontinued in Armenia on 31 August 2017) that had, amongst other things, representatives monitoring the elections. Almost all the elections that have taken place in Armenia have been fraudulent, yet the OSCE representatives failed to record them.

Domestic NGOs did not cooperate previously due to limited grants. They were busy hunting donors, and 'would put pressure on each other, even blackmail, only to get the grant'[805]. When the Coalition to Stop Violence against Women was formed more young people joined it. They were more prone to cooperation, unlike the older generation that held traditional views. Also, the new generation is better educated, the general situation in the country has changed and there is more experience in handling human rights issues. Although most focus on human rights, they rarely form coalitions:

805 Interview with a feminist activist, 27 August 2015.

> . . .because it is like this, organizations are few, everyone knows each other, there is no need to form a coalition; a coalition is formed for two reasons in Armenia, either a donor comes and says I am forming a coalition, but luckily recently there are no such donors. Well they create a senseless coalition around money and without clear goals; it is natural that in that coalition everyone starts arguing and it collapses that way by itself.
>
> (NGO representative, 11 September 2015)

It also so happens, albeit rarely, that a coalition is formed around a specific/concrete issue bringing certain NGOs together, which then work on the issue, complete it successfully and the coalition collapses naturally. The most successful NGO coalition in Armenia to date has been the 'Coalition to Stop Violence against Women'. Formed in 2010, as a reaction to the death of domestic violence victim Zaruhi Petrosyan, the Coalition 'operates on different levels, concentrating efforts on the formation of public opinion and changing the existing mentality'[806]. Their modus operandi involves public events such as press conferences, TV programs, reports, articles, marches, outdoor screenings and concerts aimed at raising awareness among women about their rights. Last but not least, the Coalition cooperates with the government, the National Assembly, international organizations, civil society and the media in Armenia for the adoption of legislation to prevent domestic violence.

As noted above, NGO coalitions are not common in Armenia. The sector suffers from corruption in addition to being viewed as foreign agents. NGOs focused on environmental issues have a leeway in the sense that they are perceived differently by the public. Moreover, environmental issues are thought of as more tangible whereas human rights are perceived within the frame of value change, therefore, not easily perceivable:

> It is a far- reaching goal; people do not understand what you are doing, what you are doing it for, especially they think whose order are you executing, which global power interests are you trying to defend here, pro-American, pro-European, etc.
>
> (Feminist activist, 27 August 2015)

Further to this point, human rights are perceived as a foreign import, a borrowing from the West 'disconnected from life'. NGO agendas are seen as installed from the West 'not at all comprehensible to the local person, they do not at all address the issues of the local person, his language, his thinking/mentality, in that sense they are very artificial and often they are grant projects right?'[807].

806 Coalition to Stop Violence against Women 2010, Armenia, accessed 15 September 2018, https://coalitionagainstviolence.org/en/home/.

807 Interview with an activist, 27 August 2015.

Foreign – funded NGO projects 'lack continuity and do not follow up and are not connected to the domestic/local setting, they did not emerge from bottom-up, from inside, i.e. the so-called civil society was not formed locally, but it is more installed from Western democracy, human rights, that is why it does not work much'[808]. Human rights NGOs are not perceived as grassroots organizations. More so, concepts such as human rights, democracy, gender, etcetera are alien to the local population and distorted in the meaning and message they convey, and that is why human rights NGOs enjoy less trust than humanitarian and/or environmental ones.

The aforementioned concepts, despite being perceived as foreign imports, also allow NGOs to survive in the Armenian setting. These NGOs operate based on the demand in the 'market'. That is to say, if at one point trafficking is 'fashionable', NGOs apply for grants based on trafficking, if the LGBTIQ+ issues are heated, then projects are submitted based on LGBTIQ+ issues. The civil society institute is not yet established in Armenia; it has long been associated with NGOs that have in turn been linked to grant-eating, propagating foreign values and so on. As a result, NGOs and the society are detached from one another. NGOs, supposedly the knowledge brokers or mediators, have failed to make foreign concepts accessible to the local population. Hence, 'gender', 'activism' to name but a few have been perceived as imposed and largely rejected. According to an NGO representative:

> It is wrong to import democracy or human rights; the person cannot understand in one day that it is already a right and it is important, it shall not be imposed on the person; rights shall be as such and not imposed on the person that you know this is a right, this is very important and since they are doing it in the EU or I don't know in any Western state, we should do too, that bottom-up approach shall be there, when there is that demand in Armenia to have that right though on paper we of course have all the rights.
>
> (4 September 2015)

6.3.3 Conceptual distortions

As noted in the previous chapter, the political field in Armenia is polarized and so is the society. The Republican Party has long had a dominant grip over power in the country. The opposition is considered unreliable, weak and is demoralized in the public eye. The government is no stranger to such perceptions either. Furthermore, there is no clear-cut distinction between pro- and anti- government (ruling party) camps. Even if certain opposition politicians are truly

808 Ibid.

regarded as such, they are still not considered as alternatives since 'the entire political environment in the country has lost its credibility'[809]. Therefore, formal civil society actors – NGOs, lawyers, journalists oppose the government by 'disturbing the system; whether anything changes or not it is important to keep the system busy, overload it with complaints and applications'[810].

The relationship between formal and informal civil society actors is both cooperative and contested. While the former interact with the state at an institutional level, the latter oppose it mainly in the street. Not all causes attract masses into the street however. For instance, justice, violated dignity are accessible to people and tend to attract bigger masses whereas 'human rights' especially in broadly defined terms 'may be comprehensible to 5000–7000 politicized, Westernized people in Armenia, not more, hence, the limited number of participants during certain protests/movements'[811]. The same argument can be made for political prisoners and domestic violence victims. These causes are considered the plight of the affected individuals and their families, whereas social and economic causes are perceived as not only self-centred but also other-centred and usually attract more people; the 'justice-injustice dichotomy is sitting in everyone's head'[812].

Despite being a party to major human rights treaties and conventions, the Armenian government has lacked the political will to incorporate those instruments into domestic settings. Moreover, 'the elites are interested in joining the EU for wealth reasons, i.e. to be able to travel freely, obtain more assets, make investments and join the civilized family of nations rather than for democracy, human rights, liberalism etc.'[813]. There is institutional and cultural deficit. Human rights culture as such is absent. NGOs are not fully independent from the state; some of them also 'play in the government camp'[814]. The only remaining counter forces are the civic initiatives but they 'do not turn into institutional power'. With the civil society or the non-state sector being unable to provide resistance and change the power relationships, 'an irreparable power imbalance is created and the state exercises more control over the active citizens not leaving much space to manoeuvre'[815].

809 Interview with a human rights lawyer, 4 September 2015.
810 Ibid.
811 Interview with a political party member, 7 September 2015.
812 Ibid.
813 Ibid.
814 Interview with a political scientist, 7 September 2015.
815 Ibid.

The NGOs, with exceptions, have largely operated as a business rather than a non-state sector. The public views them as closed institutions that are part of the system. Furthermore, their failure to internalize universal values, translate and adapt them to local traditions, values, lifestyle and mentality has meant that they have functioned within their institutional confines, distancing them further from the society at large. 'Gender', 'advocacy', 'LGBTIQ+ rights', etcetera are still incomprehensible and inaccessible to Armenian laymen despite professionalized NGOs implementing foreign-funded projects locally. Certain vulnerable groups (e.g. LGBTIQ+) and their rights are a taboo field with very few human rights defenders taking up their cause:

> ...being a human rights defender also has unpopular topics. For instance, in Armenia the protection of homosexuals' rights is considered unpopular.
>
> (Human rights defender, 9 September 2015)

In addition to being unpopular, LGBTIQ+ issues as well as those related to gender equality are considered unsafe or not harmless in the NGO circles. The government does not have a welcoming attitude to them, while the public views them as un-Armenian. As a result, while LGBTIQ+ rights are human rights, taken separately that group is located at the margins of the society having to rely on intergroup solidarity (problematic in itself) to solve their problems. It is noteworthy that perceptions of human rights among the Armenian public vary depending on the context, the situation as well as which rights are at stake. Further to this point, if taken in their entirety, human rights are understood as humans having rights, or having claims to rights ascribed to them in the domestic laws and constitution. However, if split into components, such as 'gender equality', 'LGBTIQ+ rights' etcetera, a disconnect takes place with regard to human rights in their entirety versus human rights split into components. The opposite is also true – the oft-violated rights by the Armenian state, such as property rights, right to a fair trial and the right to a peaceful assembly are more accessible and perceivable to laymen in that they are more tangible, their violation and perception thereof stem from personal experiences and the accumulated experience and knowledge contribute to the perception of the aforementioned rights.

NGOs, engaged in human rights advocacy and protection, solve particular issues. Solving particular rights issues does not lead to solving a human rights issue. Human rights advocacy and protection in Armenia, thus, do not lead to establishing a human rights culture, a human rights regime within the Armenian state, a change in the status quo. Rather, both NGOs and civic initiatives tackle *concrete* grievances. This is also due to the fact that human rights perceptions in the Armenian context are self-centred, that is, understood as interests of directly affected beneficiaries. The same is also true about the way civil society institutes are perceived:

> In Armenia when they say civil society institutes they mean NGOs and civic movements, while in the whole world when they say civil society institute they also mean political parties, that is, political parties, NGOs and different civic groups, in Armenia as a result of that fake juxtaposition civic and political parties are as if situated in a political field, when they say civil society representative they mean non-political party adherents in Armenia which is a result of distorted perceptions.
>
> (Political activist, 25 September 2015)

These distorted perceptions have led to separation of the human rights field wherein NGOs view citizens' right to vote as a political issue, therefore, a matter to be handled by the political parties, whereas they themselves engage in the protection of separate human rights violations, such as for instance, violations of the rights of political prisoners, soldiers' rights and so on. Other NGOs engage *only* in women's rights protection, or LGBTIQ+ rights protection, that is to say, human rights protection in Armenia is segmented which in itself is 'a defensive reaction because they know, that if NGOs engage in fundamental issues in the country, the authorities will target the NGOs too, like they target the opposition political parties'[816].

The NGO work remains at an institutional level, limited to the agenda and requirements of the donors. The foreign-funded projects, be it by the UN, the EU or other international organizations, fail to change the mentality of the local population, their thinking and perceptions with regard to values considered alien. As a result, NGOs get funding from abroad, implement whatever is expected from them, while the international organizations 'collect that information and strike a deal with the government'[817]. In other words, foreign-funded Armenian NGOs carry out research, prepare reports based on which the international organizations design recommendations. The latter stem from the interests of those international organizations and are used to negotiate with the authorities while the interests of the general public remain on the side. The authorities, in turn:

> When negotiating with them think how to obtain compromise in their favour, as a result, this one wins, the other one wins, the society is left with nothing, those mechanisms do not work, are harmful, dangerous and imitation largely, that is why the West is pleased

816 Interview with a political activist, 25 September 2015.
817 Ibid.

> with these authorities because they do whatever the West says, but all of it remains on paper, i.e. it remains on paper but the West is pleased because their issues are also solved.
>
> (Political activist, 25 September 2015)

The failure by domestic NGOs to serve the interests of their beneficiaries further adds to the detachment from the general public. They are looked upon as 'Armenian soldiers' servient to the West. Furthermore, grants turn out to be a goal rather than a means to solve issues. While the condition of the beneficiaries doesn't change, the supposed actors of change turn into 'VIP activists, NGO oligarchs, NGO heads who own villas abroad, who own a few apartments here etc.'[818] On the one hand, these NGOs do not become targets for the state, on the other hand:

> ...they get the money, they travel all over the world, their work is not dangerous, it is a kind of a comfort zone where the government does not touch them, their life is not in danger, they participate in parties of ambassadors with pleasure, they go to different conferences all over the world, they have fun, they get money and live on, i.e. I see it as a sort of business, nothing more.
>
> (Political activist, 25 September 2015)

There are a small number of NGOs and activists, however, who pursue genuine interests to bring about a change within the society. They are trying to challenge the 'business' aspect of local NGOs, by standing up for what is needed in Armenia rather than what the international organizations have to offer. However, they are few in number, and the international community is not interested in cooperating with them. Consequently, 'the NGO field remains monopolized because of personal and group interests as well as financial interests'[819]. Since grants are a goal, not a means, NGOs compete with one another. The NGO field in Armenia is divided amongst themselves:

> Behind the curtains they are fighting for kompromat which is not visible publicly, that is the reason for that division as well, this niche is taken for instance, you create a new one. The NGO field is very sick, everyone is a conformist there, the authorities are also happy that the NGO field is such and when that NGO field tries to get out of supervision, immediately calls are made for cooperation by the state, the NGOs immediately enter into that mood, it is a kind of party, i.e. what happens is a sad thing in reality, because it turns out that those who are supposed to bring about a change need to be changed themselves.
>
> (Political activist, 25 September 2015)

---

818 Interview with a political activist, 25 September 2015.
819 Ibid.

The 'niche' reality of NGOs keeps the field accessible to known and approved members. If training is organized somewhere, select NGO members take part. The same circle also participates in other trainings. In the end, those trainings or qualification courses do not go beyond the usual circles for two main reasons: not to allow new rivals to emerge on the scene and secondly, because those NGOs are liaised through suspicious interests. Therefore, 'if a new person enters that field he/she may have questions why it is so, that is why, the field is closed and it cannot be the other way round'[820]. The field is closed not only to those outside the select NGO circles, but to other NGOs as well. Healthy solidarity among the formal civil society sector is absent. Friction exists between ideological communities and groups too. Feminist groups as well as the LGBTIQ+ community, despite fighting for a common cause, suffer from divisions.

Most NGOs are concentrated in the capital Yerevan, and this does not allow their activities to be accessible to the regions where the level of awareness is considerably lower. There are a handful of human rights NGOs operating in the regions, servient to the needs and interests of the regional populations but in comparison to the capital city Yerevan there is still a long way to go. With NGOs failing to bring about a change in the 'Armenian reality', translating foreign values into domestic settings as well as restricted in their institutional activities, 'the street' remains a hopeful resort and space to claim rights and oppose the government. It was noted at the start of this chapter that the educational sector in Armenia is in need of reforms to educate active rather than passive citizens, instil critical thinking and shape citizens with multiple consciousnesses. Since 2007/2008 'the street' has become an attractive and crucial space for Armenians to become 'citizens'. Through contact with others, exchanges with like-minded citizens, the progressive and liberal youth in Armenia have developed legal and rights consciousness. This in turn has shifted human rights perceptions into 'it being related to everyone'. Activists, civic initiatives or as some call them civic movements – the informal non-state actors – have in some ways overshadowed the formal civil society sector and they will be the main focus in the upcoming section.

6.4 Informal non-state actors

Activism in Armenia, manifested in the form of civic initiatives, protests and demonstrations, is a spontaneous action initiated in response to or as a reaction

820 Interview with a political activist, 25 September 2015.

to social and political issues perceived as unjust, corrupt and in need of rectification. Since 2007/2008 there have been a number of such initiatives. These have largely taken place in the capital city Yerevan, likely due to the fact that 'the majority of the students and the young people are based' there, making it easy to mobilize and also perhaps because 'the administrative bodies are based in Yerevan'[821]. The first civic initiatives were organized around environmental issues such as saving Trchkan waterfall (2011), Mashtots Park (2012) and so on that would later become the cornerstones of civic initiatives. Armenia has witnessed mass protests and demonstrations before, especially in the lead up to elections, however, civic initiatives, both with regard to their format and participants as well as course of action should be distinguished. Issue-based and comprising groups of young people in their mid-20s and/or mid-30s, civic initiatives are generally short-term activities aimed at solving a particular problem. In the period 2008–2010 several such initiatives were a success, albeit marginal, gradually changing the perceptions of state-citizen relationships among the Armenian public, youth in particular:

> I think the consciousness, awareness of rights is higher, even in the regions, where there is relatively little experience, there are few organizations, but in any case people have numbers of lawyers, NGOs, if anything goes wrong with them, they are able to respond with the help of law more or less, of course it is still little, but I think there is relative change.
>
> (Feminist activist, 27 August 2015)

Environmental activism has not been about merely nature rights or nature protection. It has had a broader scope, that of civil rights, civic consciousness, actively demanding rather than passively accepting. In the case of Mashtots Park, for example, the objective was not simply for the park not to be converted into a string of boutiques, but, more importantly, it was a manifestation of civil disobedience. Furthermore, the format of the initiative to save Mashtots Park was based on openness, welcoming everyone as a participant; there was no clear-cut leader or established hierarchy. Decisions were made based on majority of votes:

> ....in Mashtots Park one was imagining that it should be a people's park, that we should ourselves design, ourselves decide what park it should be, our events should be, for others it was OK for it to become Taron's park to put it roughly, that is to say, for the city council to do it somewhere else, but for it to remain a park.
>
> (Feminist activist, 27 August 2015)

821 Interview with a human rights lawyer, 25 August 2015.

Initiators and participants in Mashtots Park were knowledgeable and well-informed about the domestic laws and constitution and made frequent references to them when interacting with the police. One of the objectives of the initiative was to make it legally "impenetrable", that is, 'not to allow things that would enable the police to interfere in legal ways'[822]. In order to achieve this objective the participants had agreed 'not to be rude to the police, not to swear at them, to do nothing uncivilized and as soon as anything went wrong' or the participants 'realized there were provocations somewhere, few of them would immediately go to handle it, to neutralise the discussion and that way an interesting process unfolded'[823]. Moreover, Save Mashtots Park initiative set a precedent in employing 'constitutionalism' as its base, in putting 'social contract' into use on site. Its participants thought of themselves as active citizens of Armenia, citizens having 'a right to directly conquer their rights'[824]. And they exercised that right in a well-developed, mature and literate manner.

6.4.1 Activists or active citizens?

However, the civic initiative to Save Mashtots Park did not succeed in setting a precedent for other civic outbreaks that followed. 'Save Teghut' initiative comes close. In general, since 2010 environmental activism has been more pronounced in Armenia. However, many environmentalists do not consider themselves activists. As in the case of concepts such as 'gender', 'activism' is also perceived as a foreign borrowing, a Western import that is alien to the Armenian reality. It is noteworthy that 'activism' bears negative connotations not only for activists themselves and the way they see themselves, but the way [perceived] activists are viewed by fellow activists. Most of the well-known and experienced activists I interviewed did not like being referred to as 'activists'. To start with, the Armenian language does not have a native equivalent to 'activist'[825]. This lack of a native equivalent leaves room for various misinterpretations. The

---

822 Interview with a lawyer, 15 September 2015.

823 Ibid.

824 Interview with a political scientist, 7 September 2015.

825 Similar problems occurred with regard to 'advocacy' as described by Armine Ishkanian in her book 'Democracy Building and Civil Society in Post-Soviet Armenia' (Routledge, 2008: 101). 'Advocacy' when translated into Armenian takes on a negative connotation and conjures up images of the repressive Soviet state that kept citizens under surveillance (*hskvumeyin*) and sought to shape their opinions through the massive state propaganda machine'. As of 2007, 'advocacy', according to Ishkanian is being translated into Armenian as 'the protection of interests' (*shaheri pashpanutyun*),

local term that has been used to describe 'activists' in Armenia is 'ashkhuzhak' or 'ashkhuzhak-payqarik', both to an extent responsible for negative perceptions of 'activists' and 'activism' in the Armenian context. 'Active' in Armenian is translated as 'ashkhuyzh', meaning energetic and/or enthusiastic, while the suffix –ak/ik is a diminutive, that when added to 'active' (ashkhuyzh) turns an 'activist' into 'a person who is part of that "tusovka" (party), turns up at all events, they even joke on Facebook, do you have an activist's diploma or not; activism has become a profession, what is activism?'[826].

The perception of 'activism' as a profession attaches expectations to those who are engaged in it. Furthermore, the term gets 'abused', with 'anyone imagining anything under "activism"' and secondly, it tends to be exclusionary in that:

> It defines a specific group of people who shall handle a certain issue, while whatever I have done, I have done it as an ordinary person, ordinary citizen and I have not done anything special and I suppose everyone can and shall do it if need be, i.e. to consider that there are certain activists who are carrying the burden of solving this and that issue is also problematic though on the other hand I understand if the field is empty, certain people appear and say we are solving this problem, those expectations arise independently of you, but I do not like that term and I personally have a problem with it, I have never called myself an activist; I may say a participant of an initiative, participant of a movement, but I do not consider myself an activist.
>
> (Activist, 27 August 2015)

The association of 'activism' and 'activists' with the West, the 'us vs them' dichotomy not only in relation to the West, Western culture, Western lifestyle but also in relation to other political events and accompanying protests at home such as the 1988[827] movement cast further doubts upon the terms 'activism' and 'activists'. These definitional problems get even more complicated when the 'civil' and the 'political' are juxtaposed and treated separately rather than as intertwined concepts. The participants at the 1988 movement did differ from those in present-day civic initiatives. To start with, 1988 'began as an ecological movement but rapidly transformed into calls for the reunification of the region of Nagorno-Karabakh in the Soviet Republic of Azerbaijan with the Soviet Republic of

---

which in her view 'again does not capture the meaning of the English word "advocacy"' (Routledge, 2008:101).

826 Interview with an activist, 25 September 2015.

827 See Mark Malkasian, *Gha-ra-bagh!: The Emergence of the National Democratic Movement in Armenia* (Wayne State University Press, 1996) for details on the 1988 movement.

Armenia and subsequent calls for Armenian independence'[828]. Although the movement initially was based on an ecological agenda without political goals, 'as it intensified with an enormous consciousness it transformed to a nationalist movement with a political and ecological agenda'[829]. The movement, although environmental in form, was national in content[830]. Through their grievances with regard to industrial pollution, the activists criticized government policy[831].

Since then Armenia has experienced several outbreaks, especially in the lead up to elections, contesting voting results, opposing political leaders deemed as illegitimate and demanding regime change. What happened in 1989 is generally not likened to contemporary civic initiatives in Armenia. 1989 'was a political liberation movement, and there were leaders whom the people were following', whereas 'the idea of leadership is rejected by most civic initiatives'[832]. Furthermore, 'activism' is largely perceived as a 'Western' term among the Armenian public, hence the rebuttal. The protesters in 1989 are talked about as a 'movement', a 'whole' without separating them from the society at large. Interestingly, activists, as they have been named following the rise in civic initiatives and protests in Armenia since 2007/2008, tend to be separated from the society at large and viewed as a separate and specific group of people charged with a mission and a duty. Failure in fulfilling perceived and expected duties leads to further singling out of this specific group with attendant labels attached to them:

> ...activism is not a profession, civic consciousness is also a bit relative, if you look the movement of 1988 when people had gathered and there was no room for a needle there, they had neither attended seminars, nor trainings organized by the USAID but it was a rights conscious society that had come with a demand, much more rights conscious than say young people who have attended a thousand trainings and seminars, who also insert a few English words in their lexicon to appear more activist.
>
> (Journalist, 4 September 2015)

Activists themselves feel uneasy with the term and opt for other ways to describe themselves and their activity. They opt for the term "active citizen", one who is motivated to handle a particular group of rights, either owing to a personal

828 Armine Ishkanian, *Democracy Building and Civil Society in Post-Soviet Armenia* (Routledge, 2008), 8.

829 Ohannes Geukjian, "The Politicization of the Environmental Issue in Armenia and Nagorno-Karabakh's Nationalist Movement in the South Caucasus 1985–1991," *Nationalities Papers* 35, no. 2 (May 2007): 233.

830 Ibid., 238.

831 Ibid.

832 Interview with a human rights defender, 31 August 2015.

motivation, because they themselves belong to a vulnerable group or because an active citizen defends their rights by defending the rights of others or 'he is an ideologist who attaches a lot of significance to that issue, understands the importance of that issue, the seriousness of the idea, it being an indicator from the perspective of social change and engages in it'[833]. Interestingly, as in the case of activists being singled out as a separate group, 'active citizens' are contrasted to passive citizens by activists to describe themselves. Their activity is one of active participation as opposed to passive acceptance, resistance versus submission to authority:

> ...the one who is active, a citizen who is there, passive sitting on his sofa in front of the TV and there is a citizen who is active and trying to bring forth some issues of public importance and trying to find solutions to those questions in some ways or get to it that those issues are handled.
>
> (Lawyer, 15 September 2015)

The activity in which an active citizen engages is supposed to be free of any kind of monetary gains. When a private gain overtakes public interests, and 'activism' pursues self-centred rather than other-centred goals, it runs the risk of being perceived as a 'profession' and subsequently refuted. Furthermore, it transfers the struggle onto a superficial level, where 'ideology' is absent and the activity is personal instead, 'the personal being the financial'[834]. The transitory nature of 'activism' is an oft-overlooked aspect that gives rise to misperceptions of the term in the Armenian context among other things. Activists are deemed as permanent, static professionals fixed in a particular time frame and setting in a ceaseless pursuit of social justice. However, 'activism' is a fluid activity alternating between active and passive periods with either one or the other being dominant at a given time. Hence, the expressions 'old activist', 'new activist', 'experienced activist' denoting particular activists, a particular time frame and setting:

> First of all activism like that, when you say old activist, Mariam has said very well that now I am not active, right she has said, well activism is not that you did something once, then you remain active for the rest of your life, because for three months you struggled in Mashtots Park, activism, you shall be active, now in this question, in that question.
>
> (Political scientist, 7 September 2015)

833 Interview with an activist, 25 September 2015.
834 Ibid.

6.4.2 Is civil also political?

Civic initiatives, outbreaks and/or resistances in Armenia recently do not necessarily and always lead to complete results, that is to say, they do not always result in positive solutions, but they indicate a process that has been initiated, that is aimed at demonstrating to the government that the citizens are disheartened and distrustful towards politicians who are no longer viewed as problem solvers. That sentiment is reflected in their announcements that their struggle is not political strongly denouncing the latter's weaknesses and by insisting that their struggle is civic they are stressing the importance of taking civic action, of being and staying active as members of citizenry that shall solve its problems relying on itself rather than on politicians. However, the contradiction lies in the fact that at the end all these young people involved in civic actions make political announcements. If the issue were solved at a state level, it would not spread onto the streets, if an issue goes into the street, it speaks of a failure at a higher level.

The loss of faith in politics following 2008 also led to political parties getting discredited in the public eye. Coupled with a weak opposition viewed as clients to the ruling regime and no political alternative in sight, 'the civil sphere' and its actors took to the scene as alternative opposing forces to the political reality in Armenia. Their objective was to conquer their rights and freedoms incrementally, through separate, small issues. A visible aspect of recent civic initiatives is their insistence on depoliticization, while at the same time having political agendas. 'Do not politicize' is a phrase one can hear during most protests taking place in Armenia. It is noteworthy that activists themselves disagree on the civil-*not*-political debate:

> Civil or political debate is absurd; under political it is assumed that the ruling regime shall step down, while the civil ones who are saying do not politicize mean do not speak about regime change; the civil or political debate has been promoted by the government itself also which has been prominently reflected in the media, that is, they are thinking let any process take place in Armenia, that's OK, only for it not to be our resignation.
>
> (Activist, 25 September 2015)

The civil-political divide is intentional in that firstly, by chanting 'don't politicize' civic initiatives detach their agendas from politics and political parties, thereby preventing alienation of potential supporters from their cause. Secondly, by detaching their civic goals from political ones they hope to be able to negotiate with the authorities and achieve at least a partial if not complete solution to the issues at stake. And finally, civic issues and agendas are considered more flexible, safe and harmless, or to use the local term 'anshar' and are not likely to get as much backlash from the authorities as political causes and agendas would. They also tend to be more clearly formulated and attract more supporters. For instance, 'transport fee shall not rise; it should be 100 AMD'[835]. Whereas political causes such as, for example, constitutional amendments, are difficult to explain to people since the latter do not have trust in the functionality of the constitution:

> The Constitution does not work, that is, the Constitution is the basic law, the laws do not function, including the Constitution, it does not function either. It is difficult to explain to the person, to make him understand that the Constitution proposes the issue of permanent legalized reproduction of the authorities; he says well they reproduce whenever they want anyway. Well it is very difficult to make them understand, while the issue of 150 dram is very easy, you do not pay 50 dram, that's it.
>
> (Lawyer, 15 September 2015)

The authorities are keen to meet civic action halfway as long as it lies within the remit of being civic; the longer it takes them to find a solution, the more politicized it will become. Different civic groups/initiatives operate on their own, they do not cooperate with each other, they do not come together to become a mass movement. This fragmentation of civic struggle works in favour of the authorities. Civic action is important as a watchdog, as a guardian over the actions and duties of the authorities, however, change is a result of political decisions and those decisions will not be citizen-centric as long as the current ruling regime stays in power.

The civil-political divide is political in and of itself. Any protest is directed at the ruling regime in the end since the need for that protest has arisen as a result of political decisions. Moreover, a civic unrest cannot be only civic or social despite claims otherwise. After all, any civic activity is carried out through exercise and enjoyment of political rights, such as freedom of assembly, right to freedom of expression, and so on. Hence, civil assembly, civil speech is by itself already political, making it 'impossible to not politicize the political'[836]. By raising issues whose solution lies within the political arena and requires action by politicians, activists do politics and engage not only in civic but also political action. A true political opposition being absent in Armenia and the civil society expected to fill the vacuum, civic activism is perceived as *that* opposition especially following 2008, and while both the public and the government consider activists doing politics, the activists themselves try to detach from that label on every occasion.

---

835 Interview with a lawyer, 15 September 2015.
836 Interview with a feminist activist, 27 August 2015.

The civil-political artificial divide is maintained in 'media outlets, in the social media, in speeches, and it is also a tool of manipulation'[837]:

> Political parties are discredited. Civic initiatives contribute to imitation; the authorities carry out imitation – look we have freedom of speech, look we have civic movements, look we have free media which is not free at all in reality and on the one hand those civic movements are positive, on the other hand, they indeed contribute to power imitation.
>
> (Activist, 25 September 2015)

Decisions to join civic initiatives or protests are usually based on one's perceptions as a citizen, one with specialized knowledge and skills that can contribute to the solution of the problem at stake. Joining a particular civic initiative does not necessarily lead to joining every other as well, since each pursues a certain goal, such as, for instance, 'saving a waterfall', or 'contributing to the mining in this or that area to be terminated'[838] and so on.

There is progress amongst the youth as to how they perceive themselves within the Armenian state and as members of active citizenry who should get involved in the civil sector in Armenia and contribute to the public good rather than strive for private gains. However, issue-specific civic initiatives each concentrate on a particular problem and gather around that problem. The issue of 'the masses' arises in that they do not develop into a mass movement and each operates within their niche and that leads to fragmentation within the civil sphere. However, despite their marginal success, civic struggles, initiatives or protests have revealed a new generation, new political generation, not from a physical point of view but from an ideological perspective.

Activism is not only transitory but dynamic as well. Those dynamisms are manifested not only in the activities undertaken by activists but in whatever paths activists follow once they stop being active and adopt not so active lifestyles or, rather, continue their activity on different platforms. Some of them become politicized in the sense that they become members of political parties, some quit activism in general and others continue to organize tours and expeditions while still engaging in matters related to nature. There are also activists who join environmental struggles/activism not necessarily being environmentalists themselves. The latter engage in environmental struggles when there is a common objective and the stated ideas resonate with them and their ideological inclinations such as, for example 'the right to a healthy environment'. Perceptions

837 Interview with a journalist, 17 September 2015.
838 Interview with a human rights lawyer, 25 August 2015.

of rights and the accompanying activist struggles move back and forth between broad and specific causes, claims and demands:

> Different people were involved in the environmental movements of 2008, 2009, 2010. There were groups that were for instance doing expeditions, they simply had love for nature, but other than that they were not politicized, for example, the fact that HPP was being built on Trchkan, the fact that Teghut was turning into a mine, that one group of people did not see for instance the economic policy behind it; I don't know the class issues, that is why, it was simply an issue of nature destruction.
>
> (Feminist activist, 27 August 2015)

Mashtots Park has been the best example/case thus far in terms of statements that were made as well as the standpoints different participants expressed them from – social, economic or political. It revealed not only the interconnectedness of the social, the economic and the political but also the intertwined nature of economic, social, cultural, civil and political rights. The latter have been exercised to voice social and economic concerns. As such, social and economic rights have been more underlined in civic struggles and, as was noted earlier, they have echoed the despair of a large number of people. Furthermore, social and economic rights are more tangible and their deprivation highlights political issues:

> . . .for me personally for instance those organizations that are only busy with monitoring elections or those that are monitoring the violations of the rights of political prisoners, in general prisoners' rights are not appealing. They are doing an important work, there's nothing wrong with it, but I don't know I am more interested in social, economic issues, also because those inequalities are visible there and to an extent also the roots, where political issues originate from.
>
> (Feminist activist, 27 August 2015)

6.4.3 Electric Yerevan protests

Electric Yerevan, locally known as 'No to Plunder' was one of several protests marking the Armenian political scene since the early 2000s. More specifically, it belongs to the series of mass protests domestically termed as 'civic initiatives', that is, protests initiated and led by a group or groups of young people that attract more supporters as they proceed. The protests started on June 20, 2015 lasting until 11 September 2015. On June 17, Armenia's Public Services Regulatory Commission (PSRC) announced that the Electricity Networks of Armenia (ENA) would be allowed to raise the electricity fees in Armenia by another 16 %, starting August 1[839]. The fee increase would amount to an estimated $85 a year

---

839 Markar Melkonian, "No to Plunder, No to Maidan," *Hetq*, 26 June 2015, accessed

for an average household[840]. Poor households already struggling to cover the costs of housing, public transportation, healthcare, and higher education, would now have to pay more than 50 % for electricity than they did three years ago[841].

June 22, 2015 was notable for the escalation of protests against the stated decision when several thousand protesters set off from Yerevan's Liberty Square to march towards the Presidential Palace on Baghramyan Avenue[842]. They were met with 'a large phalanx of police' that 'brought the march to a halt'[843]. A sit-in followed. As the night approached 'the hundreds of demonstrators on Baghramyan were singing and dancing, calling on residents of Yerevan to join them'[844]. However, in the early hours at approximately 5:30 a.m. riot police began moving towards the crowd, using water cannons against the protesters[845]. Police officers in civilian clothes dragged people away from the scene with batons[846]. As a result, 25 people were hospitalised and 237 arrested. Journalists were also targeted by the police; several had their equipment confiscated or damaged[847]. Amnesty International called on the Armenian authorities to 'urgently ensure an impartial, independent and thorough investigation into allegations that police used excessive force – including dousing people with water cannon – to disperse a mainly peaceful demonstration before arresting more than 200 protesters on the streets of the capital Yerevan'[848]. Denis Krivosheev, Deputy Europe and Central Asia Programme Director at Amnesty International stated that:

> For the Armenian authorities to disperse what was up until then a peaceful demonstration is a heavy-handed tactic that must be avoided to protect the right to freedom of

18 October 2018, http://hetq.am/eng/news/61154/.

840 Ibid.

841 Ibid.

842 Ibid.

843 Ibid.

844 'Electricity Protest in Yerevan Turns Violent as Police Use Water Canons to Disperse Crowds,' *CIVILNET*, 23 June 2015, accessed 11 October 2018, https://www.civilnet.am/news/2015/06/23/electricity-protest-yerevan-turns-violent-water-cannons/272683.

845 'Day-by-day #Electric Yerevan,' *CIVILNET*, 27 June 2015, accessed 11 October 2018, https://www.civilnet.am/news/2015/06/27/day-by-day-electricyerevan/273182.

846 Ibid.

847 Ibid.

848 "Armenia: Investigate Alleged Police Abuses after Protesters Doused with Water Cannon and Arrested," *Amnesty International*, 23 June 2015, accessed 15 October 2018, https://www.amnesty.org/en/latest/news/2015/06/armenia-investigate-alleged-police-abuses-after-protesters-doused-with-water-cannon-and-arrested/.

> expression and assembly. Video footage showing high-powered jets from water cannon flinging peaceful protesters to the ground is a cause for concern.[849]

The heavy-handed dispersal of protesters, nevertheless, did not thin the circles of demonstrators. On the contrary, from 6 p.m. on June 24, 2015, more people joined in for an evening of chanting, singing and dancing[850]. As the closure of Baghramyan Avenue entered its fourth day, the president's office issued a statement that following a meeting between the then President Serzh Sargsyan and Russian transport minister Maxim Sokolov, Sargsyan recommended the creation of a Russian-Armenian inter-governmental commission to undertake an independent audit of the Russian-owned Electric Networks of Armenia[851].

On Saturday, 27 June 2015, at about 1:00 a.m. several protesters decided to block Mashtots and Tumanyan avenues, prompting the then 'Police Chief Vova Gasparyan to yell uncontrollably at organizers and say that the police did not want to move in, but would have to take measures if those adjacent streets would not be cleared of protesters'[852]. As the situation escalated, police reinforcements were brought in[853]. Confrontation took place between the police forces and the protesters. The protests gradually died down. While the intended audit announced by Serzh Sargsyan concluded that 'the electricity tariff was in fact warranted'[854]. The government approved the sale of Electricity Networks of Armenia (ENA) to the Tashir Group[855]. The Armenian government and the Tashir Group then announced that 'they would jointly subsidize the difference between the previous and current electricity prices for households and small businesses, but only until July 31, 2016, and only to a certain amount (those who exceed the limit will pay the new price on their entire bill)'[856].

Electric Yerevan was one of a series of protests that have marked 'a tradition of dissent and contention against government abuses, which include successful

849 Ibid.

850 'Day-by-day #Electric Yerevan,' *CIVILNET*, 27 June 2015, accessed 15 October 2018, https://www.civilnet.am/news/2015/06/27/day-by-day-electricyerevan/273182.

851 Ibid.

852 Ibid.

853 Ibid.

854 Nona Shahnazarian, "'Here Is Not Maidan, Here Is Marshal Baghramian': The 'Electric Yerevan' Protest Movement and Its Consequences," *PONARS Eurasia*, January 2016, accessed 17 October 2018, http://www.ponarseurasia.org/memo/here-not-maidan-here-marshal-baghramian-electric-yerevan-protest.

855 Ibid.

856 Ibid.

protests against mining projects in Armenia's north and planned transport fare hikes for Yerevan'[857]. Like previous protests or, as they are locally termed, 'civic initiatives', Electric Yerevan was organized in an informal way by a group of young 'activists', later joined by an estimated 20,000 people[858]. In addition to offline activities, online platforms were created and made available to mobilize, inform fellow citizens about planned activities, raise the awareness about the protests, as well as acquaint people with certain laws whenever and wherever required. One such big online platform is the public group 'We are against the electricity price hike' on Facebook, comprising some 20,600 members. The group has been active since 2014 and was created in order to 'Fight against electricity price hike and prevent it'. The group serves as a platform to 'share information, spread awareness among the public, express opinions, organize discussions and make suggestions'. Additionally, it posts announcements about upcoming events, short videos from the scene where events are taking place as well as updates about government decisions with regard to grievances and claims that have been raised in relation to issues put forward during protests.

Protests in the offline field, which I will term 'the street' to denote the public space where interactions, confrontations, exchange of ideas, discussions and action take place, usually take the form of rallies, demonstrations, sit-ins, marches, blocking streets and sometimes hunger strikes. Both online and offline fields have been actively used by activists/protesters in Armenia in recent years. The key differences between the two fields owe to visibility that exposes the individual in the offline field/the street, thereby putting the resources they have in peril, while online activity is invisible and given the relatively free online media in Armenia, it enables more people to get involved. However, as much as online media facilitates civic engagement, it at the same time makes them more vulnerable and aware that once their online activity takes to the street they may risk exposure and repercussions. This is why apart from public posts and discussions, there also exist closed groups that only approved people/members have access to, which enables like-minded and trustworthy individuals to come together and design plans of action. These plans of action are then executed in the street bringing together people who share a feeling of apathy, despair because they all have problems in their homes but:

857 Karena Avedissian, "The Power of Electric Yerevan," *openDemocracy*, 6 July 2015, accessed 17 October 2018, https://www.opendemocracy.net/karena-avedissian/electrified-yerevan.

858 Ibid.

> When there is a public space, public sphere, public field, a space where you can speak, that is, complain, if only to one another, those spaces do not exist or are very few now, very few, maximum say kitchens, houses, workplace perhaps but not everywhere.
>
> (Activist, 27 August 2015)

Public space makes an individual a part of a collective with a shared feeling, both positive and negative, ranging from love for their country, its future, frustrations with state officials to ideological similarities, such as feminist causes, economic inequalities, etcetera. A remarkable feature of civic activities in the Armenian setting has been increasing knowledge and awareness of domestic laws and the constitution which has empowered the citizens vis-à-vis state authorities. Domestic laws and constitution have served as 'a sword to attack and defend'[859] and many a time during protests they have been referenced by activists when confronting the police. On the other hand, the police have confronted the protesters with counter frames, one of the infamous ones being the installation of 'agitators' among activist circles or protest groups to provoke the police, thereby causing public disorder forcing the riot police to intervene. This counter tactic has been put to use during several protests, most notoriously during the 2016 Yerevan Hostage Crisis when 'police used stun grenades, which wounded dozens of demonstrators and some journalists, some severely. The police also beat journalists and protesters and detained dozens of people'[860]. Unidentified men in civilian clothes also took part in detaining protesters, beating them, also beating journalists, damaging and taking their equipment[861]. Victims were dragged, punched, kicked and beaten with wooden clubs[862]. Some suffered injuries to their faces, arms, hands, shoulders, backs, and legs[863].

Mass protests in Armenia have generally encountered violent intervention on the part of the police. Nonetheless, 'the street' remains the space where resident-to-citizen making takes place. The street is the only option left when all other options have been exhausted:

> We don't have much choice, that is the only thing that is left because your voice is not heard, neither by the legislative body, nor by the executive, if it is heard, very formal, it

859 Interview with a former MP and public activist, 25 August 2015.

860 "Armenia: Excessive Police Force at Protest," *Human Rights Watch*, 1 August 2016, accessed 18 October 2018, https://www.hrw.org/news/2016/08/01/armenia-excessive-police-force-protest.

861 Ibid.

862 Ibid.

863 Ibid.

> has an imitative nature, that is why people take to the streets, because there are no other places where their voice will be heard, that is the only available option...
>
> (Activist, 27 August 2015)

6.4.4 Exercising rights in 'The Street'

The street is not just an empty and abstract space where crowds gather and enter into motion towards a certain direction. The street is filled for a specific objective, which may or may not be achieved in the end. However, the street can also be gradually emptied as a result of internal frictions, political manoeuvres and external forces. The already noted Electric Yerevan protest is a case in point. Spiked by the intended electricity price hike, Electric Yerevan marked deep-seated issues in the Armenian political reality. Namely, pervasive corruption, bribery and nepotism being common practice among government officials, persistent limits on press freedom, judiciary that suffers from a lack of independence and transparency as well as prosecutorial bias, arbitrary rulings, extensive use of pre-trial detention, and artificially low acquittal rates amongst others[864]. Electric Yerevan protests demonstrated once again persistent issues in relation to police misconduct, including arbitrary arrests without warrants, beatings during arrest and interrogation, and the use of torture to extract confessions[865].

Protesters took to the streets demanding a repeal of the electricity tariff hike, review of the current fare and holding the police accountable for the excessive use of force on 23 June 2015[866]. Chants such as 'no to plunder' and 'we are the owners of our country' accompanied the protests along with posters reading 'Get out of your home, join us, NOT plunder', 'I'm not anti-system, the system is anti me', 'The more you water us, the more we will grow', 'Baghramyan will never become Maydan', 'My name is fight, my end victory', 'High Voltage' and so on. While these posters were designed to highlight the objectives of the protest, they were also intended to attract supporters and they acquired new objectives as the protests proceeded. 'The more you water us, the more we will grow' was aimed at the police and their use of water cannons to disperse the demonstrators on 23 June 2015. 'Baghramyan will never become Maydan' together with 'This is not

---

864 'Freedom in the World: Armenia,' *Freedom House*, 2015, accessed 18 October 2018, https://freedomhouse.org/report/freedom-world/2015/armenia.

865 Ibid.

866 Karena Avedissian, "The Power of Electric Yerevan," *openDemocracy*, 6 July 2015, accessed 17 October 2018, https://www.opendemocracy.net/karena-avedissian/electrified-yerevan.

Maydan, this is Marshal Baghramyan' was aimed at Russian and Western media likening Electric Yerevan to colour revolutions in other post-Soviet states, as well as presenting it as either anti-Russian or meddled with by the West. Reacting to Electric Yerevan, several Russian MPs called on the Armenian government to expel the American ambassador, claiming that US diplomats were trying to "incite another colour revolution"[867]. In turn, Tevan Pogosian, an Armenian MP stated that the situation had been caused by the poor management of the Electric Networks of Armenia and that 'instead of improving management, some people were looking for "Maidans" '[868].

Reflecting on the 'danger of lazy analogies' Sergei Markedonov noted that since Kyiv's 'EuroMaidan' 'most opposition activity in the post-Soviet space is viewed through "Ukrainian lens" '[869]. Such moves, however, shift 'the domestic political agenda in any given country to the background'. Instead, domestic politics is made a sacrifice to 'geopolitical determinism', according to which 'any crisis in former Soviet territories are merely a reflection of the "proxy war" between America and Russia'[870]. The demonstrators themselves insisted the protests focused on issues a little closer to home, such as failings of the Armenian government and, more essentially, the hold that corruption has over broad swaths of governance and everyday life[871].

The protests were notable in attracting large masses, using eye-catching posters, songs and dances as well as forming barricades between the police and the demonstrators by arranging public trash bins between them, thereby highlighting the distance that exists between the citizens and the state. The police are viewed as a brutal force that executes the president's orders and generally creates negative feelings among the public. Since the infamous events of

---

867 Roland Oliphant, "Armenia's "Electric Yerevan" Protests Enter Seventh Day," *Telegraph*, 25 June 2015, accessed 18 October 2018, https://www.telegraph.co.uk/news/worldnews/europe/armenia/11699692/Armenias-Electric-Yerevan-protests-enter-seventh-day.html.

868 Ibid.

869 Sergei Markedonov, "What Armenians Are Protesting (and What They're Not)," *openDemocracy*, 24 June 2015, accessed 18 October 2018, https://www.opendemocracy.net/sergei-markedonov/what-armenians-are-protesting-and-what-they%E2%80%99re-not-protesting.

870 Ibid.

871 Michael Cecire, '"Electric Yerevan" Protests Put Spotlight on Armenia's Corruption,' *World Politics Review*, 15 July 2015, accessed 18 October 2018, https://www.worldpoliticsreview.com/articles/16232/electric-yerevan-protests-put-spotlight-on-armenia-s-corruption.

1 March 2008[872] when mass protests met with a heavy-handed response leading to 10 deaths, including 8 civilians and 2 policemen, the police have been an intervening force during large-scale protests in Armenia[873]. The distance and mistrust between the protesters and the police has grown deeper with each protest and the first time that attempts were made to identify the police as citizens and 'one of us' was during 2016 Yerevan Hostage Crisis protests and 2018 mass protests that led to the resignation of Serzh Sargsyan which will be discussed in more details later.

In contrast to 'Save Mashtots Park' civic initiative, which is viewed by many as the most literate, mature and organized civic activity in Armenia, Electric Yerevan suffered from a lack of exit strategy and a clear agenda. During such civic initiatives as 'Save Mashtots Park' and 'I will only pay 100 dram' participants constantly said what they were thinking and why, why they thought what they were saying was correct and what it was they were proposing, while Electric Yerevan lacked a plan of action and although Baghramyan Avenue remained blocked for almost two weeks, the activity died down in the end. It comprised several key organizers but gained wide public support as it went on.

Generally, civic activities in Armenia have been directed at the government, its policies and the many decays that have been characterising it since independence. Some civic initiatives have had specific demands such as 'de-privatize public transport system and return public property to the community', 'install a complex and integrated public transport system in the city of Yerevan, including alternative means of transportation', 'implement strict monitoring over transport companies, so that they provide quality, safe and civilized services in the meantime ensuring the labour rights and appropriate working conditions for drivers and other members of staff', 'creation and reinforcement of drivers' unions'[874] and the participants have acted in accordance with designed strategies and plan of action to achieve the intended goals. Others, such as Electric Yerevan have set up the demands but failed to act strategically throughout the duration of

---

872 United States Department of State, *Bureau of Democracy, Human Rights and Labor, Country Reports on Human Rights Practices for 2008*, ARMENIA, 25 February 2009, accessed 10 June 2018, https://www.state.gov/j/drl/rls/hrrpt/2008/eur/119066.htm.

873 Nadja Douglas, "The Culture of Policing in Armenia," No. 3/2018 (August 2018), ZOiS Report, accessed 8 November 2018, https://www.zois-berlin.de/fileadmin/media/Dateien/ZOiS_Reports/ZOiS_Report_3_2018.pdf.

874 '"Vtcharum enq 100 dram" nakhadzernutyan haytararutyuny,' [Announcement of "We pay 100 dram" initiative] *Hetq*, 26 July 2013, accessed 21 October 2018, http://hetq.am/arm/news/28378/vtcharum-enq-100-dram-nakhadzernutyan-haytararutyuny.html.

the protests. Yerevan Hostage Crisis 2016 protests followed a similar path. Civic activities are not unilinear collective actions formed around a static spirit of unison, but rather what starts as collective breaks down into individual characteristics with accompanying consequences.

Electric Yerevan comprised a group of several young people in their late 20s – early 30s that were the core of the protests; they were the initiating group making announcements, decisions and so on. Activists that had taken part in previous protests and civic initiatives reported that Electric Yerevan was masculinized and the decision-making was concentrated at the hands of the initiating group with other activists being free to join the protests but not allowed to have a say in organizational or strategic matters. The involvement of more experienced activists would add to the quality of the protests, further enhancing and reinforcing them. However, most civic initiatives usually contain a nucleus, that is, a key or core group of initiators that lead the protests attracting supporters along the way. Mobilizing around issues of concern has not been a difficult task. Affective emotions have proved to be a powerful step in the creation of outrage and the fixing of blame[875]. The ruling regime in Armenia has been distrusted by the public[876] and has aroused negative emotions for reasons discussed in Chapter 5. And the series of protests that have occurred in the country, whether social, political or environmental, have had a clear target: the current regime must go away for want of a more democratic government and better governance. In this regard, protests have managed to mobilize people rather quickly; however, rupture has taken place as a result of viewpoints, indecision as to what to do next and how to make the protests more sustainable:

> ...you know during that period what was a weak side in our movements, that when some, in general it is like that in the world, it is very easy to mobilize against something, to say we do not want this, both the fascist may not want for the electricity price to increase and the LGBT activist, the anarchists, the feminist groups, everyone may not want it to increase, but what to do afterwards, always conflicts arise there, because of viewpoints.
>
> (Feminist activist, 27 August 2015)

Civic initiatives in Armenia have, as a matter of fact been organized by several like-minded individuals who have come together to pursue their common

875 James M. Jasper, "The Emotions of Protest: Affective and Reactive Emotions in and around Social Movements," *Sociological Forum* 13, no. 3 (September, 1998): 406.

876 Yevgenya Paturyan, "(Dis)trusting People and Political Institutions in Armenia," *Caucasus Analytical Digest* 31 (2011): 6–10.

interests, such as, preserve the environment, stop mining in rural areas, preserve a waterfall and so on[877]. The outlooks and behaviour of some of these actors have been shaped by ideational factors, 'ranging from culture and ideology to aspirations and principled beliefs, onto cause-effect knowledge of specific policy problems'[878]. However, the reverse has also been the case, that is, the possession or enjoyment of human rights has led individuals to only use them for their own benefit. This loss of sense of obligation for the human rights of others has been viewed not only as a betrayal of the human rights concept[879] but also blurred the boundaries within which activism is perceived in Armenia:

> Civic activism is a way to collect social capital; even without doing anything, being at the relevant place at the relevant time allowed to quickly collect social capital which then was not correctly diversified. Stardom issues arise which disrupt the connection between the rest of the community and the activist becomes a sort of a dinosaur...
>
> (Activist, 31 August 2015)

Collective action frames involve identity construction; therefore, internal rifts between activists and/or protest groups can prove disruptive to the overall end result. Collective resistance is a joint action that thrives on the 'we' feeling of the resisting group. At the start 'we', a politically defined group seeks rights and when '"we" succeeds in obtaining rights it loses its "we-ness" and dissolves into individuals'[880]. However, the 'we-ness' needs to first be maintained throughout the resistance phase in order to conquer the claimed rights before dissolving into individuals. If 'we-ness' dissolves into individuals before the claimed rights are conquered or the intended goals are achieved, the protest, resistance, civic action or any other civic activity risks disruption and gradual abatement:

> Where is Electric's thing, agenda, what agendas have been set up after Mashtots Park, what strategies have been designed? Well we should self-criticism, but as soon as you get to that stage when you should make an assessment everyone where they have been

---

877 Armine Ishkanian, Evelina Gyulkhandanyan, Sona Manusyan and Arpy Manusyan, "Civil Society, Development and Environmental Activism in Armenia," (2013), accessed 23 October 2018, http://eprints.lse.ac.uk/54755/1/Ishkanian_Civil_Society_Development_Enviromental_Activism_America_2013.pdf.

878 John Gerard Ruggie, "What Makes the World Hang Together? Neo-utilitarianism and the Social Constructivist Challenge," *International Organization* 52, no. 4 (1998): 879.

879 Marie-Bénédicte Dembour, "What Are Human Rights? Four Schools of Thought," *Human Rights Quarterly* 32, no. 1 (2010): 8.

880 Wendy Brown, "States of Injury: Power and Freedom in Late Modernity," (Princeton University Press, 1995): 98, quoted in Costas Douzinas and Conor Gearty, eds. *The Meanings of Rights: The Philosophy and Social Theory of Human Rights* (Cambridge University Press, 2014), 115.

active does not want to be pointed out and they personally, that is the fanaticism, they take it personally, but I was active in Mashtots Park or in 100 or Pak Shuka, well if I tell you something, we want to evaluate, etc. you already take it personally not to be criticized because no you did well, but it cannot be like that, it shall be done, that assessment shall be done and to see where you are, together, separately we make analysis, etc. but together, those who want to work in this sphere, let's say OK now we are here, and want to get here, right?

(Political Scientist, 7 September 2015)

The 'Save Mashtots Park' initiative, notwithstanding issues of its own, set a precedent for civic action where citizens learnt to 'conquer their rights themselves'. They were able to organize around preserving Mashtots Park and interact with the police through the language of law and constitution. The activists engaged in the initiative were inclusive and open to different views and suggestions. However, that positive dynamic did not lead to fundamental changes since it did not alter the power relationship. The other actor, the state and its authorities, used the initiative in their favour since electoral campaigns were under way at the time. They allowed the action to proceed in order to 'demonstrate that there is freedom of speech, expression, peaceful assembly and protest and to boost their publicity during that period to attract voters'[881]. In the end, Mashtots Park was saved but activists became victims of a 'propaganda machine' setting the stage of the well-known 'do not politicize' slogan, wherein issues at stake are apolitical in nature. In the period between 2008 to 2016, 'various civic initiatives in Armenia tried to raise awareness of local problems and solve some of them, but there were no mass protests that could challenge the government and spark major changes in society'[882]. Most of the raised problems were social and environmental issues[883]. And even though they recorded some successes, the activity did not turn into institutional power:

...preparedness, Constitution, what it says, how you are doing it, what issue in which way, you design a strategy, you assess that strategy all the time, you succeeded here, you did not there, that is to say, the problem is not necessarily 'Serzh go away'. The matter is

881 Interview with a political party member, 7 September 2015.

882 Gohar Saroyan, "Depoliticising Protests in Armenia," *openDemocracy*, 6 June 2016, accessed 23 October 2018, https://www.opendemocracy.net/od-russia/gohar-saroyan/depoliticising-protest-in-armenia.

883 The situation changed in April 2018 when Nikol Pashinyan initiated and led mass protests which in the end forced the resignation of Serzh Sargsyan. This event will be discussed separately in another section.

> to solve that problem and change power relationships, to go a step further for you to be able to solve bigger questions. That is not happening.
>
> (Political scientist, 7 September 2015)

Civic struggle in Armenia has largely been understood in terms of street struggle and, particularly with the advent of civic initiatives as novel components of Armenian civil society[884], the NGOs – older and formal forms of civil society – have been pushed into the background playing the role of auxiliaries. However, civic activism itself seems to not have progressed beyond 'the street'. It has not set precedents, has lacked sustainability and has been localized mainly in the city of Yerevan. Furthermore, the different civic initiatives have been confined to themselves and have not come together to form a big movement. In that regard, rights consciousness has been segmented manifesting itself in relation to separate rights but absent in a broader term:

> For instance, environmentalists are fighting only for the environment, and don't care about anything else, it (rights consciousness) is more relevant to established societies when you have solved your fundamental issue and then you start defending the dog's tail's rights, but when you have not solved your right to free choice, fundamental rights and you switch to segmentation the field ruptures, if you look in that context there is increase in segmented rights consciousness.
>
> (Activist, 25 September 2015)

6.4.5 Segmentation and exclusivity of activism in Armenia

Activism in the Armenian context is segmented not only in terms of rights consciousness but also suffers from inclusivity issues. It resembles 'a club', 'a party' and is crystallized and narrowed to a select few. There are exceptions of activists who consider themselves active or concerned citizens of Armenia and stay true to their ideology and principles and fight for what they believe in, such as nature protection for example. However, personal interests, material gains and career prospects do play a role too. The latter is among reasons that 'activism' is discredited in Armenia and 'activists' are considered enthusiasts that cannot advance beyond 'the social' let alone change 'the political'. Existing within its own confines, activism presents a type of monopoly, is exclusive rather than inclusive and cannot seriously challenge the political reality in Armenia. Furthermore,

---

884 Yevgenya Jenny Paturyan and Valentina Gevorgyan, "Civic Activism as a Novel Component of Armenian Civil Society," (2016). Turpanjian Center for Policy Analysis. Yerevan, Armenia, available at: http://tcpa.aua.am/files/2012/07/English-3.pdf.

there is some cooperation between NGOs and activists but cooperation on a professional level is lacking:

> If you want to create a judicial precedent, you should . . . appropriate lawyers etc., if you want to have an economic precedent, you should something else etc., and there we come to something else, that the connection between professional community, those who have professional knowledge and activism is very weak and it is weak in the sense that, it is weak in intercommunity sense, where lots and lots of different specialists are directly engaged in, they were themselves initiating I don't know the pension things, for example Synopsys was doing that, but I am speaking about institutional relations, that is, roughly speaking, I am a group here, I decide that for my needs I need one economist, one lawyer, one this, one that and I send out a conditional so-called inquiry somewhere saying people will you come to provide us with consultation, services?
>
> (Activist, 31 August 2015)

The lack of cooperation on a professional level as well as internal frictions among activist circles confine civic activism or the so-called street struggle to the street, square, park, that is, the specific locale where civic action, activity, protest and/or resistance take place. This also makes it easier for the authorities to counter activists with means of their own, contain the protests and disperse the protesters. Tactics that have been used by the authorities to handle different protests have ranged from creating disruptions without necessarily resorting to violence, spreading misinformation about protest participants and their objectives, creating fragmented relationships to entering into separate relationships with this or that group:

> . . .a group arrives which takes the agenda into a different direction, not roughly to be discovered and pushed away, but turning a bit this way, a bit that way, a network is formed, for example, now a network of opinion leaders is operating in Armenia, conditionally speaking, that is based within the pro-government discourse, but. . . but it is quite popular among the non-governmental community.
>
> (Activist, 31 August 2015)

The perception of rights in narrow terms in the Armenian context turns the struggle for rights into an exclusive domain and runs the risk of activists being perceived as 'political puppets', manipulated by the ruling regime and not including in their circles those that hold alternative views or are critical of civic struggles in one way or another. This phenomenon shall certainly not be generalized to include all the civic initiatives that have been organized in Armenia to date. Feminist and environmental groups are generally viewed as more welcoming and inclusive. In this regard, environmental struggles that took place in Teghut, Trchkan for instance, are considered good examples that could have set precedents for inclusivity and transcendence, but as was mentioned earlier, activism in Armenia is segmented:

> The activist for me is the one who has no limitations in the sense that he perceives the human being as the highest value and fights, that is, although yes he has his narrow scope, is fighting for the trees, but he does not exclude, the activist should carry that discourse school in himself, that is, it is more that feminist idea, he may even not consider himself a feminist but should be guided by that idea, I don't know what our activists are doing.
>
> (Human rights defender and activist, 23 September 2015)

Citizens' perceptions of rights, the rule of law and lawfulness have changed over the years, in particular since the infamous events of 2008; however, the authorities' tactics to counter dissent have changed too. In other words, while activists have learnt lessons from each civic initiative, struggle, activity, the authorities have in turn acquired new means to contain those very struggles, stifle the protests and discredit the activists and 'activism' itself in the public eye. Activists have been depicted in a negative light in the pro-government media, presented as glory-hunters, stirrers of public disorder, fame seekers who use their public profile to obtain funds and scholarships to study abroad, etcetera. While it would be short-sighted to frame all activists in Armenia as altruists and other-centred, only guided by perceptions of their own rights and the rights of others, it would also be short-sighted to frame all of them as pretenders and engaging in citizen activism guided solely by personal interests and gains. Generalizations of this kind would not only negate the rise of active citizenry in Armenia, however segmented it is, they would also undermine individual idiosyncrasies that form part of any collective action, revealing a process that is uneven, prone to disruption and contingent upon intersubjective as well as idiosyncratic factors.

As indicated extensively in Chapter 5, the state is a powerful actor in the Armenian political reality and it has contributed to [mis]perceptions of activism in Armenia. Through both the media as well as the police it has been a disruptive force in stifling protests and establishing its own precedents in tackling dissent. Activist struggles, in turn, have enabled abatement through predictability coupled with a lack of agenda, strategy, constituency, education within activist struggles themselves, failure to attract supporters and sustainability:

> Creativity is needed in protests/disobedience; nowadays in many cases the struggle in Armenia dies down a bit, decreases because it follows the same pattern – rallies, posters and Serzh go away, naturally in many cases that Serzh go away is an important component but there shall also be solutions.
>
> (Human rights defender and activist, 23 September 2015)

By 'solutions' most of the knowledge brokers and intermediaries, that is, presumed actors of change I interviewed, understood achievements of citizen activism beyond the street, beyond 'the social', change in power relationships and the political reality which according to them is difficult to attain since 'actors operate within a specific framework which is already given', that is, 'whatever they are doing is already within the established rules and conditions of the game'[885] and this is where the civil society reaches its limits. Furthermore, the opposition is weak in Armenia, perceived in terms of clients and conformists. Similarly, the NGO field (with few exceptions) suffers from grant chasing and detachment from the community, rarely to be seen on protest sites, which, on the one hand, has to do with their work taking place at an institutional level, in offices, rather than in the street and on the other hand, their visibility in the street would put their work at peril since the NGOs have been government targets for a while depicted as bearers of foreign agendas, living on Western money to name but few.

Political parties, on the other hand, have been suffering from a loss of image and inability to act as counter power to the ruling Republican Party. In order to dissociate themselves from political parties and present their struggles as genuine, legitimate and honest, activist circles have made calls for 'depoliticization' of protests, confining themselves to 'the social' in and of itself has not moved them beyond 'the street'. During Electric Yerevan protests in the summer of 2015 as well as the protests that started following the 2016 Yerevan Hostage Crisis, some political party figures arrived at protest sites and made themselves visible. This was not perceived by activists as support for the ideas and claims they were making, but rather, as attempts by political parties to hijack the protests and use them in their favour, on the one hand to save their image, on the other hand, to gain power should the protests succeed:

> . . .for instance, an X party saw Mashtots Park; they did not think what I should do to work with them with a little bit more long-term principle, to see what they need, let's say an atmosphere of mutual trust, long, in general creating an atmosphere of trust is a long-term process isn't it? You do not do a thing immediately with a magic stick, but no, instead one can faster, easier, you have the hotbed of activism, you can immediately put your hands on it, or extract energy from it, short-term, quickly right? And the irrational thing is that lots of activists became victims of that propaganda machine, you

885 Interview with an activist, 27 August 2015.

know what, do whatever you want, only do not politicize, it is a very common thing, propaganda...

(Activist, 31 August 2015)

6.5 2016 Summer protests

2016 was also notable for negative developments in relation to human rights practices, including, significant limitations on the freedom of assembly through excessive use of force in some instances and especially against representatives of certain opposition groups and their supporters[886]. The year started with the arrest and imprisonment of Founding Parliament activist Gevorg Safaryan after a minor scuffle with a police officer and in June of the same year Founding Parliament leader Zhirayr Sefilian was arrested[887]. The latter's supporters took over the Erebuni police station in Yerevan on 17 July 2016 demanding the resignation of President Serzh Sargsyan and the release of all political prisoners[888]. Three hours into the siege, the group released a video statement addressing the people:

> Dear friends, citizens, Armenian nation, it has begun, we are doing this for you, we have resorted to this step for you. Go out to the streets! We demand that all political prisoners be set free, Jirayr Sefilian, Gevorg Safaryan, Valodia Avedisyan, Shant Haroutyunyan and friends. Everyone, with no exception. And with the precondition that they be brought here. Armenian people, it depends on you... go out to the street. We are a single unit and we cannot reach our goal alone. There is no other way; we had to resort to this step. Our request is that you not leave us alone in this matter for which we are putting our lives at stake[889].

A water cannon and armed police could be seen at several locations. Also, roads leading to Yerevan had been blocked from all directions with cars being searched and turned back[890]. Social media and the websites of media outlets reporting on the developments were being made inaccessible and/or shut down[891]. Sefilian,

886 "Nations in Transit 2017 (Armenia)," *Freedom House*, accessed 23 October 2018, https://freedomhouse.org/report/nations-transit/2017/armenia.

887 Ibid.

888 "Daredevils of Sassoun: The Hostage Crisis in Yerevan as It Developed," *CIVILNET*, 20 July 2017, accessed 25 October 2018, https://www.civilnet.am/news/2017/07/20/Dardevils-of-Sassoun-the-Hostage-Crisis-in-Yerevan-as-It-Developed/318741.

889 "What Happened Today in Yerevan and Why (Developing)," *CIVILNET*, 17 July 2016, accessed 25 October 2018, https://www.civilnet.am/news/2016/07/17/what-happened-today-in-yerevan-and-why-developing/296980.

890 Ibid.

891 Ibid.

whose release was one of the main demands of Sasna Tsrer group, is a prominent figure within the country thanks to his role in the 1988–1994 conflict between Azerbaijan and Armenia over Nagorno-Karabakh[892]. Sefilian initially entered the political arena by mobilizing over Nagorno-Karabakh war veterans and voicing their complaints over poor housing, healthcare, and unemployment[893]. Seeking to widen his support base he then launched 'Founding Parliament' along with several like-minded public figures from a variety of backgrounds[894].

The incident reflected broader grievances that the Armenian population has had towards the ruling system, namely, poverty, corruption, rights violations, fraudulent elections to name but few. The siege shall be looked upon within the context of the 4-day war in Karabakh between 1–5 April 2016. The group, describing themselves as Daredevils of Sassoun, in reference to an Armenian epic tale from the Middle Ages about a generation of men fighting for Armenian independence[895], claimed that 'peaceful means of protest and mobilisation had failed and for that reason, they had come to the conclusion that the only way to save the future of the [Armenian] nation and the homeland was through popular revolt and an armed rebellion'[896].

In addition to the incident being termed as an armed rebellion and therefore, quite different from the civic activities that had taken place in Armenia since 2007/2008 and unlike human rights defenders who 'speak the language of human rights and democracy and are often presented by the authorities and in the Armenian media as grant-eaters who promote western/foreign values and norms'[897], Sasna Tsrer group used 'the language of nationalism and national pride'[898]. Public support for the group and their ideology varied, depending on which groups one considers under 'public'- formal civil society actors, informal

---

892 Charles Recknagel, 'Explainer: What Is Armenia's "Founding Parliament" Movement?' *Radio Free Europe Radio Liberty*, 18 July 2016, accessed 25 October 2018, https://www.rferl.org/a/armenia-founding-parliament-explainer-sefilian/27865671.html.

893 Ibid.

894 Ibid.

895 Ibid.

896 Armine Ishkanian, "From Civil Disobedience to Armed Violence: Political Developments in Armenia," *openDemocracy*, 19 July 2016, accessed 25 October 2018, https://www.opendemocracy.net/od-russia/armine-ishkanian/from-civil-disobedience-to-armed-violence-political-developments-in-armen.

897 Ibid.

898 Ibid.

civil society actors, the media, or the public at large. Formal civil society actors, that is, NGOs, as they are referred to within the scope of this research, focused on police actions, condemning the excessive use of force against the protesters, including holding policemen engaged in violence towards and inhumane treatment of citizens responsible[899]. Informal civil society actors, that is, the activists who adhere to liberal ideas and the human rights discourse and who are considered bearers of Western values, supported the group but not their ideology which they viewed as militarist and contrary to their own perceptions and practice of peaceful protests. It is noteworthy that this was particularly visible among feminist and LGBTIQ+ activists, fighting for the rights of women and sexual minorities, two of the most vulnerable groups in Armenia.

The way the group was framed in the media and the social media where the developments were actively discussed and debated ranged from 'terrorists', 'criminals', 'heroes' to 'armed rebels'. Whichever frame was used depended on the motive which in turn includes 'the construction of appropriate vocabularies of motive'[900], that is, wording the problem in ways that attracts the supporters and puts the struggle into a certain perspective. 'Terrorists', defined as people that 'use unlawful violence and intimidation, especially against civilians, in the pursuit of political aims' arouse negative emotions and would thus, make the group look as violent agents rather than heroes and justify police intervention. However, the 'terrorist' frame soon died down 'due to the everyday presence of large masses supporting the group in the streets', consequently leading to 'terrorist' frame 'being ousted from media circulation under pubic pressure'[901]. Breaking the silence on 22 July 2016, the then President Serzh Sargsyan made a public announcement, using the frame 'armed group':

> I call upon the gunmen to show restraint and to refrain from endangering others' lives with their provocative actions. The hostages must be set free. The armed group has to lay down their arms. The situation will be resolved strictly within Armenia's Constitution

---

899 '"Ynddem kananc nkatmamb brnutyan koaliciayi" haytararutyuny,' [Announcement of the "Coalition to Stop Violence against Women"] *Hetq*, 26 July 2016, accessed 26 October 2018, https://hetq.am/hy/article/69400.

900 Robert D. Benford and David A. Snow, "Framing Processes and Social Movements: An Overview and Assessment," *Annual Review of Sociology* 26, no. 1 (2000): 617–618.

901 "Human Rights Defenders, Activism, and the Media: Cases, Challenges and Solutions," Yerevan, Socioscope Societal Research & Consultancy Center NGO, 2017, accessed 26 October 2018, http://socioscope.am/wp-content/uploads/2017/10/ACT17_pdf-for-internet.pdf.

> and laws. Any attempts at personal reprisal will be prevented in accordance with the law[902].

Furthermore, Serzh Sargsyan underlined that 'the further development of that mindset was fraught with very dangerous consequences for our country and statehood'[903]. Serzh Sargsyan is a man known for his connections to Nagorno-Karabakh like the Daredevils of Sassoun. However, unlike the group whose members are considered 'heroes', Sargsyan is widely considered as an autocrat heading a criminal-oligarchic regime. In fact, national security and statehood have been popular terms employed by Sargsyan and his predecessors to extend their power. Through these counter frames the ruling regime has sought to 'rebut, undermine, or neutralize a person's or group's myths, versions of reality, or interpretive framework'[904]. Moreover, the Sargsyan administration has engaged in framing contests with informal civil society actors who have attempted 'to ward off, contain, limit, or reverse potential damage to the movement's previous claims or attributes'[905] by circulating alternative frames to affect public perceptions of these actors. These alternative frames have been in the form of labelling activists as 'Western agents', 'destroyers of Armenian values' as well as media manipulations by spreading misinformation and through fake social media user profiles channel public debates into directions conducive to the government's agenda.

The armed group did not follow the then President Sargsyan's announcement, and on the same day, 22 July 2016, the Civil Contract Party headed by Nikol Pashinyan started holding meetings on Khorenatsi Street[906]. Pashinyan announced that he had been, was and would be there as long as the citizens of Armenia needed him to be[907]. On 23 July 2016, the armed group accused

902 "Armenian President Finally Breaks Silence Over Yerevan Hostage Situation," *Epress.am*, 22 July 2016, accessed 27 October 2018, https://epress.am/en/2016/07/22/armenia-president-finally-breaks-silence-over-yerevan-hostage-situation.html.

903 Ibid.

904 Robert D. Benford, "Framing Activity, Meaning and Social Movement Participation: The Nuclear Disarmament Movement," PhD thesis (University of Texas, Austin, 1987): 75, quoted in Robert D. Benford and David A. Snow, "Framing Processes and Social Movements: An Overview and Assessment," *Annual Review of Sociology* 26, no. 1 (2000): 626.

905 Ibid.

906 'Daredevils of Sassoun: The Hostage Crisis in Yerevan as It Developed,' *CIVILNET*, 20 July 2017, accessed 27 October 2018, https://www.civilnet.am/news/2017/07/20/Dardevils-of-Sassoun-the-Hostage-Crisis-in-Yerevan-as-It-Developed/318741.

907 Ibid.

Pashinyan of using their action for his own personal and political gain[908]. Pashinyan in turn, was believed to act as a mediator and try to not allow the public's emotions to lead to unpredictable outcome. However, as has been the case during previous collective activities on the Armenian scene, and as was mentioned in previous chapters, political discussions and debates during mass protests tend to develop along personal rather than ideological lines.

On 23 July 2016, Nikol Pashinyan announced that he was leaving Khorenatsi Street, fulfilling the request of the armed group[909]. He stated that the platform would be empty for anyone who wanted to rule but that no one should think they can force his team to abandon their principles. During the days of his presence in the arena of the protests, Pashinyan was trying to quieten the public, in order to prevent clashes with the police which is exactly the threshold that in the past has led the protests to die down. The authorities have so-called tolerated public assemblies to a certain point in time, be it for 10 days or 14 days relying on public emotions or euphoria to die down and for the public to stop joining the protests.

However, should the protests or public assemblies extend beyond the tolerable 10–14 days, the police tends to intervene with force to disperse the protesters. Furthermore, Pashinyan was one of the lead figures during the infamous 2008 protests that resulted in 10 deaths, including 8 civilians and 2 policemen. Having the experience of 2008, Pashinyan might have been genuinely eager to prevent similar clashes during the protests of July 2016 and using his political experience try to attract more supporters to the cause of the Daredevils of Sassoun, however, his calls that 'the police are our brothers' further enlarged the gap between those that were supporting his presence during the protests and those that wanted to see him leave the scene. This led to fragmentation among the public and heated discussions took place on the social media and among the circles of active citizenry.

The police have long been viewed as an entity separate from the citizenry. They have been viewed as citizenry within citizenry in the sense that they have forcefully dispersed the protests causing bodily harm and injuries to citizens and instead of being considered representatives of the law and order, they have been deemed above that same law and order alongside state authorities[910]. Therefore,

908 Ibid.

909 Artak Hambardzumyan, 'Pashinyane parzabanum e te inchu chi masnakcum Azatutyan hraparaki hanrahavaqnerin,' [Pashinyan Explains Why He Is not Taking Part in the Assemblies at Freedom Square] *Radio Liberty*, 4 August 2016, accessed 30 October 2018, https://www.azatutyun.am/a/27900041.html.

910 Tamar Shirinian and Nelli Sargsyan, "The Armenian Violence Question: A Conversation on Means and Social Change," *Public Seminar*, 13 December 2016,

Pashinyan's 'the police are our brothers' triggered mixed reactions and he himself then became identified with that very police and the regime the latter serve and whatever peaceful objectives Pashinyan had in mind were dissolved into affective emotions of hostility creating outrage[911].

On 24 July 2016 the protests on Khorenatsi Street in support of Sasna Tsrer gain momentum[912]. The National Security Service presents the articles with which the armed group members may be charged and calls for surrender[913]. On 25 July 2016 the rallies gain more crowds, and the need to provide Sasna Tsrer with food is raised. It is noteworthy that this further enlarged the gap between 'us' the protesters and 'them' the state/police wherein the latter were being deemed as inhumane and degrading in their treatment towards the armed group. On the evening of July the 25th, 2016 shooting erupts between the armed group and the police forces[914] resulting in injuries to 2 members of Sasna Tsrer.

At dawn on 26 July 2016 a citizen named Arthur Sargsyan breaks the police chain to take food to the armed group and remains in the territory of the regiment[915]. Sargsyan later was named the 'Bread Bringer'. Protests continued on the following days resulting in arrests and detention of protesting citizens. On July 29, 2016 'police fired stun grenades into peaceful crowds in the neighbourhood of the seized police station, causing demonstrators to sustain first and second degree burns and fragmentation wounds'[916]. The police made no attempts for 'less violent crowd control means, and did not make any meaningful effort to warn crowds to disperse or about their plans to use force'[917]. Instead, 'law enforcement officers surrounded protesters with the apparent aim of punishing, injuring, and

---

accessed 27 October 2018, http://www.publicseminar.org/2016/12/the-armenian-violence-question/.

911 James M. Jasper, "The Emotions of Protest: Affective and Reactive Emotions in and around Social Movements," *Sociological Forum* 13, no. 3 (September, 1998): 406.

912 "Daredevils of Sassoun: The Hostage Crisis in Yerevan as It Developed," *CIVILNET*, 20 July 2017, accessed 27 October 2018, https://www.civilnet.am/news/2017/07/20/Dardevils-of-Sassoun-the-Hostage-Crisis-in-Yerevan-as-It-Developed/318741.

913 Ibid.

914 Ibid.

915 Ibid.

916 "Armenia: Events of 2016," *Human Rights Watch*, accessed 27 October 2018, https://www.hrw.org/world-report/2017/country-chapters/armenia.

917 Ibid.

detaining them, thereby ending the protests'[918]. Between 17 and 30 July 2016, more than 700 persons were detained by the police in relation to the standoff between the police and Sasna Tsrer armed group[919]. Many of them were denied their basic rights, including access to a lawyer of their choosing and the opportunity to inform a relative of their detention and whereabouts[920]. Detainees were also beaten, in some cases severely, and not allowed to get prompt medical care for their injuries[921].

Police actions were questioned and criticized by local NGOs as well as international human rights organizations. Transparency International Anti-Corruption Center released a statement on the effectiveness of the international assistance in police sector reforms[922]. The statement was addressed at the OSCE Office in Yerevan (closed on 31 August 2017) engaged in police reforms particularly since 2008 when 'its assistance focused on policing public assemblies'[923]. The statement further claimed that 'the Armenian people have witnessed increasingly aggressive and unlawful behaviour of the policemen'[924]. And lastly, the statement was raising a number of questions with regard to the level of efficiency of implementation of police reforms, the extent to which the performance of the Armenian police structures corresponded with the OSCE's values of security and policing and aimed reforms, the extent to which the spent resources were considered to be effective given that the mode of police actions had not recorded any change since 2008 and, last but not least, what the OSCE thought of the enlargement of Armenia's police establishment and the emerging 'police state' and what steps had been taken to prevent such a development and to ensure compliance of the institution to democratic principles[925]. Transparency International concluded that the efforts made by the OSCE as well as other international organizations

918 United States Department of State, *Bureau of Democracy, Human Rights and Labor, Country Reports on Human Rights Practices for* 2016, ARMENIA, 3 March 2017, accessed 27 October 2018, https://www.state.gov/j/drl/rls/hrrpt/2016/eur/265392.htm

919 Ibid.

920 "Armenia: Events of 2016," *Human Rights Watch*, accessed 27 October 2018, https://www.hrw.org/world-report/2017/country-chapters/armenia.

921 Ibid.

922 "Statement on the Effectiveness of the International Assistance in Police Sector Reforms," *Transparency International Anti-Corruption Center*, 22 July 2016, accessed 28 October 2018, https://transparency.am/en/news/view/1550.

923 Ibid.

924 Ibid.

925 Ibid.

invested in police reforms in Armenia had failed and that all international assistance to the sector be suspended until there is serious reconsideration of the role of the police within Armenia's governance system[926].

In 2015 when I conducted my fieldwork in Armenia following Electric Yerevan protests, discontent with police reforms as well as their efficiency was raised by my key informants. Active citizens from all walks of life, feminists, LGBTIQ+ activists, journalists, political scientists et alia questioned police reforms, international organizations, the Armenian authorities and human rights protection in Armenia:

> Well you know human rights application in Armenia is generally converted into a fictive phenomenon in the government circles and state officials and they make it an object of sale, they always negotiate with abroad, they get some money, grants and they turn it into a theatre, whenever necessary the so-called human rights are protected, whenever unnecessary and it affects their personal interest, financial interest they forget about that same value since there exists the instinct to protect a personal interest and group protection of one another, since huge finances are there, that is, human value, human rights in the streets are of course not protected, of course they are violated every day, of course they step over it all, of course there is also the opposite side that rights should be conquered step by step, it is not Europe that should come and give them to you, every day you conquer them with hard work.
>
> (Journalist, 17 September 2015)

Perceptions of human rights as everyday hard work and the consciousness to construct them from below have been reflected in eruptions of public discontent targeted at the Armenian government and its many policies not deemed human-centric but as detached from citizens' needs and interests. The active citizens of Armenia have attempted, through a process of contestation to make and remake human rights within a certain social and political context. They have done so 'as rational agents with physical bodies, minds, continuity of consciousness, and a capacity for moral agency' capable of 'constructing social norms (such as human rights) for themselves'[927].

Civic outbreaks in the form of peaceful protests have been more pronounced since 2007/2008. In this regard the incident in July 2016 did not start as a

---

926 Ibid.

927 Benjamin Gregg, *Human Rights as Social Construction* (Cambridge University Press, 2011), 42; Rainer Forst, "The Basic Right to Justification: Towards a Constructivist Conception of Human Rights," *Constellations* 6, no. 1 (1999): 35–60; Sally Engle Merry, "Transnational Human Rights and Local Activism: Mapping the Middle," *American Anthropologist* 108, no. 1 (March, 2006): 38–51.

peaceful protest. Rather, in order to ensure the safety of Sasna Tsrer armed group and show support for their demands, people took to the streets in large numbers. The protests did not have a clear structure, agenda and/or strategy. Commenting on the "Founding Parliament" of Jirair Sefilyan, which Sasna Tsrer are affiliated with, Haykak Arshamyan, analyst at Regional Studies Center in Yerevan, Armenia, noted that[928]:

> They refuse [to participate in] the election process as it is today in Armenia due to violence and non-transparency in the system. And their program is that this government should resign and we should have a transition government and new elections. Their ideas are a bit complicated and unclear.

Activists on the social media were wondering whether there was a platform where people were discussing what was happening. Some were also noting that 2016 events 'were not Electric Yerevan and there was no way one could even try to depoliticize things'. Discussions were raising the question as to why more people were not joining the protest, separating Sasna Tsrer armed group as people whose life, safety and security should be guaranteed from their agenda and the direction into which the protests were moving. On July 31, 2016 Varuzhan Avetisyan, member of Sasna Tsrer announced that they would lay down their weapons and surrender to security forces to avoid bloodshed[929]. The trials of the group commenced in June 2017. Observers noted a number of concerns such as 'defence lawyers facing difficulties accessing the court building due to unprecedented, selective verification procedures carried out by court bailiffs'[930]. Also, some lawyers 'experienced difficulties in accessing their clients whilst in pre-trial detention and there were attempts by detention security staff to interfere with confidential attorney-client case material'[931].

The protests that followed in support of Sasna Tsrer in the summer of 2016 bore similarities with Electric Yerevan in terms of a lack of a clear strategy and long-term vision that would lead to sustainability. Intervention by police to disperse the protesters signified the abatement of the protests while the indecision

928 "RSC Staff on Armenian Hostage Standoff," *Regional Studies Center*, 18 July 2016, accessed 30 October 2018, https://regional-studies.org/news/media/548-180716.

929 "Daredevils of Sassoun: A Timeline," *EVN Report*, 17 July 2017, accessed 30 October2018,https://www.evnreport.com/politics/daredevils-of-sassoun-a-timeline

930 "Behind the Glass Wall – The Right to a Fair Trial in the Sasna Tsrer Cases," Report of a fact-finding mission to Armenia, 15 March 2018, accessed 30 October 2018, http://prwb.am/new/wp-content/uploads/2018/03/Armenia_report_2018-1.pdf.

931 Ibid.

whether to remain on Baghramyan Avenue or move to Opera Square signified the divisions that existed between different groups of protesters. And like in the summer of 2015, the active phase of protests lasted 14 days. Sasna Tsrer relied on people rather than on the political opposition to consolidate around their demands. This is not entirely surprising however. As has been noted more than once in this writing, the political opposition in Armenia has been weak for years, which is one of the main reasons that civic initiatives and protests have become popular and attractive, even more trustworthy than the political opposition.

Despite marginal successes, civic activism, be it in the form of protests, resistance or disobedience, was considered exhausted already in 2015 when I spoke to different active citizens in Armenia that had been part of various civic initiatives. They noted despair with each failure where exhaustion meant civic activism as means to change the status quo and affect political changes in the country would not be achieved unless there was a politically organized force in place to present itself as an alternative and mobilize people around one clearly defined agenda:

> . . . it reaches a point that turns into raw political processes, outbreaks, you bring the question again out into the street but from the perspective of a dogma around regime change. And you are not able to form serious agendas and do serious mobilizations, design serious strategies and change the power relationship.
>
> (Political scientist, 7 September 2015)

The above-mentioned critique relates to civic activism and outbreaks which, it is worth noting again, cannot result in tangible success unless the grievances and claims that are set forth are not presented as 'against' something or someone, but 'for' something or someone. The protests in support of Sasna Tsrer group lacked a politically formulated and presented content. Instead, the speeches were filled with patriotic content, anger and even hostility. And while the latter emotions were push factors that brought people out into the streets, they also acted as factors that eventually led to abatement, further retarding the process of political change through civic outbreaks. And as was noted in 2015, the protests in the summer of 2016 lacked creativity and to an extent suffered from predictability enabling the police to 'open the valve of the filled up basin successfully':

> Sadly I see it drop by drop but the basin can also be filled drop by drop, of course it would be good to fill with a big pipe but we can what we are able. But the basin fills up,

fills up, I see that it is filling up, the important thing is that the valve does not get opened by someone. In this case they were able to open the valve very successfully.

(Environmental activist, 9 September 2015)

6.6 2018 April protests

Prior to discussing the 2018 April protests that resulted in the resignation of Serzh Sargsyan, it is useful to note the key political events that took place in the year of 2017. As was already indicated in the previous chapters, in late 2015 constitutional changes were approved through voting, transforming Armenia from a semi-presidential to a parliamentary republic[932]. No further presidential elections would be held, and once Sargsyan completed his term in 2018, executive power would be transferred to a prime minister, who is appointed by the National Assembly[933]. Sargsyan could not be prevented through legal requirements, and given that his Hayastani Hanrapetakan Kusaktsutyun (HHK) maintained a majority in the National Assembly in the 2017 polls, he was likely to assume the position of prime minister[934]. The National Assembly elections that took place in April were marred by credible allegations of vote-buying, voter intimidation, and abuse of administrative resources by the ruling party[935].

Also in 2017 a trial began for members of the armed group Sasna Tsrer. Four of the members charged for alleged crimes committed during the July 2016 armed takeover of a Yerevan police station claimed that police beat them in the court building in June[936]. Officers removed the men from the courtroom after an argument broke out between them and police[937]. The men claimed that police beat them in basement holding cells[938]. Authorities opened an investigation but no criminal charges were brought with some officers allegedly to have participated in the beatings remaining on duty in the courtroom[939]. In 2017, court hearings commenced in the case against Marina Poghosyan, a human rights defender and director of the NGO Veles, known for exposing government corruption and

932 "Freedom in the World 2018: Armenia," *Freedom House*, accessed 30 October 2018, https://freedomhouse.org/report/freedom-world/2018/armenia.

933 Ibid.

934 Ibid.

935 Ibid.

936 "Armenia: Events of 2017," *Human Rights Watch*, accessed 30 October 2018, https://www.hrw.org/world-report/2018/country-chapters/armenia.

937 Ibid.

938 Ibid.

939 Ibid.

providing legal aid to victims of human rights violations[940]. Ms. Poghosyan had been charged with extortion in 2015 after she alleged that former government officials were running a money laundering scheme[941]. Her trial was linked to her work exposing corruption by local human rights defenders[942]. On 30 April, Poghosyan reported that a fake Facebook profile had been created under her name and used to send sexually explicit photos and videos to her contacts to smear her reputation[943].

As Serzh Sargsyan finished his term as president, it was expected that on April 14, 2018, the ruling Republican Party of Armenia would nominate him, the head of the party, for the positon of prime minister[944]. However, on March 31, 2018, opposition MP Nikol Pashinyan began a two-week nationwide walk to protest the potential nomination of Sargsyan, travelling to seven cities, nearly 210 kilometres[945]. The protests that followed comprised demonstrations, sit-ins, student protests, civil disobedience, online activism, boycotts of business and general strike. Some of the methods used were familiar from previous protests, but the 2018 spring protests used additional means that proved key in their eventual success. The timeline of these protests was provided at the end of Chapter 5. In this section I will focus on the main aspects of the protests, the interactions between the key actors as well as the ways in which 2018 spring protests were different from their predecessors and how those differences guaranteed their success in the end.

The lead figure of the protests, Nikol Pashinyan, 'had been a fixture in Armenian opposition circles for two decades'[946]. A journalist by profession, 'Nikol Pashinyan has a long history of engaging in protest and politics in Armenia'[947]. Both as a journalist and an MP, Pashinyan has been known for his vocal criticism

940 "Armenia 2017/2018," *Amnesty International*, accessed 30 October 2018, https://www.amnesty.org/en/countries/europe-and-central-asia/armenia/report-armenia/.

941 Ibid.

942 Ibid.

943 Ibid.

944 "What You Need to Know about Demonstrations in Yerevan," *CIVILNET*, 14 April 2018, accessed 30 October 2018, https://www.civilnet.am/news/2018/04/14/What-you-need-to-know-about-demonstrations-in-Yerevan/333498.

945 Ibid.

946 Emil Sanamyan, "Saint Nick of Armenia: How Protest Leader Nikol Pashinyan "Rescued" Armenia and Made It Merry," 5 May 2018, accessed 30 October 2018, https://www.opendemocracy.net/od-russia/emil-sanamyan/saint-nick-of-armenia-how-nikol-pashinyan-rescued-armenia-and-made-it-merry.

947 Eurasia Partnership Foundation, "Velvet Revolution and Political Developments in Armenia. Briefing Book," September 2018, p. 3, available at: https://hkdepo.am/up/

of the government[948]. In 1995 he was dismissed from the journalism faculty of the Yerevan State University over his criticism of university corruption and went into opposition journalism full-time[949]. Seeking to challenge the status quo, Pashinyan became a vocal opponent of ex-president Levon Ter-Petrosyan's return to politics. The latter was a candidate in the 2008 presidential elections alongside Serzh Sargsyan who was running as a successor to Kocharyan[950]. Official results declared Sargsyan the winner; however, Ter-Petrosyan claimed victory himself and launched a protest campaign. In response, Kocharyan, the outgoing president ordered police to disperse protesters and introduced a state of emergency[951]. As a result of street clashes, ten people were killed, of which eight civilians and two security personnel in what became known as "March 1 events," the bloodiest in Armenia's politics since independence[952].

Pashinyan became a fugitive for over a year, eventually turning himself over to the police and was sentenced to seven years in prison on charges of provoking mass riots[953]. He was released on amnesty in 2011. A year later he was elected to parliament on the list of Ter-Petrosyan-led Armenian National Congress (ANK), but the two soon fell out[954] and during the 2013 presidential election Pashinyan backed Raffi Hovhannisyan's campaign. His separation from ANK was met with vicious criticism from political circles. During his time as MP in the National Assembly Pashinyan continued to vociferously and publicly criticize government policies[955]. Later on, 'under Armenia's system of proportional representation (awarding seats in the Assembly to representatives of parties polling at least 5 % of the vote), he was elected as the leader of the tiny "Civil Contract" party,

docs/Armenia_Briefing_Book_Velvet_Revolution_and_Political_Developments_September%2013_2018.pdf.

948 Ibid.

949 Ibid.

950 Ibid.

951 "Eight Killed in Armenia Protest," *The Guardian*, 3 March 2008, accessed 30 October 2018, https://www.theguardian.com/world/2008/mar/03/1.

952 Emil Sanamyan, "Saint Nick of Armenia: How Protest Leader Nikol Pashinyan "Rescued" Armenia and Made It Merry," 5 May 2018, accessed 30 October 2018, https://www.opendemocracy.net/od-russia/emil-sanamyan/saint-nick-of-armenia-how-nikol-pashinyan-rescued-armenia-and-made-it-merry.

953 Ibid.

954 Ibid.

955 Ibid.

and managed to get reelected over a ten-year period, despite his persistent opposition to the Russian influence over Armenia, which remains considerable'[956].

On 13 April 2018 demonstrators started rallying and blocking streets in central Yerevan[957]. Waving Armenian flags, they clogged Marshal Baghramian Avenue, which leads to the National Assembly building, stopping traffic in the process[958]. They were met with riot police that prevented them from advancing further toward parliament and later rolled out razor wire to hold the surging crowd back, with some local media reporting the use of tear gas and stun grenades as well[959]. On 16 April 2018 the police issued a statement calling the protests illegal and warning that 'law enforcement had the authority to forcibly "discontinue" street gatherings accompanied by "collective breaches of public order" '[960]. The police justified their likely intervention by 'disproportionate restriction of the rights of others' brought about by the protesters. On the same day, 'the protests saw their first violence, with several clashes between police and protesters resulting in injuries to 46 people, including six police officers'[961]. Pashinyan announced about rallies that would include paralysing the entire Yerevan and all the streets, including blocking state agencies. He also informed about the initiation of a velvet revolution committee in the coming days that would lead the movement.

As the protests went on, one of Yerevan's main bridges was blocked on April 20 by three heavy trucks after the crowd reached it early in the afternoon[962]. The truck drivers left their vehicles parked there and joined the "Reject Serzh" marchers headed toward parliament[963].

---

956 Daniel L. Feldman and Haris Alibašić, "The Remarkable 2018 'Velvet Revolution': Armenia's Experiment Against Government Corruption," *Public Integrity* 21 (2019): 425.

957 'Protesters, Armenian Riot Police Clash Over Nomination For Prime Minister,' *RFE/RL's Armenian Service*, 16 April 2018, accessed 20 October 2018, https://www.rferl.org/a/armenia-opposition-activists-block-roads-bridge-subway-in-yerevan-protesting-sarkisian-expected-shift/29169981.html.

958 Ibid.

959 Ibid.

960 Ibid.

961 Grigor Atanesian, "Thousands of Protesters Shut Down Armenia's Capital, Dozens Injured in Clashes," *Eurasianet*, 16 April 2018, accessed 30 October 2018, https://eurasianet.org/thousands-of-protesters-shut-down-armenias-capital-dozens-injured-in-clashes.

962 Alan Crosby, "Armenian Protests Smell Like Teen Spirit," *RFE/RL's Armenian Service*, 20 April 2018, accessed 30 October 2018, https://www.rferl.org/a/this-round-of-armenian-protests-smells-like-teen-spirit/29182665.html.

963 Ibid.

On 22 April 2018 a meeting took place between Serzh Sargsyan and Nikol Pashinyan, where the former told the latter that 'A party that scored 8 percent in [parliamentary] elections can't speak on behalf of the people'[964]. Sargsyan then walked out of the meeting room at Yerevan's Marriott Hotel. Later on the same day Pashinyan was detained. His detention, however, did not stifle the protests. On the contrary, tens of thousands of people filled the Republic Square[965]. On 23 April 2018, protests resumed and talks circulated about former and current members of the Armenian armed forces, including participants of the 2016 April War having joined the rallies[966]. Later that day Serzh Sargsyan resigned from the position of prime minister to the surprise of many not only domestically but abroad as well[967]. What followed was a nationwide celebration with 'strangers hugging and congratulating one another, cars honking their horns, and shops running out of champagne. Everybody celebrated in their own way: some put tables in the streets and marked the occasion traditionally, with vodka and a barbecue, while others danced to Berlin-style techno music in bars. Still, the happiness seemed universal'[968].

2018 April protests bear similarities with previous protests and civic initiatives. However, there are a number of differences that guaranteed their eventual success

---

964 "Armenia: Opposition Leader Pashinian Detained after Abortive Meeting with PM," *Deutsche Welle*, 22 April 2018, accessed 30 October 2018, https://www.dw.com/en/armenia-opposition-leader-pashinian-detained-after-abortive-meeting-with-pm/a-43486135.

965 Karlen Aslanian, "Huge Crowds Keep Up Pressure on Armenian PM," *Radio Liberty*, 22 April 2018, accessed 30 October 2018, https://www.azatutyun.am/a/29185545.html.

966 "Unarmed Soldiers Join Anti-Government Protests in Armenia," *Reuters*, 23 April 2018, accessed 1 November 2018, https://www.reuters.com/article/us-armenia-politics-protests-army/unarmed-soldiers-join-anti-government-protests-in-armenia-idUSKBN1HU15U?utm_campaign=trueAnthem%3A+Trending+Content&utm_content=5addc74504d3014ac94e325b&utm_medium=trueAnthem&utm_source=facebook.

967 Andrew Roth, "Shock as Armenia's Prime Minister Steps Down after 11 Days of Protests," *The Guardian*, 23 April 2018, accessed 1 November 2018, https://www.theguardian.com/world/2018/apr/23/serzh-sargsyan-resigns-as-armenias-prime-minister-after-protests.

968 Mikayel Zolyan, 'Armenia's "Permanent Revolution": Why Do the Protests Continue in Yerevan?' *openDemocracy*, 25 April 2018, accessed 1 November 2018, https://www.opendemocracy.net/en/odr/armenia-s-permanent-revolution-why-do-protests-continue-in-yerevan/.

and the resignation of Serzh Sargsyan. The emphasis on non-violence, restraint and discipline was visible in previous civic activities, however, the authorities in fact succeeded in instigating disorder, creating divisions among activists and in the end breaking down the protests. The inexperience of the activists did play a role, a factor that made a difference in April 2018. As was noted above, Pashinyan has a political background and is a known opposition figure for his vocal speeches against the government and the ruling party. Furthermore, having experienced protests and public unrest before, he used the lessons learnt in a literate and well-thought-out manner, providing the content that had been missing from other protests, and it is the manner and the content of the protests that resonated with a lot of people, and the number of the protesters grew every day. In 2015, several of my key informants remarked that a student movement had been absent in Armenia and that as long as the consciousness of opposing university heads and taking the protest into the universities failed, change would be delayed in Armenia. In April 2018, students and young people in their late teens formed an important part of the protests[969].

The generation that was born and grew up in post-Soviet Armenia is 'unhindered by censorship and supported by social media, has the ability and flexibility to mobilize and get organized in order to channel not only their own frustration but also the frustration of their parents'[970]. Furthermore, as autonomous agents, this post-Soviet or independent Armenian generation has, owing to increased travel, study abroad opportunities, access to the World Wide Web and last but not least, through the 'street', that is, coming into contact with both like-minded as well as other thinkers in a public space been able to critically reflect outside the conditions within which they have been socialized, as well as sufficiently distance themselves from habits to re-examine them[971]. Once exposed to alternatives, otherness and ways of thinking and doing different from what they are accustomed to, these agents distance themselves from the routines, habits and beliefs. In such cases, they will be capable of drawing comparisons, reflecting on two different realities and drawing inferences regarding their society's

969 Bradley Jardine, "Armenian Youth, the 'Engine of the Revolution,' Fight for a Fairer Society," *eurasianet*, 7 May 2018, accessed 12 December 2019, https://eurasianet.org/armenian-youth-the-engine-of-the-revolution-fight-for-a-fairer-society.

970 Asbed Kotchikian, "It's the People, Stupid: Debunking the Myths on Protests in Armenia," *Hetq*, 19 April 2018, accessed 1 November 2018, https://hetq.am/en/article/87561.

971 Rob Stones, "Rights, Social Theory, and Political Philosophy, a Framework for Case Study Research," In *Rights: Sociological Perspectives*, ed. Lydia Morris (Routledge, 2006).

'historically fashioned social inheritance, that is, its historically situated ideals, customs, beliefs, institutions, and practices'[972].

> I think that it has been more friends, environment, my education in the AUA, travelling a lot that have conditioned my participation and activism as of late and it is there that I have changed through real experience, that is, you do something in practice and thereby you change, you do something and that something changes you and it is there that you extract knowledge from, you extract knowledge from that experience and not that you read a book and. . .
>
> (Activist, 27 August 2015)

The 'us vs them' dichotomy is reproduced through constant comparisons with the Soviet generation, that is, the parents of active Armenian citizens who lived in a period where social and economic rights were granted at the expense of civil and political rights and where education was not meant to challenge the existing regime. In addition, the 'us vs them' dichotomy is multi-layered, and constant comparisons exist not only between generations, but between activists and citizens themselves, and as in the case of April 2018 events in particular, between 'the Serzh era' and the 'Nikol era', between 'the home' and 'the street', 'the university', 'the home' and 'the street':

> Perhaps I became more of a citizen in the street, I was working as a journalist for Hetq, and there I got to know people, I covered the actions they organized, I participated in them later, I made friends and that's where my connection with people was created, not that we are friends, classmates, fellow students, we are people who are concerned about a problem and we think that it is related to everyone and that is where it started yes, the street has given me more than the university.
>
> (Environmental activist, 11 September 2015)

'The home' in this instance is not only 'the family', but also 'the local'. Civic initiatives or street protests have been able to attract large masses precisely owing to this factor, that is, the raised issues have echoed with ordinary people through employing a language those people understand and framing causes in terms that make the plight of ordinary people more tangible. The 2018 April protests further highlighted this aspect. The protests led by Nikol Pashinyan redefined 'democratization' which since the 1990s had been associated with Western donors and projects funded by them and implemented in Armenia. Marching along the streets with a megaphone, Pashinyan could be heard saying 'Come out into the street and stand up for your rights, come out into the street and stand up for your freedom, come out into the street and stand up for your homeland'. These

972 Ibid., 140–141.

calls were triggers for citizens to exercise their individual agency and take to the streets not only as rights-bearers but also duty-holders. The latter has generally been used in terms of 'the state' having a duty towards its citizens. However, what was discernible in the 2018 April protests in Armenia was the consciousness of 'building one's country', 'turning one's country into a lawful state', and 'taking a responsibility for one's country'[973].

The contention between the local and the global was manifested in the ways the protesters attempted to draw the attention of the international media to the protests, their use of slogans, posters and even the song that was made the anthem of 2018 April protests. The barricades between the police and the protesters have been a known aspect of protests in Armenia. Those barricades were still persistent in April 2018, as the police has acted as a disruptive force during protests and not been identified with the citizenry at large. While the protesters marched carrying such posters as 'I am Nikol', 'I am also Armenian, arrest me too', 'I reject the deceiving and threatening Serzh', 'Armenian policemen, we are peaceful, what about you?', 'Don't scare us with March 1' Pashinyan himself, criticized for calling the police 'our brothers' during 2016 summer protests, insisted on the police being 'one of us' and requested that the protesters not curse, swear at or act violently towards the police. On the one hand, this tactic would indeed live up to the claims that the protests were peaceful, thereby preventing police intervention, on the other hand, it might (and did in the end) melt the ice between the police and the protesters, making them participants in the 'citizen-making' in the streets.

The 2018 Velvet Revolution brought together both known and unknown/new faces. Previously there were grievances and frustrations that the already existing civic initiatives did not come together to form a bigger and a massive movement to counter the grip that the Republican Party had over power in Armenian politics. Both completed as well as ongoing civic initiatives had achieved marginal success and recorded some victories but those had addressed specific problems and once the government made concessions, the protests would gradually die down. In the spring of 2018 however, the protests acquired mass character and comprised both new people as well as participants from previous movements, such as Voch Talanin (No to Plunder), No Pasaran, Electric Yerevan, Mashtots Park, all of which are thought to have led up and contributed to 2018 Velvet

973 Shushanik Minasyan, "The Velvet Revolution – A New Path for Armenia," in *Armenian Developments: Perspectives of Democratization and the Role of the Civil Society*, eds. Wolfram Hilz and Shushanik Minasyan (Baden-Baden, 2019), 119–132.

Revolution[974]. The latter included the lessons learnt from those protests in terms of the tactics as well as the strategies to counter the police should they attempt to disperse the protesters. The accumulated experience of both the protesters and the police came into play during the mass protests in the spring of 2018. The 2018 Velvet Revolution was notable for its emphasis on positivity which 'was taken from the No Pasaran mobilisation, where it worked and brought results'[975]. The car processions, for instance, were taken from the Voch Talanin movement[976].

The political reality in Armenia had been diagnosed prior to April 2018 – 'over the past two decades the oligarchic regime, by seizing both the political and economic sectors, used brute force and economic repression to extend and consolidate its hold on power. Oligarch politicians, such as MP Samvel Aleksanyan (Lfik Samo) and former Prime Minister Hovik (the Mouse) Abrahamyan, are much-reviled figures in Armenian society. As part of the RPA led government, they have operated with impunity, intimidation, and violence, propagating a politics of fear'[977]. They had also been identified as 'the source(s) of causality, blame, and/or culpable agents'[978] and were thus the responsible entities for the 'Armenian reality' that was to be remedied. At the start of his announced march in the city of Gyumri, the second largest city in Armenia, Pashinyan stated that 'this was a move against Serzh Sargsyan, against the RPA', the culpable agents responsible for the situation in Armenia and the sources to blame for popular grievances. Additionally, he constructed appropriate vocabularies of motive, that is, worded the problem in ways that attracted supporters and put the struggle into a certain perspective[979]:

> Today the largest mass protest in the history of the 3-rd Armenian Republic is taking place. The protest was announced only 6 hours ago. Many were wondering why we

974 Karena Avedissian, "A Real Revolution? Protest Leader Armen Grigoryan on What's Happening in Armenia," *openDemocracy*, 30 April 2018, accessed 17 January 2020, https://www.opendemocracy.net/en/odr/real-revolution-protest-leader-armen-grigoryan-on-what-s-happening-in-ar/.

975 Ibid.

976 Ibid.

977 Armine Ishkanian, "A Revolution of Values: Freedom, Responsibility and Courage in Armenia's Velvet Revolution," *openDemocracy*, 3 May 2018, accessed 1 November 2018, https://www.opendemocracy.net/od-russia/armine-ishkanian/revolution-of-values-freedom-responsibility-and-courage-in-armenias-velve.

978 Robert D. Benford and David A. Snow, "Framing Processes and Social Movements: An Overview and Assessment," *Annual Review of Sociology* 26, no. 1 (2000): 616.

979 Ibid., 617–618.

> decided to hold it in the Republic Square. We did it in order to demonstrate that the Republic of Armenia exists, that the RA citizen exists, that the biggest square has filled up against Serzh Sargsyan. This movement has one leader and that leader is you and that leader is you (stated Pashinyan pointing to groups of people).

Pashinyan's speeches contained emancipatory elements that affected his supporters not only emotionally but also revealed the components necessary for a human rights respecting state. In other words, when addressing the crowd gathered in the Republic Square Pashinyan would formulate his ideas in terms of thinly formulated human rights, that is, he would opt for the lower-level components to give human rights a concrete meaning, that is, human rights as democratic governance, social justice, economic equality, constitutional order, independent judiciary and accountable politicians. The latter was particularly reflected in the way he communicated with his supporters not only in the Square or in the Street but online as well. Pashinyan and his team paid attention to complaints and criticism addressed to them on the social media and publicly addressed those during subsequent rallies. One such instance involved reckless driving without number plates that jeopardized the spirit and objective of the protests and that reportedly had no connection with the movement as many insisted. Pashinyan, addressing the public the next day in the Republic Square, urged everyone not to drive without number plates and for cars not to enter the Square:

> We shall not allow people to make use of this and turn this into an uncontrollable situation. I call out to you to temporarily stop these processes only in Yerevan, so that during constant traffic it becomes clear more quickly who is driving with concealed number plates or without them.

Pashinyan further called out to people to self-organize and stop cars without number plates and urge them to travel with those. According to him, driving without number plates was the same as taking part in protests wearing masks. Pashinyan insisted that the struggle of their movement was for lawfulness; therefore, such manifestations were intended to smear it. Through his transparent and accountable communication with the public Pashinyan seemingly drew comparisons between himself and the ruling authorities, demonstrating that he was democratic and connected to the people who had put their trust in him. His use of online platforms such as Facebook Live 'to tell his followers how to conduct themselves and explain the decisions he was making' reflected 'the aspirations of transparency and openness'[980].

---

980 Tigran Amiryan, "Culture of Protest: The Symbols of Armenia's Velvet Revolution," *The*

The success of the 2018 mass protests was also due to good organising amongst other things, with 'the rallies being much more interesting and energetic' in contrast to the formerly 'boring opposition rallies that felt like 45- minute lectures'[981]. The liberating/emancipatory messages that Pashinyan was sending throughout the course of the protests transcended to the students, a key group that mobilized around Pashinyan's agenda and tried to revolutionize the educational culture in Armenia, one of submission and passive acceptance rather than challenging the authority, the lecturers and so on. Posters such as 'Free, Independent Student' could be seen in the Square while Pashinyan himself when addressing the public in the Republic Square after rallies every evening could be heard saying: 'To freedom, to the Republic of Armenia, to Yerevan, the capital of Armenians, to the Republic of Artsakh and us and our children who live and will continue to do so in a free and happy Armenia'.

The geography of the protests also extended to include other cities and even villages in Armenia and went out of the boundaries of Armenia to include protests in front of Armenian embassies in several cities all over the world with large Armenian communities such as Glendale, California, Moscow, Marseille, Toronto, Montreal, Sochi, Vancouver, Athens, London, Berlin, Buenos Aires, Chicago and Sao Paulo. The diaspora was involved not only financially and morally; some even went to Armenia from abroad to join the protests[982]. The geography during previous protests was rather sporadic and asymmetrical, that is to say, compared to the regions, the processes were evolving at a different pace in Yerevan. Since late 2014 and already in 2015 more activity has been visible in Gyumri and Vanadzor. And during the protests in April 2018 mass civil disobedience protests took place in the regions, including blocking highways, interstate roads, student protests and so on. The extension or spillover of protests into the regions has to do with the presented agenda and how well it resonates with the general public. Furthermore, the language or vocabulary that was used such as freedom, social equality and absence of corrupt practices among others, are all components of human rights that the majority of Armenians value in contrast to other concepts, such as gender and/or activism that are deemed imported

---

Calvert Journal, 9 June 2018, accessed 17 December 2019, https://www.calvertjournal.com/articles/show/10318/culture-of-protest-symbols-of-armenia-velvet-revolution.

981 Karena Avedissian, "A Real Revolution? Protest Leader Armen Grigoryan on What's Happening in Armenia," *openDemocracy*, 30 April 2018, accessed 17 January 2020, https://www.opendemocracy.net/en/odr/real-revolution-protest-leader-armen-grigoryan-on-what-s-happening-in-ar/.

982 Ibid.

from abroad and respectively not embraced. Human rights after all, is an interwoven concept; it is complete in the entirety with its components, that is, if one component fails, the entirety ceases to be complete, thereby risking to push the concept out of meaning and applicability. Constitutional order, independence of the judiciary, absence of corrupt practices, free and fair elections, democratic governance, responsibility of the state towards the citizens, as well as the duty of the citizens towards one another to name but few are all important components of human rights and for making the latter a reality, a tangible concept, rather than just an abstract theory. It is this perception and thin formulation of rights that lay at the core of April 2018 protests.

The April 2018 protests were 'probably the most gender-balanced protests in Armenia' to date, there being 'almost as many women on the streets as men and at certain points the women even outnumbered men (especially given that men were more likely to be detained or beaten up by the police)'[983]. The protesters were 'organisationally sophisticated, grassroots-driven, with an extraordinary degree of self-governance'[984]. On 22 April 2018, after Pashinyan was detained, contrary to the government's expectations that the protests would die down, more people took to the streets. The decentralized structure of the protests as well as the high level of discipline by both the leaders and participants reduced the risk of police intervention and made it difficult for them to disperse the protests. The protesters would block various streets, sometimes even unblocking some and blocking others in what looked like a 'cat-and-mouse game' with the police. The high level of self-organization by protest participants and Pashinyan's tactic of leading the protests into different directions demobilized the police[985].

A key feature of the 2018 April protests was the eventual riddance of the perception of activists as rights conquerors for ordinary citizens or active citizens conquering rights for passive residents resulting in citizens of different

983 Mikayel Zolyan, "Armenia's 'Permanent Revolution': Why Do the Protests Continue in Yerevan?" *openDemocracy*, 25 April 2018, accessed 1 November 2018, https://www.opendemocracy.net/od-russia/mikayel-zolyan/armenia-s-permanent-revolution-why-do-protests-continue-in-yerevan.

984 Anna Ohanyan, "A Very Potent Protest Movement Is Emerging in Armenia," *Aljazeera*, 21 April 2018, accessed 1 November 2018, https://www.aljazeera.com/indepth/opinion/potent-protest-movement-emerging-armenia-180419135116999.html.

985 "Analytical Report: From Shrinking Space to Post-Revolutionary Space: Reimagining the Role and Relations of Civil Society in Armenia," Yerevan, Socioscope Societal Research & Consultancy Center NGO, 2018, p. 29, available at: http://socioscope.am/wp-content/uploads/2019/01/Socioscope-report_15.01_spread-eng.pdf.

professions and ideologies moving from the periphery to the centre and merging into a big whole, thereby making the protests more 'popular' than 'activist'. Compared to previous protests, 'activists' and 'activism' were not pronounced in April 2018. This is not to say that they had no contribution to the protests and the respective outcome. What this says, however, is that 'activists' were part of 'the people', of one big whole comprising ordinary citizens with the consciousness to change the social and political reality they live in and improve the human condition not only for themselves, but for their families, children, grandchildren, fellow students, fellow citizens and so on. If previously activists, the main initiators of civic activities, be those protests, demonstrators, rallies or sit-ins were held accountable for failures and perceived as Western-oriented careerists somewhat detached from the general citizenry and considered citizens of a different class, in the course of the protests in April 2018 activists from previous protests and civic initiatives also joined[986].

However, interactions unfolding on the social media between various groups contained the term 'citizen' to address one another as well as the general public. Posts such as 'You are the leader, go out into the street' as well as observations by activists participating in the protests further underlined the reduction of the distance between activists and ordinary citizens, the former turning into ordinary citizens and the latter turning into activists. Furthermore, participants in the 'Love and Peace Revolution' as Pashinyan termed the protests of April 2018 felt responsibility as individual citizens and collectively as citizenry and through travel back and forth between both their individual and collective consciousness and as individual and collective agents managed to replace old perceptions with new ones in the social and political reality in Armenia.

The 2018 April protests were sophisticated and inclusive. Unlike previous protests where a lot of activity was taking place online, the main activity was taking place offline, in the streets, in the square. The online platforms, that is, social media was used for urgent messages, notifications, posting photos as well as videos to expose rights violations by the police and to prevent the spread of misinformation. Social media has been used by the government formerly to spread misinformation in order to create divisions between activists and discredit them in the public eye. This time in order to circumvent social media

986 Karena Avedissian, "A Real Revolution? Protest Leader Armen Grigoryan on What's Happening in Armenia," *openDemocracy*, 30 April 2018, accessed 18 December 2019, https://www.opendemocracy.net/en/odr/real-revolution-protest-leader-armen-grigoryan-on-what-s-happening-in-ar/.

surveillance and possible government interference, protest participants communicated with one another through applications in regard to meeting spots, tactics and strategies. Lessons learnt from previous protests further empowered the participants and old tactics of intimidation on the part of the government failed to work this time[987].

Serzh Sargsyan resigned on 23 April 2018 following almost a fortnight of protests. It is noteworthy that his resignation came on the eve of the commemoration of genocide victims of 1915. This might have contributed to his decision to leave power without violence or bloodshed, contrary to how he came to power in 2008. Last but not least, 'previous civic initiatives were mostly reactions to government decisions or events, rather than pro-active goals of changing the Armenian reality'[988]. Many activists 'would position themselves as "outside of politics," although some of the issues they raised were inherently political'[989]. The protests of April 2018 were political from the start, 'incensed by poverty, corruption, and the fact that the economy is dominated by oligarchs who are close to political leadership. Then there is the lack of accountability for law enforcement's abuses, lack of judicial independence, and other human rights issues, including protecting minorities and ensuring justice for domestic violence survivors'[990]. As Pashinyan became prime minister of Armenia on 9 May 2018, he stated 'No more bribes, no more monopolies, human rights will be protected, rule of law will prevail!'[991] It remains to be seen how Pashinyan and his new government, expected to be formed following snap elections early December 2018, are going to implement the promised political agenda.

987 "Freedom on the Net 2018 – Armenia," *Freedom House*, 1 November 2018, accessed 6 January 2020, https://www.refworld.org/docid/5be16b2a3.html; Karlen Aslanian, "Social Media Key to Armenian Revolution, Says Pashinian," *Radio Liberty*, 31 January 2019, accessed 6 January 2020, https://www.azatutyun.am/a/29744146.html.

988 Yevgenya Jenny Paturyan, "Armenian Civil Society: It Is not All about NGOs," *Caucasus Analytical Digest* No. 73 (26 May 2015): 3.

989 Ibid.

990 Anahit Chilingaryan, "Protest Leader Becomes Armenia's Prime Minister," *Human Rights Watch*, 9 May 2018, accessed 1 November 2018, https://www.hrw.org/news/2018/05/09/protest-leader-becomes-armenias-prime-minister.

991 Ibid.

6.7 Concluding remarks

In this chapter I have addressed both formal and informal civil society actors, in the form of NGOs and activists, the roles of both in improving the human rights situation in Armenia as well as the differences between them. In addition, I have demonstrated how both actors interact with the state and how that interaction affects their efforts to set up human rights claims and get the government to perform its duties. While negative rights assume inaction on the part of the state, police interference, often through employing brutal force, has been the common practice in Armenia. The perception of NGOs as representatives of the Armenian civil society has given way to civic initiatives as new (informal) civil society actors oriented towards short-term goals and solutions, independent of external funding, comprising groups of young people who are legally and politically aware and knowledgeable about domestic laws and constitution as well as their rights and responsibilities as citizens.

These conscious citizens have taken to the streets on more than one occasion to contest government policies, decisions and systemic corruption, among others. Despite marginal success, the civil has not turned into a political struggle, and activism in Armenia has been manifested through sporadic outbreaks and suffers from internal divisions and detachment from the general public. Coupled with misperceptions surrounding 'activism' and misrepresentation of activists in the Armenian media and by government circles, activist struggles have not progressed beyond 'the street'. This has led to activists feeling uneasy about the term, some even leaving public space and adopting more passive lifestyles. The Armenian non-state sector reveals the tense relationship between subjectivities in collective action. It also reveals the ways publicly active citizens are perceived by one another and the society at large.

As attempts to bring about incremental changes in the social and political life in Armenia seemed to slow down further, 'activism' dissolved in citizenry, 'I' became 'We' and the gap between active citizens and passive residents became less visible in the Spring of 2018 when, headed by opposition politician Nikol Pashinyan, hundreds of thousands of Armenians took part in protests against the premiership of Serzh Sargsyan, eventually forcing the latter to step down. The 2018 April protests, which Pashinyan himself has termed 'Velvet Revolution' or 'Revolution of Peace and Love', encompassed a myriad of actors and brought them all into one big whole of 'active citizenship'. The protests, while using some of the lessons learnt from previous civic actions, had additional dimensions that ensured their success – that of active participation of various actors rather than a select few, conquering rights not only for oneself but for others and, last but not least, countering the government's frames with more sophisticated ones to enforce the latter's failure.

7 Conclusions

This research project has aimed at exploring and explaining the roles of non-state actors in improving the human rights situation in Armenia. It has also pursued the goal of revealing the human rights perceptions and practices of those same actors and the ways in which they interact with one another as well as with the government and the citizenry at large. The findings demonstrate, as argued extensively in Chapter 6, that formal and informal non-state actors in Armenia differ with regard to their roles, human rights perceptions and practices and the ways of interaction with one another, the government and the citizenry at large. While formal civil society actors, that is NGOs, operate at an institutional level and are funded by external/foreign donors and are, as a result, not at liberty to operate outside those institutional confines, informal civil society actors operate in a 'loose' fashion, in that they do not depend on funding but instead initiate, assemble and act spontaneously and are more confrontational in their interactions with the government.

The concept of human rights has been treated as a contested one along with activism throughout this research. At first sight this account may strike as pessimistic, however, it has been the intention and the objective of this study to demonstrate that human rights are prone to transformation not only as tools used against government abuse but also contested as practice. Furthermore, as was noted at the beginning of the writing, there is no one single and clear-cut lens through which one can study human rights. Neither has this research attempted to create such a theory. Rather, human rights have been approached through a specific lens, the lens of sociology, by placing the key actors at the centre, looking at claims-making and rights struggle as constantly tested, challenged, appropriated, resisted and/or rejected.

This research has revealed where and how the battle for human rights takes place. It has engaged the key actors prominent in that struggle, the government, the police, the courts and the knowledge brokers, translators or mediators, those actors that are equipped with the necessary human rights knowledge and advocacy, awareness-raising skills to not only counter the power of the state and its institutions but to also act as a sort of 'bridge' between the state, the citizenry at large and larger international institutions and networks. The research has not provided either a state-centric or an actor-centric account of either exercise or violation of human rights in the Armenian context. Rather, the research has put both actors vis-à-vis one another to critically study and question the power dynamics, the relationships, the roles and activities of both taken separately as well as in interaction with one another.

The results reveal the ways in which human rights, their perceptions as well as practices, are manifest in the Armenian context, the ways in which they are shaped and reshaped by their very bearers and the ways in which they get manipulated and distorted by powerful actors and are at the same time picked up by other actors who fight for their 'conceptual restoration' and give rights a meaning. Relying on the goodwill of states to comply with internationally recognized human rights standards ascribed in international human rights treaties and conventions rarely works since states slip through the loopholes of that very system, justifying violations through culture, traditions, sovereignty and, more often than not, getting away with breaches and abuse.

Democratic and accountable governments that observe the rule of law, constitutional arrangements, as well as have established independent judiciary do not need to be reminded of human rights standards, since those standards are internalised and incorporated into domestic laws. Contrarily, less democratic governments are not only prone to frequent rights violations, but also need to be reminded of their domestic and international obligations and it is well documented that states prone to rights violations rarely give in to naming and shaming. Cases of successful naming and shaming, as well as international sanctions forcing rights violating states to respect them are far and few in between. Notable examples are such states as Russia, China and Iran that, unless standing to lose from international criticism, are usually immune to naming and shaming. What these states do is turn the criticism around and point to human rights abuses and issues in other countries.

In January 1993, 'Khamenei proclaimed that Iran was standing by all the innocent Muslims in the world, which angered "despotic powers;" the latter in turn showed their enmity by making baseless claims that Iran was violating human rights.'[992] Khamenei further asserted that 'America's claims to lead the world and its interference in the affairs of other countries amount to bullying'[993]. Following the 1993 Human Rights Conference in Vienna, 'in which the United States had pressed for the universality of human rights, an Iranian Deputy Foreign Minister insisted that "[h]uman rights has come to mean Western culture and that human rights is a tool [for Western powers] to whitewash their

992 Ann Elizabeth Mayer, "Universal Versus Islamic Human Rights: A Clash of Cultures or a Clash with a Construct?" *Michigan Journal of International Law* 15 (1993): 318.
993 Ibid.

intervention and aggression against the weaker countries." '[994] In response to a global human rights survey issued by the State Department criticizing China and other countries, in particular China's severe crackdown on the legal community and "extralegal measures" of enforced disappearances and house arrest against government critics, China stated: "The United States made comments on the human-rights situation in many countries while being tight-lipped about its own terrible human-rights record and showing not a bit of intention to reflect on it"[995]. China pinpointed the ' "wanton infringement" of civil rights and "rampant gun-related crimes" in the United States'[996]. These are but two examples of countries not giving in to criticism of their human rights record. As noted in Chapter 5, Armenia has also signed and ratified a number of human rights instruments and is a member of several international organizations. However, its human rights record since independence has fallen short of fulfilling the obligations under those treaties and conventions.

Given the above, this research has focused on human rights as a language used by competing interest groups and in doing so investing meaning in it[997]. That language 'provides us with a set of ethical validity claims which we as individuals and on behalf of ourselves and others make against society as a whole'[998]. The human rights language 'can be and is used to justify numerous competing positions – the debate over abortion is often couched in terms of the 'right to life of the unborn child' (when does a human 'begin'?) against the 'right to choice of the mother' (the sovereignty of the body), while rights-language is central to the positions of both those who favour censoring hate speech and those who oppose it. The language of rights is appropriated to serve a particular ideological position; it does not do so automatically'[999]. It is these competing positions and/or frames that this research has explored and found out that each of the actors in Armenia, whether state or non-state, employ varying and divergent frames when a rights claim is made and the government is challenged.

---

994 Ibid.

995 Eric Baculinao, "China on U.S. Criticism on Human Rights: 'Hold up a Mirror,' " *NBC NEWS*, 14 April 2016, accessed 16 December 2018, https://www.nbcnews.com/news/china/china-u-s-criticism-human-rights-hold-mirror-n555826.

996 Ibid.

997 Darren O'Byrne, "On the Sociology of Human Rights: Theorising the Language-Structure of Rights," *Sociology* 46, no. 5 (2012): 835–836.

998 Ibid.

999 Ibid.

The research has applied the theoretical debates about the sociology of rights to the study of human rights actors in Armenia, bearing in mind national particularities and the historical, cultural and religious backgrounds as well as socio-economic factors while at the same time demonstrating how these factors act as stumbling blocks or are used as excuses by the Armenian state not to carry out its duty. Interestingly, the actors of change that lie at the core of this research have turned to those same factors to counter the state, by questioning the validity of the state's claims in regard to those factors, as well as the areas where the state has failed in its duty and have pressed for redress and change through using public assemblies, protests and demonstrations as platforms for their speech and actions. Being faced with Soviet residues in such areas as education, health, governance, as well as consequences of the collapse of the Soviet Union with major impact upon the economy, later on having to deal with the rise of oligarchs and nouveau riches, power grab and consolidation in the hands of a few at the expense of the rest of society, a decay that has characterized not only Armenia but other post-Soviet states as well, the non-state actors in Armenia have gradually and incrementally moved onto the periphery opening way to ordinary individuals, politically, socially, legally and rights conscious citizens assembling in public spaces for 'a confrontational dialogue' with the government and its institutions. Consequently and particularly in the course of the 2018 Velvet Revolution the notion of 'the citizen' transformed in Armenia. 'Bystanders' became active participants, passive residents turned into active, informed and concerned citizens and the 'I' turned into 'We'.

There has been a shift from submission to resistance, rights talk to rights action, travel back and forth between individuals and collectives as well as the local to the global and back. Findings have revealed tension between Western and Armenian perceptions of certain rights-related concepts. The resistance to such concepts and their use or replacement with other concepts in confrontations with the state as well as when interacting with other non-state actors emphasizes the importance of language in rights struggle, the ways in which actors put that language into use as well as how that language is shaped and reshaped in the course of communicative action. Be it in regard to 'gender', 'democracy', 'activism' to name but a few, embrace and appropriation has been slow if not rejected altogether precisely because they have not sounded close to home, have not arisen out of local understandings and demands.

The Armenian citizens, especially the younger generation, those that have travelled and studied abroad, participated in different civic protests are familiar with and aware of their basic human rights, treaties and conventions. They have accumulated the necessary knowledge, skills and experience to counter the government and to extend their knowledge, skills and experience to fellow citizens. However, human rights perceptions and practices between the state and non-state actors in Armenia are more local than global, more particular than universal, manifest in speech and action, confrontations, resistances and interactions in 'The Street'. This is not to say that 'the universal' has no appeal to local struggles. It does have an appeal but the latter shall not be exaggerated since without local resonance with universal human rights ideas, rights will remain just an aspirational model, an abstract notion with no content or substance.

Challenges ahead

The 2018 Velvet Revolution started with Pashinyan's 'protest walk across the country, sparking increasingly large marches, strikes, and civil disobedience, enlisting tens of thousands of Armenians infuriated by dishonesty and inequality under the long-dominant Republic Party'[1000]. The background of Pashinyan as well as his team is different from the previous elite. In contrast to the latter, 'which was associated with the communist party or komsomol, participated in the hot stage of the war in NK in 1990–1994, and had inherited the Soviet lack of ethical values, particularly vis-à-vis corruption' Pashinyan and his team 'are closely related to the civil society of Armenia'[1001]. Furthermore, 'many of them have studied in the West or both in the West and Russia, and represent the young generation of leaders (Pashinyan is the oldest one in his team so far, and he is 43 years old) who have no qualities associated with the homo sovieticus and who have become conscious citizens during the independence times'[1002].

Pashinyan was both popular and garnered a lot of support in the course of 2018 mass protests owing to his focus on 'combatting corruption, establishing social equality, dismantling monopolies, creating a competitive marketplace, calling for snap parliamentary elections, improving national security and engaging in electoral reform'[1003]. However, Pashinyan's newly formed government may be more vulnerable than expected. His 'mission to eradicate corruption and relieve the pressure of Armenia's economic suppression may also result

---

1000 Daniel L. Feldman and Haris Alibašić, "The Remarkable 2018 'Velvet Revolution': Armenia's Experiment Against Government Corruption," *Public Integrity* 21 (2019): 425.

1001 Eurasia Partnership Foundation, "Velvet Revolution and Political Developments in Armenia. Briefing Book," September 2018, p. 8, available at: https://hkdepo.am/up/docs/Armenia_Briefing_Book_Velvet_Revolution_and_Political_Developments_September%2013_2018.pdf.

1002 Ibid.

1003 Ibid., 5.

in heavy opposition by former heads of Sargsyan's regime'[1004]. Furthermore, there have been shifts in the civil society as well, with some currently employed in government positions, while others preferring activist work and 'remain[ing] vocal in their criticism of government policies'[1005]. The previous two decades were notable for more adversarial and antagonistic state-society relations[1006]. Despite an increasing number of civic initiatives and protests the former ruling elites only made limited concessions which did not lead to any political changes or eradication of unlawful and corrupt practices whose nature has been systemic in Armenia. The accumulated knowledge and experience of the past protests proved significant in the 2018 Velvet Revolution. Since then 'civil society in Armenia has taken two divergent pathways. The first pathway is characterized by the entry of civic activists into institutionalized politics, and the second pathway has involved activists' steadfast refusal to engage in institutionalized politics and to instead continue to work within civil society'[1007].

Motivations for either joining the executive or legislative branches of government or continuing to operate in the civil society differ among activists. For some it was 'the desire to scale up their efforts and contribute to Armenia's socioeconomic and political development' in addition to 'their continued sense of ownership and responsibility for the revolution'[1008]. Those who preferred to remain civil society actors deemed it 'important to remain outside of institutionalized politics so as to maintain their independence and autonomy'[1009]. Others, on the other hand, were 'driven by their ideological opposition to what they perceive as the growing neoliberal turn taken by the Pashinyan government'[1010]. Apart from 'progressive, rights-seeking organizations', the 'civil society space in post-revolutionary Armenia is also a sphere of action for conservative, right-wing, (ultra)nationalist groups'[1011]. The latter compete against and oppose liberal and left-leaning groups whose agendas are considered a threat to Armenian values

---

1004 Ibid.

1005 Armine Ishkanian and Sona Manusyan, "The Postprotest Context in Armenia: Divergent Pathways for Civic Actors," *Carnegie Europe*, 24 October 2019, available at: https://carnegieeurope.eu/2019/10/24/postprotest-context-in-armenia-divergent-pathways-for-civic-actors-pub-80143.

1006 Ibid.

1007 Ibid.

1008 Ibid.

1009 Ibid.

1010 Ibid.

1011 Ibid.

and patriarchy that is considered 'unresolved' by feminist groups[1012]. Whereas 'the closeness between strangers in the streets and the genuine solidarity between lay people during the revolution are acknowledged, they don't seem backed by change of patriarchal political values, which makes some even hesitate in naming the process revolutionary'[1013].

The current government led by Pashinyan faces a number of challenges both domestically as well as abroad. At home 'years of rule by a criminally corrupt regime have saddled Armenia with a legacy of injustice, high levels of poverty and a heavy debt burden'[1014]. Furthermore, most of the country's 'domestic business concerns are controlled by people connected to the former authorities, as are many of the broadcast and online media which have already begun a campaign of criticizing and distracting the government with minor scandals, undermining its ability to set a clear agenda'[1015]. Elimination of corruption and restoration of justice are amongst the priorities of Pashinyan's government, however, the 'new leadership has yet to move convincingly beyond select, high-profile cases to address the issue in a comprehensive way'[1016]. Similar issues still persist in such areas as 'tax and customs policy, education, regional development', as well as 'constitutional and legal changes needed to address two dangerous legacies of the previous regime: the overconcentration of power in the prime minister, and an electoral system designed to perpetuate single-party dominance'[1017].

The aforementioned obstacles are 'exacerbated by the top-heavy nature of Armenia's new leadership. Pashinyan trusts only a small circle of allies, mostly those from his political party, Civil Contract, and those who were active in the protests that eventually brought him to power'[1018]. Moreover, decision-making has been difficult with regard to the Amulsar gold mine and the

---

1012 Socioscope Societal Research & Consultancy Center NGO, "Analytical Report. From Shrinking Space to Post-Revolutionary Space: Reimagining the Role and Relations of Civil Society in Armenia," 2018, available at: http://socioscope.am/wp-content/uploads/2019/01/Socioscope-report_15.01_spread-eng.pdf.

1013 Ibid., 39.

1014 Miriam Lanskoy and Elspeth Suthers, "Armenia's Velvet Revolution," *Journal of Democracy* 30, no. 2 (2019): 95.

1015 Ibid.

1016 Ibid., 96.

1017 Ibid.

1018 Joshua Kucera and Ani Mejlumyan, "Pashinyan Allies Lament Slow Pace of Change in the New Armenia," *eurasianet*, 14 October 2019, accessed 17 January 2020, https://eurasianet.org/pashinyan-allies-lament-slow-pace-of-change-in-the-new-armenia.

Istanbul Convention – environmental and gender-related issues that present a tough test to the current government. Environmentalists and grassroots activists oppose the exploitation of the Amulsar mine citing harm to the environment. Pashinyan, in turn, 'has made attracting foreign investment key to reviving Armenia's economy, and backing out of the project – carried out by a company based in the U.S. and registered in the UK – would send a bad signal to other potential investors'[1019]. After Pashinyan announced that 'a long-awaited environmental report indicated that "the mine should be exploited", many of his allies, including government officials, publicly objected that his reading of the report was too optimistic and the prime minister two weeks later walked back the approval, asking the Environment Ministry to gather more data'[1020].

The Istanbul Convention has also posed a tough challenge. While backed by many of the new senior officials as well as Armenia's partners in the West, 'some of the convention's provisions, such as a statement that gender is socially constructed and a requirement to implement the convention's ideas in the education system, have given ammunition to opponents who seek to turn the country's social conservative population against it'[1021]. The Convention was signed by the previous government but is yet to be ratified by Pashinyan's government. The latter have publicly expressed their intention to proceed with ratification, however, 'soon after pushback, including from the influential church, the My Step coalition decided to hold off'[1022].

Abroad, 'Armenia's challenges include closed borders with Turkey, the simmering Nagorno-Karabakh conflict, and continued Russian influence'[1023]. Unlike Ukraine or Georgia, however, 'Armenia has taken a more conciliatory attitude toward Russia'[1024]. This is problematic in view of both expected

---

1019 Ibid.

1020 Ibid., see also Ani Mejlumyan, "Following Outcry, Armenian Government Steps Back on Controversial Mine Project," *eurasianet*, 5 September 2019, accessed 17 January 2020, https://eurasianet.org/following-outcry-armenian-government-steps-back-on-controversial-mine-project.

1021 Joshua Kucera and Ani Mejlumyan, "Pashinyan Allies Lament Slow Pace of Change in the New Armenia," *eurasianet*, 14 October 2019, accessed 17 January 2020, https://eurasianet.org/pashinyan-allies-lament-slow-pace-of-change-in-the-new-armenia.

1022 Ibid.

1023 Miriam Lanskoy and Elspeth Suthers, "Armenia's Velvet Revolution," *Journal of Democracy* 30, no. 2 (2019): 96.

1024 Ibid.

and intended changes. The Russian influence over and control of key sectors of the Armenian economy, including gas and electricity distribution is one[1025]. The other is 'the military base operated by Russian forces in Gyumri, patrolling Armenia's borders with Turkey and Iran' in addition to 'a considerable percentage of Armenian citizens either residing in Russia permanently or migrating there on a seasonal basis'[1026]. Last but not least, 'Russia also serves as the dominant arbiter of the Nagorno-Karabakh conflict. The Kremlin could use any of these levers to cripple Armenia'[1027]. It remains to be seen if and how the Pashinyan government is able to reduce the Russian influence by deepening the country's relationships with other partners. It is also worthwhile to observe if and how the Pashinyan government installs strong and effective safeguards against official corruption, reforms the judicial system and adopts legislation in areas of controversy and resistance such as domestic violence, mining etcetera.

Implications for further research

The findings of this research can be used for comparative studies of other civic protests and struggles not only within Armenia but outside of it as well. They may also be useful for longitudinal studies regarding social and political developments in 'post-revolutionary' or 'New Armenia' as it is termed locally. It will be interesting to follow how the newly formed government headed by prime-minister Nikol Pashinyan proceeds to implement the promises made during the 2018 April protests and in case there are failures, how the public, the key non-state actors react to his governance.

These research findings will prove useful and helpful for future studies of interactions between state and non-state actors, the use of human rights language as well as new frames and counter frames that will be employed by formal and informal civil society actors to demand the newly formed government to act upon its intentions. As the NGOs have been pushed into the background and independent activists as well as ordinary citizens have moved forward, future studies could examine the ways in which the roles of these non-state actors shape and evolve around Pashinyan's government. Since many civil society members have now been appointed in government positions, a vacuum has been created in the civil society sector as highlighted by other scholars[1028].

1025 Ibid., 97.

1026 Ibid.

1027 Ibid.

1028 Armine Ishkanian, "Armenia's Unfinished Revolution," *Current History* 117, no. 801 (2018): 271–276.

Future studies could prove helpful as to the directions the civil society shifts to and the ways in which it interacts with the new government, as well as challenges and counters it. Reduction in human rights violations or improvement in the status of human rights in Armenia, in particular in social and economic rights, women's rights, coupled with attention to LGBTIQ+ issues are a matter of longitudinal research and would benefit from this research both theoretically as well as empirically.

Bibliography

Abadjian, Vahram. "Kakistocracy or the True Story of What Happened in the Post-Soviet Area," *Journal of Eurasian Studies* 1, no. 2 (2010): 153–163.

Agbakwa, Shedrack C. "Reclaiming Humanity: Economic, Social and Cultural Rights as the Cornerstone of African Human Rights," *Yale Human Rights and Development Journal* 5 (2002): 177.

Aguilar, Gaby Oré. "The Local Relevance of Human Rights: A methodological Approach," Institute of Development Policy and Management (IOB), Discussion Paper/2008.04.

Ahmed, Faiz. "Judicial Reform in Afghanistan: A Case Study in the New Criminal Procedure Code," In Goodale, Mark, and Sally Engle Merry, eds. *The Practice of Human Rights: Tracking Law between the Global and the Local*. Cambridge University Press, 2007.

Alexander, Jeffrey C. *The Civil Sphere*. New York: Oxford University Press, 2006.

Alexopoulos, Golfo. "Soviet Citizenship, More or Less: Rights, Emotions, and States of Civic Belonging," *Kritika: Explorations in Russian and Eurasian History* 7, no. 3 (2006): 487–528.

Amendments to the Constitution of the Republic of Armenia (2015). Retrieved 21 August 2018 from http://www.parliament.am/parliament.php?id=constitution&lang=eng#1.

Amiryan, Tigran. "Culture of Protest: The Symbols of Armenia's Velvet Revolution." *The Calvert Journal* (9 June 2018). Retrieved 17 December 2019 from https://www.calvertjournal.com/articles/show/10318/culture-of-protest-symbols-of-armenia-velvet-revolution.

Amnesty International. Will Human Rights Survive Illiberal Democracy (2015) [Online]. Retrieved February 2018 from https://www.amnesty.nl/content/uploads/2015/10/illiberal-democracy-PDF-20mrt.pdf?x65409.

Amnesty International. Armenia 2017/2018. Retrieved 30 October 3018 from https://www.amnesty.org/en/countries/europe-and-central-asia/armenia/report-armenia/.

Amos, Jennifer. "Embracing and Contesting: The Soviet Union and the Universal Declaration of Human Rights, 1948–1958," In Hoffman, Stefan-Ludwig, ed. *Human Rights in the Twentieth Century*. New York: Cambridge University Press, 2010.

Amos, Owen. "Rights and Wrongs." In Mooney, Annabelle. "Human Rights: Law, Language and the Bare Human Being," *Language & Communication* 32, no. 3 (2012): 169–181.

ANI Armenian Research Center. Artagaght. Hayastani bnakchutyune 2017-i hunvar-mart amisnerin nvazel e 4.600- ov. [Migration. Armenia's Population Has Decreased by 4.600 during January-March 2017] (28 June 2017). Retrieved 22 August 2018 from http://www.aniarc.am/2017/06/28/migration-2017-january-march/.

ANI Armenian Research Center. Serzh Sargsyani nakhagahutyan amen or Hayastanic heracel ev chi veradardsel 102 mard. [On each day of Serzh Sargsyan's Presidency 102 People Have Left Armenia and not Returned] (12 November 2018). Retrieved 15 January 2019 from https://www.aniarc.am/2018/11/12/102-persons-each-day-serzh-sargsyan-in-numbers/.

An-Na'im, Abdullahi Ahmed. "Toward a Cross-Cultural Approach to Defining International Standards of Human Rights: The Meaning of Cruel, Inhuman, or Degrading Treatment or Punishment." In Mark, Goodale ed. *Human Rights: An Anthropological Reader*. Oxford: Blackwell, 2009.

An-Na'im, Abdullahi Ahmed. "An Inclusive Approach to the Mediation of Competing Human Rights Claims," *Constellations* 20, no. 1 (2013): 7–17.

Armaline, William T., Davita S. Glasberg, and Bandana Purkayastha. *The Human Rights Enterprise: Political Sociology, State Power, and Social Movements*. Polity Press, 2015.

Armenia Joins Eurasian Union. *Radio Liberty* (3 January 2015). Retrieved 21 August 2018 from https://www.azatutyun.am/a/26774782.html.

Armenia: Investigate Alleged Police Abuses after Protesters Doused with Water Cannon and Arrested. *Amnesty International* (23 June 2015). Retrieved 15 October 2018 from https://www.amnesty.org/en/latest/news/2015/06/armenia-investigate-alleged-police-abuses-after-protesters-doused-with-water-cannon-and-arrested/.

Armenia: Opposition Leader Pashinian Detained after Abortive Meeting with PM.. *Deutsche Welle* (22 April 2018). Retrieved 30 October 2018 from https://www.dw.com/en/armenia-opposition-leader-pashinian-detained-after-abortive-meeting-with-pm/a-43486135.

Asian Development Bank. *Civil Society Briefs (ARMENIA)* (2011). Retrieved 27 July 2015 from https://www.adb.org/sites/default/files/publication/29304/csb-arm.pdf.

Aslanian, Karlen. Huge Crowds Keep Up Pressure on Armenian PM. *Radio Liberty* (22 April 2018). Retrieved 30 October 2018 from https://www.azatutyun.am/a/29185545.html.

Aslanian, Karlen. Social Media Key to Armenian Revolution, Says Pashinian. *Radio Liberty* (31 January 2019). Retrieved 6 January 2020 from https://www.azatutyun.am/a/29744146.html.

Atanesian, Grigor. Thousands of Protesters Shut Down Armenia's Capital, Dozens Injured in Clashes. *Eurasianet* (16 April 2018). Retrieved 30 October 2018 from https://eurasianet.org/thousands-of-protesters-shut-down-armenias-capital-dozens-injured-in-clashes.

Atkinson, Joshua D. *Journey into Social Activism: Qualitative Approaches.* New York: Fordham University Press, 2017.

Avedissian, Karena. The Power of Electric Yerevan. *openDemocracy* (6 July 2015). Retrieved 17 October 2018 from https://www.opendemocracy.net/karena-avedissian/electrified-yerevan.

Avedissian, Karena. A Real Revolution? Protest Leader Armen Grigoryan on What's Happening in Armenia. *openDemocracy* (30 April 2018). Retrieved 18 December 2019 from https://www.opendemocracy.net/en/odr/real-revolution-protest-leader-armen-grigoryan-on-what-s-happening-in-ar/.

Baculinao, Eric. China on U.S. Criticism on Human Rights: 'Hold up a Mirror.' *NBC NEWS* (14 April 2016). Retrieved 16 December 2018 from https://www.nbcnews.com/news/china/china-u-s-criticism-human-rights-hold-mirror-n555826.

Baghdasaryan, Milena. "The Practice of Political Rights and Patron-Client Relations: A Case Study of a Party in Armenia," *Citizenship Studies* 21, no. 8 (2017): 1034–1051.

Baird, Natalie. "To Ratify or Not to Ratify – An Assessment of the Case of Ratification of International Human Rights Treaties in the Pacific," *Melbourne Journal of International Law* 12 (2011): 249.

Beetham, David. *Democracy and Human Rights.* Polity Press, 1999.

"Behind the Glass Wall – the Right to a Fair Trial in the Sasna Tsrer Cases," Report of a fact-finding mission to Armenia (15 March 2018). Retrieved 30 October 2018 from http://prwb.am/new/wp-content/uploads/2018/03/Armenia_report_2018-1.pdf.

Bell, Daniel A., and Joseph H. Carens. "The Ethical Dilemmas of International Human Rights and Humanitarian NGOs: Reflections on a Dialogue between Practitioners and Theorists," *Human Rights Quarterly* 26, no. 2 (2004): 300–329.

Bell, Lynda S. "Who Produces Asian Identity? Discourses, Discrimination, and Chinese Peasant Women in the Quest for Human Rights." In Donnelly, Jack, ed. *Universal Human Rights in Theory and Practice.* Cornell University Press, 2003.

Benford, Robert D., and David A. Snow. "Framing Processes and Social Movements: An Overview and Assessment," *Annual Review of Sociology* 26, no. 1 (2000): 611–639.

Benford, Robert. "Framing Activity, Meaning and Social Movement Participation: The Nuclear Disarmament Movement," Unpublished Ph.D. dissertation, University of Texas-Austin, 1987. In Benford, Robert D., and David A. Snow. "Framing Processes and Social Movements: An Overview and Assessment," *Annual Review of Sociology* 26, no. 1 (2000): 611–639.

Benhabib, Seyla. "Political Geographies in a Global World: Arendtian Reflections," *Social Research* 69, no. 2 (2002): 539–566.

Benton, Ted. "Do We Need Rights? If so, What Sort?" In Morris, Lydia, ed. *Sociological Perspectives*. Routledge, 2006.

Berlin, Isaiah. *Two Concepts of Liberty: An Inaugural Lecture Delivered before the University of Oxford on the 31st of October 1958*. Clarendon, 1959.

Berman, Harold J. "The Dilemma of Soviet Law Reform," *Harvard Law Review* 76, no. 5 (1963): 929–951.

Berman, Mitchell N. "Aspirational Rights and the Two-Output Thesis," *Harvard Law Review Forum* 119 (2005): 220.

Besson, Samantha. "Human Rights and Democracy in a Global Context: Decoupling and Recoupling," *Ethics and Global Politics* 4, no. 1 (2011): 19–50.

Bittner, Stephen V. *The Many Lives of Khrushchev's Thaw: Experience and Memory in Moscow's Arbat*. London: Cornell University Press, 2008.

Brauman, Rony. "Controversies within Health and Human Rights," Address at the Carnegie Council on Ethics and International Affairs (February 14, 2001), available at: https://www.carnegiecouncil.org/studio/multimedia/20010214-controversies-within-health-and-human-rights. In Bell, Daniel A., and Joseph H. Carens. "The Ethical Dilemmas of International Human Rights and Humanitarian NGOs: Reflections on a Dialogue between Practitioners and Theorists," *Human Rights Quarterly* 26, no. 2 (2004): 300–329.

Braun, Virginia and Victoria Clarke. "Using Thematic Analysis in Psychology," *Qualitative Research in Psychology*, 3, no. 2 (2006): 77–101.

Brennan, Katherine. "The Influence of Cultural Relativism on International Human Rights Law: Female Circumcision as a Case Study," *Law & Inequality* 7 (1988): 367.

Brown, Michael. "Cultural Relativism 2.0," *Current Anthropology* 49, no. 3 (2008): 363.

Brown, Wendy. "States of Injury: Power and Freedom in Late Modernity," In Douzinas, Costas, and Conor Gearty, eds. *The Meanings of Rights: The Philosophy and Social Theory of Human Rights*. Cambrdige University Press, 2014.

Buechler, Steven M. "New Social Movement Theories," *The Sociological Quarterly* 36, no. 3 (1995): 441–464.

Buergenthal, Thomas. "The UN Human Rights Committee," *Max Planck YBUNL* 5 (2001): 341.

Bulghadaryan, Naira. Hayastanic Evradataran nerkayacvats dimumneri tive krknaki pakasel e. [There Has Been Double Decrease in the Number of Applications Submitted to the European Court from Armenia] *Radio Liberty* (26 January 2018). Retrieved 21 August 2018 from https://www.azatutyun.am/a/29000023.html

Burford, Russel E. "Getting the Bugs out of Socialist Legality: The Case of Joseph Brodsky and a Decade of Soviet Anti-Parasite Legislation," *The American Journal of Comparative Law* 22 (1974): 465–508.

Byrnes, Andrew C. "The other Human Rights Treaty Body: The Work of the Committee on the Elimination of Discrimination against Women," *The Yale Journal of International Law* 14 (1989): 1.

Campbell, Tom. *The Political Approach to Human Rights: Matching Human Rights Morality with Human Rights Mechanisms* [Online]. Retrieved June 2017 from https://www.scribd.com/document/111674326/Matching-Human-Rights-Morality-With-Human-Rights-Mechanisms-1.

Cardenas, Sonia. *Conflict and Compliance: State Responses to International Human Rights Pressure*. University of Pennsylvania Press, 2007.

Carreira da Silva, Filipe. "Outline of a Social Theory of Rights: A Neo-Pragmatist Approach," *European Journal of Social Theory* 16, no. 4 (2013): 457–475.

Caroli, Dorena. "Bolshevism, Stalinism, and Social Welfare (1917–1936)," *International Review of Social History* 48, no. 1 (2003): 27–54.

Cecire, Michael. "Electric Yerevan" Protests Put Spotlight on Armenia's Corruption. *World Politics Review*. Retrieved 18 October 2018 from https://www.worldpoliticsreview.com/articles/16232/electric-yerevan-protests-put-spotlight-on-armenia-s-corruption.

Chilingaryan, Anahit. Protest Leader Becomes Armenia's Prime Minister. Human Rights Watch (9 May 2018). Retrieved 1 November 2018 from https://www.hrw.org/news/2018/05/09/protest-leader-becomes-armenias-prime-minister.

Clark, Ann Marie. *Diplomacy of Conscience: Amnesty International and Changing Human Rights Norms*. Princeton University Press, 2001.

Clark, Tom. "On 'Being Researched': Why Do People Engage with Qualitative Research?" *Qualitative Research*, 10, no. 4 (2010): 399–419.

Coalition to Stop Violence against Women 2010, Armenia. Retrieved 15 September 2018 from https://coalitionagainstviolence.org/en/home/.

Cohen, Stanley. "Government Responses to Human Rights Reports: Claims, Denials, and Counterclaims," *Human Rights Quarterly* 18 (1996): 517.

Cohen, Stephen. "The Significance of 'In the Name of Civil Liberties,'" *Law and Philosophy* 7, no. 3 (1988–1989): 375–394.

Coleman, Doriane Lambelet. "The Contradiction between Soviet and American Human Rights Doctrine: Reconciliation Through Perestroika and Pragmatism," *Boston University International Law Journal* 7 (1989): 61.

Collier, David, and Steven Levitsky. "Democracy with Adjectives: Conceptual Innovation in Comparative Research," *World Politics* 49, no. 3 (1997): 430–451.

Collins, Randall. "Stratification, Emotional Energy, and the Transient Emotions," In Jasper, James M. "The Emotions of Protest: Affective and Reactive Emotions in and around Social Movements," *Sociological Forum* 13, no. 3 (1998): 397–424.

Colomer, Joseph M. "Exit, Voice, and Hostility in Cuba," *International Migration Review* 34, no. 2 (2000): 423–442.

Council of Europe. *European Convention for the Protection of Human Rights and Fundamental Freedoms, as amended by Protocols Nos. 11 and 14*, ETS 5 (4 November 1950). Retrieved 21 August 2018 from http://www.refworld.org/docid/3ae6b3b04.html.

Cranston, Maurice. *What Are Human Rights?* New York: Taplinger, 1973.

Crosby, Alan. Armenian Protests Smell Like Teen Spirit. *RFE/RL's Armenian Service* (20 April 2018). Retrieved 30 October 2018 from https://www.rferl.org/a/this-round-of-armenian-protests-smells-like-teen-spirit/29182665.html.

Cutler, Robert M. "Soviet Dissent under Khrushchev: An Analytical Study," *Comparative Politics* 13, no. 1 (1980): 15–35.

Danial, Sandra. "Cultural Relativism vs Universalism: Female Genital Mutilation, Pragmatic Remedies," *The Journal of Historical Studies* 2, no. 1 (2013): 1–10.

Danish Immigration Service. *Armenia: State Actors, Political Situation, Vulnerable Groups and Citizenship* (2016). Retrieved 21 August 2018 from http://www.refworld.org/docid/583c4aec4.html.

Daredevils of Sassoun: A Timeline. *EVN Report* (17 July 2017). Retrieved 30 October 2018 from https://www.evnreport.com/politics/daredevils-of-sassoun-a-timeline.

Daredevils of Sassoun: The Hostage Crisis in Yerevan as It Developed. *CIVILNET* (20 July 2017). Retrieved 25 October 2018 from https://www.civilnet.am/news/2017/07/20/Dardevils-of-Sassoun-the-Hostage-Crisis-in-Yerevan-as-It-Developed/318741.

Davenport, Christian. "Human Rights and the Democratic Proposition," *The Journal of Conflict Resolution* 43, no. 1 (1999): 92–116.

Day-by-day #Electric Yerevan. *CIVILNET* (27 June 2015). Retrieved 11 October 2018 from https://www.civilnet.am/news/2015/06/27/day-by-day-electricyerevan/273182.

de Azevedo, Marco Antonio Oliveira. "Rights as Entitlements and Rights as Claims," *Veritas (Porto Alegre)* 55, no. 1 (2010): 164–182.

De Mesquita, Bruce Bueno, George W. Downs, Alastair Smith, and Feryal Marie Cherif. "Thinking inside the Box: A Closer Look at Democracy and Human Rights," *International Studies Quarterly* 49, no. 3 (2005): 439–457.

De Sousa Boaventura, Santos. "The Rise of the Global Left: The World Social Forum and Beyond," In Nash, Kate. "Human Rights, Movements and Law: On not Researching Legitimacy," *Sociology* 46, no. 5 (2012): 797–812.

Dean, Richard N. "Beyond Helsinki: The Soviet View of Human Rights in International Law," *Virginia Journal of International Law* 21 (1980): 55.

Defeis, Elizabeth F. "Human Rights and the European Court of Justice: An Appraisal," *Fordham International Law Journal* 31 (2007): 1104.

Deflem, Mathieu, and Stephen Chicoine. "The Sociological Discourse on Human Rights: Lessons from the Sociology of Law," *Development and Society* 40, no. 1 (2011): 101–115.

Delmas, Candice. "Disobedience, Civil and Otherwise," *Criminal Law and Philosophy* 11, no. 1 (2017): 195–211.

Dembour, Marie- Bénédicte. "What Are Human Rights – Four Schools of Thought," *Human Rights Quarterly* 32 (2010): 1.

Demonstrations in Yerevan: Chronicle of April 14. *CIVILNET* (14 April 2018). Retrieved 22 August 2018 from https://www.civilnet.am/news/2018/04/14/Demonstrations-in-Yerevan-Chronicle-of-April-14/333656.

Dobson, Miriam. "The Post-Stalin Era: de-Stalinization, Daily Life, and Dissent," *Kritika: Explorations in Russian and Eurasian History* 12, no. 4 (2011): 905–924.

Donnelly, Jack. "Human Rights as Natural Rights," *Human Rights Quarterly* 4, no. 3 (1982): 391.

Donnelly, Jack. *Universal Human Rights in Theory and Practice*. Cornell University Press, 2003.

Douglas, Nadja. The Culture of Policing in Armenia No. 3/2018. *ZOiS Report* (August 2018). Retrieved 8 November 2018 from https://www.zois-berlin.de/fileadmin/media/Dateien/ZOiS_Reports/ZOiS_Report_3_2018.pdf.

Douzinas, Costas, and Conor Gearty, eds. *The Meanings of Rights: The Philosophy and Social Theory of Human Rights*. Cambridge University Press, 2014.

Du Plessis, Max. "The Universal Aspirations of the International Criminal Court," *African Security Review* 11, no. 4 (2002): 115–118.

Dubet, Francois, and Henri Lustiger Thaler. "Introduction: The Sociology of Collective Action Reconsidered," *Current Sociology* 52, no. 4 (2004): 557–573.

Dudwick, Nora. "Political Transformations in Postcommunist Armenia: Images and Realities," In Dawisha, Karen, and Bruce Parrott, eds. *Conflict, Cleavage and Change in Central Asia and the Caucasus*. Cambridge University Press, 1997.

Eight Killed in Armenia Protest. *The Guardian* (3 March 2008). Retrieved 30 October 2018 from https://www.theguardian.com/world/2008/mar/03/1.

Electricity Protest in Yerevan Turns Violent as Police Use Water Canons to Disperse Crowds. *CIVILNET* (23 June 2015). Retrieved 11 October 2018 from https://www.civilnet.am/news/2015/06/23/electricity-protest-yerevan-turns-violent-water-cannons/272683.

Engel, David M., and Frank W. Munger. "Rights of Inclusion: Law and Identity in the Life Stories of Americans with Disabilities," In Silbey, Susan S. "After Legal Consciousness," *Annual Review of Law and Social Science* 1 (2005): 323–368.

Epress.am. Armenian President Finally Breaks Silence Over Yerevan Hostage Situation (22 July 2016). Retrieved 27 October 2018 from https://epress.am/en/2016/07/22/armenia-president-finally-breaks-silence-over-yerevan-hostage-situation.html.

Eurasia Partnership Foundation. Velvet Revolution and Political Developments in Armenia. Briefing Book. September 2018. Retrieved 17 January 2020 from https://hkdepo.am/up/docs/Armenia_Briefing_Book_Velvet_Revolution_and_Political_Developments_September%2013_2018.pdf.

Evans, Tony. "If Democracy, then Human Rights?" *Third World Quarterly* 22, no. 4 (2001): 623–642.

Evrard, John T. "Human Rights in the Soviet Union: The Policy of Dissimulation," *DePaul Law Review* 29 (1979): 819.

Fairchild, Mildred. "Social-Economic Classes in Soviet Russia," *American Sociological Review* 9, no. 3 (1944): 236–241.

Farer, Tom J. "Elections, Democracy, and Human Rights: Toward a Union," *Human Rights Quarterly* 11, no. 4 (1989): 504.

Feldman, Daniel L. and Haris Alibašić. "The Remarkable 2018 'Velvet Revolution': Armenia's Experiment against Government Corruption." *Public Integrity* 21 (2019): 420–432.

Ferris-Rotman, Amie. Armenia's Charismatic Opposition Leader Whips up Pressure after Talks Break Off. *The Washington Post*, (25 April 2018). Retrieved 22 August 2018 from https://www.washingtonpost.com/world/europe/armenias-charismatic-opposition-leader-whips-up-pressure-after-talks-break-off/2018/04/25/e158f47a-488d-11e8-8082-105a446d19b8_story.html?utm_term=.5e1a34025e9d.

Fireside, Harvey. *Soviet Psychoprisons*. London: W.W. Norton & Company, 1979.

Forst, Rainer. "The Basic Right to Justification: Towards a Constructivist Conception of Human Rights," *Constellations* 6, no. 1 (1999): 35–60.

Forst, Rainer. "The Justification of Human Rights and the Basic Right to Justification: A Reflexive Approach," *Ethics* 120, no. 4 (2010): 711–740.

Forsythe, David. *Human Rights and World Politics*. University of Nebraska Press, 1989.

Franklin, James C. "Shame on You: The Impact of Human Rights Criticism on Political Repression on Latin America," *International Studies Quarterly* 52, no. 1 (2008): 187–211.

Freedom House (2015). Freedom in the World: Armenia. Retrieved 18 October 2018 from https://freedomhouse.org/report/freedom-world/2015/armenia.

Freedom House (2017). Nations in Transit 2017 (Armenia). Retrieved 23 October 2018 from https://freedomhouse.org/report/nations-transit/2017/armenia.

Freedom House. Freedom in the World 2018: Democracy in Crisis (2018) [Online]. Retrieved January 2019 from https://freedomhouse.org/sites/default/files/FH_FITW_Report_2018_Final_SinglePage.pdf.

Freedom House. Freedom in the World 2018: Armenia. Retrieved 30 October 2018 from https://freedomhouse.org/report/freedom-world/2018/armenia.

Freedom House. Freedom on the Net 2018 – Armenia. Retrieved 6 January 2020 from https://www.refworld.org/docid/5be16b2a3.html.

Freedomhouse.org. Freedom in the World 2017| Populists and Autocrats: The Dual Threat to Global Democracy (2017) [Online]. Retrieved December 2018 from https://freedomhouse.org/sites/default/files/FH_FIW_2017_Report_Final.pdf.

Freeman, Michael, "The Philosophical Foundations of Human Rights," *Human Rights Quarterly* 16, no. 3 (1994): 491.

Freire, Maria Raquel, and Licínia Simão. "The Armenian Road to Democracy – Dimensions of a Tortuous Process. CEPS Working Document No. 267, May 2007." (2007): 28.

Frezzo, Mark. *The Sociology of Human Rights*. Polity Press, 2015.

Fryer, Eugene D. "Soviet Human Rights: Law and Politics in Perspective," *Law and Contemporary Problems* 43 (1979): 296.

Gathii, James Thuo. "Defining the Relationship between Human Rights and Corruption," *University of Pennsylvania Journal of International Law* 31 (2009): 125.

Gerards, Janneke H., and Lize R. Glas. "Access to Justice in the European Convention on Human Rights System," *Netherlands Quarterly of Human Rights* 35, no. 1 (2017): 11–30.

Gerlant, Uta. "'The Law Is Our Only Language': Soviet Dissidents and Human Rights," In Huhle, Rainer (Hg.). *Human Rights and History. A Challenge for Education*. Berlin: Stiftung "Erinnerung, Verantwortung und Zukunft", 2010.

Geukjian, Ohannes. "The Politicization of the Environmental Issue in Armenia and Nagorno-Karabakh's Nationalist Movement in the South Caucasus 1985–1991," *Nationalities Papers* 35, no. 2 (2007): 233–265.

Gevorgyan, Valentina. The Next Step in the Development of Armenian Civil Society (2017). Retrieved 28 July 2018 from http://www.osf.am/wp-content/uploads/2017/11/The-Next-Step-in-the-Development-of-Armenian-Civil-Society-paper.pdf.

Ghosal, Sarbani Guha. "Human Rights: Concept and Contestation," *The Indian Journal of Political Science* 71, no. 4 (2010): 1103–1125.

Gill, Graeme. "Nationalism and the Transition to Democracy: The Post-Soviet Experience," *DEMOKRATIZATSIYA: WASHINGTON-* 14, no. 4 (2006): 613.

Ginsburg, Tom, and Tamir Moustafa. *Rule by Law: The Politics of Courts in Authoritarian Regimes*. Cambridge University Press, 2008.

Giragosian, Richard. "From Partisan Confrontation to Political Stalemate: The Struggle for Stability in Armenia," In Hug, Adam, ed. *Spotlight on Armenia*. London: Foreign Policy Centre, 2011.

Glendon, Mary Ann. “The Forgotten Crucible: The Latin American Influence on the Universal Human Rights Idea,” *Harvard Human Rights Journal* 16 (2003): 27.

Goffman, Erving. “Frame Analysis: An Essay on the Organization of the Experience,” In Benford, Robert D., and David A. Snow. “Framing Processes and Social Movements: An Overview and Assessment,” *Annual Review of Sociology* 26, no. 1 (2000): 611–639.

Good, Colleen. “Human Rights and Relativism,” *Macalester Journal of Philosophy* 19, no. 1 (2010): 4.

Goodale, Mark. “Toward a Critical Anthropology of Human Rights,” *Current Anthropology* 47, no. 3 (2006): 485–511.

Goodale, Mark. “Introduction: Locating Rights, Envisioning Law between the Global and the Local.” In M. Goodale and S. E. Merry, eds. *The Practice of Human Rights: Tracking Law between the Global and the Local*. Cambridge University Press, 2007: 1–38.

Goodale, Mark. “Human Values and Moral Exclusion,” *Ethics & Global Politics* 9, no. 1 (2016): 32957.

Goodhart, Michael. “Neither Relative nor Universal: A Response to Donnelly,” *Human Rights Quarterly* 30, no. 1 (2008): 183–193.

Gordon, Joy. “The Concept of Human Rights: The History and Meaning of Its Politicization,” *Brooklyn Journal of International Law* 23, no. 3 (1998): 689.

Gordon, Neve, and Nitza Berkovitch. “Human Rights Discourse in Domestic Settings: How Does It Emerge?” *Political Studies* 55, no. 1 (2007): 243–266.

Gready, Paul. “The Politics of Human Rights,” *Third World Quarterly* 24, no. 4 (2003): 745–757.

Greer, Steven. “What’s Wrong with the European Convention on Human Rights?” *Human Rights Quarterly* 30, no. 3 (2008): 680–702.

Gregg, Benjamin. *Human Rights as Social Construction*. Cambridge University Press, 2011.

Habermas, Jurgen. “The Theory of Communicative Action,” In Buechler, Steven M. “New Social Movement Theories,” *The Sociological Quarterly* 36, no. 3 (1995): 441–464.

Hafner- Burton, Emilie M. *Making Human Rights a Reality*. Princeton University Press, 2013.

Hakobyan, Lusine, et al. Armenian Civil Society: From Transition to Consolidation, *Analytical Country Report. CIVICUS Civil Society Index. Yerevan, Armenia: Counterpart International*. Retrieved 22 August 2018 from http://program.counterpart.org/Armenia (2010).

Hakobyan, Lusine, et al. CIVICUS Civil Society Index Rapid Assessment: Armenia Country Report (2014). Retrieved 22 August 2018 from https://www.civicus.org/images/Civicus-Report_August-2014_FFinal.pdf.

Hambardzumyan, Artak. Pashinyane parzabanum e te inchu chi masnakcum Azatutyan hraparaki hanrahavaqnerin. [Pashinyan Explains Why He Is not Taking Part in the Assemblies at Freedom Square] *Radio Liberty* (4 August 2016). Retrieved 30 October 2018 from https://www.azatutyun.am/a/27900041.html.

Handerson, Conway W. "Conditions Affecting the Use of Political Repression," *The Journal of Conflict Resolution* 35, no. 1 (1991): 120–142.

Hasselbacher, Lee. "State Obligations Regarding Domestic Violence: The European Court of Human Rights, due Diligence, and International Legal Minimums of Protection," *Northwestern Journal of International Human Rights* 8 (2009): 190.

Haule, Romuald R. "Some Reflections on the Foundation of Human Rights – Are Human Rights an Alternative to Moral Values?" *Max Planck Yearbook of United Nations Law Online* 10, no. 1 (2006): 367–395.

Hauser, Gerard A. "The Moral Vernacular of Human Rights Discourse," *Philosophy & Rhetoric* 41, no. 4 (2008): 440–466.

Hawkins, Darren G. *International Human Rights and Authoritarian Rule in Chile*. University of Nebraska Press, 2002.

Hellbeck, Jochen. "Speaking Out: Languages of Affirmation and Dissent in Stalinist Russia," *Kritika: Explorations in Russian and Eurasian History* 1, no. 1 (2000): 71–96.

Helsinki Citizens' Assembly Vanadzor Office. *Situation of Human Rights Defenders in Armenia in 2013 Report* (29 September 2014). Retrieved 21 August 2018 from http://archive.hcav.am/wp-content/uploads/2014/09/HRD-Eng-Final2.pdf.

Helsinki Committee of Armenia. *Human Rights in Armenia* (2014). Retrieved 21 August 2018 from http://armhels.com/wp-content/uploads/2015/02/Ditord-69-Eng.pdf.

Higgins, Tracy E. "Anti-Essentialism, Relativism, and Human Rights," *Harvard Women's Law Journal* 19 (1996): 89.

Hirschl, Ran. "Negative Rights vs. Positive Entitlements: A Comparative Study of Judicial Interpretations of Rights in an Emerging Neo-Liberal Economic Order," *Human Rights Quarterly* 22 (2000): 1060.

Hirschman, Albert O. *Exit, Voice, and Loyalty: Responses to Decline in Firms, Organizations and States*. Harvard University Press, 1970.

Hofrenning, Daniel JB. "Human Rights and Foreign Aid: A Comparison of the Reagan and Carter Administrations," *American Politics Quarterly* 18, no. 4 (1990): 514–526.

Horn, Anita Sophia. "Moral and Political Conceptions of Human Rights: Rethinking the Distinction," *The International Journal of Human Rights* 20, no. 6 (2016): 724–743.

Hornsby, Robert. *Political Protest and Dissent in the Khrushchev Era*. Diss. University of Birmingham, 2009.

Horvath, Robert. "Breaking the Totalitarian Ice: The Initiative Group for the Defense of Human Rights in the USSR," *Human Rights Quarterly* 36, no. 1 (2014): 147.

Howard, Marc M. "The Weakness of Postcommunist Civil Society," *Journal of Democracy* 13, no. 1 (2002): 157–169.

Howard, Rhoda E. "Cultural Absolutism and the Nostalgia for Community," *Human Rights Quarterly* 15 (1993): 315.

Howard, Rhoda E. "Human Rights and the Culture Wars: Globalization and the Universality of Human Rights," *International Journal* 53, no. 1 (1998): 94–112.

Howard-Hassmann, Rhoda E. *In Defense of Universal Human Rights*. Polity Press, 2018.

Hug, Adam, ed. *Spotlight on Armenia*. London: Foreign Policy Centre, 2011.

Human Rights Council. Report of the Special Rapporteur on the Situation of Human Rights Defenders (23 December 2010), Margaret Sekaggya, Addendum, Mission to Armenia. Retrieved 21 August 2018 from http://www2.ohchr.org/english/bodies/hrcouncil/docs/16session/A-HRC-16-44-Add2.pdf.

Human Rights Defender of the Republic of Armenia. Retrieved 21 August 2018 from http://www.ombuds.am/en/defender/history.html.

Human Rights Watch. Armenia: Excessive Police Force at Protest (1 August 2016a). Retrieved 18 October 2018 from https://www.hrw.org/news/2016/08/01/armenia-excessive-police-force-protest.

Human Rights Watch. Armenia: Events of 2016 (2016b). Retrieved 27 October 2018 from https://www.hrw.org/world-report/2017/country-chapters/armenia.

Human Rights Watch. Armenia: Events of 2017. Retrieved 30 October 2018 from https://www.hrw.org/world-report/2018/country-chapters/armenia.

Hunt, Alan. "Rights and Social Movements: Counter-Hegemonic Strategies," *Journal of Law and Society* 17 (1990): 309.

Hunt, Murray. "The European Convention on Human Rights," *Yearbook of European Law* 22, no. 1 (2003): 483–497.

Ibhawoh, Bonny. "Cultural Relativism and Human Rights: Reconsidering the Africanist Discourse," *Netherlands Quarterly of Human Rights* 19, no. 1 (2001): 43–62.

Ignatieff, Michael. *Human Rights as Politics and Idolatry*, ed. Amy Gutmann. With commentary by K. Anthony Appiah, David A. Hollinger, Thomas W. Laqueur, and Diane F. Orentlicher. Princeton: Princeton University Press, 2001.

Ignatieff, Michael. *Human Rights as Politics and Idolatry*. Princeton University Press, 2003.

Ishkanian, Armine. *Democracy Building and Civil Society in Post-Soviet Armenia*. Routledge, 2008.

Ishkanian, Armine, et al. Civil Society, Development and Environmental Activism in Armenia (2013). Retrieved 12 April 2015 from http://eprints.lse.ac.uk/54755/1/Ishkanian_Civil_Society_Development_Enviromental_Activism_America_2013.pdf.

Ishkanian, Armine. "Challenging the Gospel of Neoliberalism? Civil Society Opposition to Mining in Armenia," In Thomas Davies, Holly Eva Ryan, Alejandro Milcíades Peña (ed.) *Protest, Social Movements and Global Democracy Since 2011: New Perspectives* (Research in Social Movements, Conflicts and Change, Volume 39) Emerald Group Publishing Limited, (2016a), pp. 107–136.

Ishkanian, Armine. From Civil Disobedience to Armed Violence: Political Developments in Armenia. *openDemocracy* (19 July 2016b). Retrieved 25 October 2018 from https://www.opendemocracy.net/od-russia/armine-ishkanian/from-civil-disobedience-to-armed-violence-political-developments-in-armen.

Ishkanian, Armine. "Armenia's Unfinished Revolution," *Current History* 117, no. 801 (2018a): 271–276.

Ishkanian, Armine. A Revolution of Values: Freedom, Responsibility and Courage in Armenia's Velvet Revolution. *openDemocracy* (3 May 2018b). Retrieved 1 November 2018 from https://www.opendemocracy.net/od-russia/armine-ishkanian/revolution-of-values-freedom-responsibility-and-courage-in-armenias-velve.

Ishkanian, Armine and Sona Manusyan. The Postprotest Context in Armenia: Divergent Pathways for Civic Actors. *Carnegie Europe* (24 October 2019). https://carnegieeurope.eu/2019/10/24/postprotest-context-in-armenia-divergent-pathways-for-civic-actors-pub-80143 (accessed 17 January 2020).

Jardine, Bradley. Armenian Youth, the 'Engine of the Revolution,' Fight for a Fairer Society. *Eurasianet* (7 May 2018). Retrieved 12 December 2019 from https://eurasianet.org/armenian-youth-the-engine-of-the-revolution-fight-for-a-fairer-society.

Jasper, James M. "The Emotions of Protest: Affective and Reactive Emotions in and around Social Movements," *Sociological Forum* 13, no. 3 (1998): 397–424.

Jonas, Susanne. *The Battle for Guatemala: Rebels, Death Squads, and U.S. Power*. Boulder: Westview Press, 1991.

Judgments and Decisions in Respect of Armenia. Retrieved 21 August 2018 from http://agent.echr.am/en/judgments/judgmentsanddecisionsinrespectofarmenia.html.

Juviler, Peter H. *Freedom's Ordeal: The Struggle for Human Rights and Democracy in Post-Soviet States*. University of Pennsylvania Press, 1998.

Keith, Linda Camp. "The United Nations International Covenant on Civil and Political Rights: Does It Make a Difference in Human Rights Behavior?" *Journal of Peace Research* 36, no. 1 (1999): 95–118.

Keller, H., and Ulfstein, G., eds. *UN Human Rights Treaty Bodies: Laws and Legitimacy*. Cambridge University Press, 2012.

Kelly, Tobias. "The UN Committee against Torture: Human Rights Monitoring and the Legal Recognition of Cruelty," *Human Rights Quarterly* 31, no. 3 (2009): 777–800.

Kline, George L. "Socialist Legality and Communist Ethics," *Natural Law Forum* 8 (1963): 21.

Korey, William. *NGOs and the Universal Declaration of Human Rights: A Curious Grapevine*. New York: St. Martin's Press, 1998.

Kotchikian, Asbed. It's the People, Stupid: Debunking the Myths on Protests in Armenia. *Hetq* (19 April 2018). Retrieved 1 November 2018 from https://hetq.am/en/article/87561.

Kowalewski, David. "Religious Belief in the Brezhnev Era: Renaissance, Resistance and Realpolitik," *Journal for the Scientific Study of Religion* 19, no. 3 (1980): 280–292.

Krastev, Ivan, and Stephen Holmes. "Imitation and Its Discontents," *Journal of Democracy* 29, no. 3 (2018): 117–128.

Krishnadas, Jane. "The Sexual Subaltern in Conversations "Somewhere in Between": Law and the Old politics of Colonialism," *Feminist Legal Studies* 14 (2006): 53–77.

Kucera, Joshua, and Ani Mejlumyan. Pashinyan Allies Lament Slow Pace of Change in the New Armenia. *eurasianet* (14 October 2019). https://eurasianet.org/pashinyan-allies-lament-slow-pace-of-change-in-the-new-armenia (accessed 17 January 2020).

Kurkchiyan, Marina. “The Armenian Media in Context: Soviet Heritage, the Politics of Transition, Democracy, and the Rule of Law,” *Demokratizatsiya* 14, no. 2 (2006).

Laclau, Ernesto. “Emancipation(s),” In Morris, Lydia, ed. *Sociological Perspectives*. Routledge, 2006.

Langlois, Anthony J. “Human Rights without Democracy? A Critique of the Separationist Thesis,” *Human Rights Quarterly* 25, no. 4 (2003): 990–1019.

Langston, Joy. “Breaking out Is Hard to Do: Exit, Voice, and Loyalty in Mexico’s One-Party Hegemonic Regime,” *Latin American Politics and Society* 44, no. 3 (2002): 61–88.

Lanskoy, Miriam, and Elspeth Suthers. “Armenia’s Velvet Revolution.” *Journal of Democracy* 30, no. 2 (2019): 85–99.

Levitsky, Steven, and Lucan Way. “The Rise of Competitive Authoritarianism,” *Journal of Democracy* 13, no. 2 (2002): 51–65.

Liakhov, Peter and Knar Khudoyan. How Citizens Battling a Controversial Gold Mining Project Are Testing Armenia’s New Democracy. *openDemocracy* (7 August 2018). Retrieved 14 February 2019 from https://www.opendemocracy.net/od-russia/peter-liakhov-knar-khudoyan/citizens-battling-a-controversial-gold-mining-project-amulsar-armenia.

Lutz, Ellen L., and Kathryn Sikkink. “Internaitonal Human Rights Law and Practice in Latin America,” *International Organization* 54, no. 3 (2000): 633–659.

MacFarquhar, Neil. He Was a Protester a Month Ago. Now, Nikol Pashinyan Leads Armenia. *The New York Times* (8 May 2018). Retrieved 22 August 2018 from https://www.nytimes.com/2018/05/08/world/europe/armenia-nikol-pashinyan-prime-minister.html.

Mahmood, Saba. “Feminist Theory, Embodiment and the Docile Agent: Some Reflections on the Egyptian Islamic Revival,” *Cultural Anthropology* 16, no. 2 (2001): 202–236.

Maliks, Reidar, and Johan Karlsson Schaffer, eds. *Moral and Political Conceptions of Human Rights: Implications for Theory and Practice*. Cambridge University Press, 2017.

Malkasian, Mark. *Gha-ra-bagh!: The Emergence of the National Democratic Movement in Armenia*. Wayne State University Press, 1996.

Mamulyan, Araks, and Gagik Aghbalyan. 1 mln evroyic avel Hayastane vtcharel e Mardu iravunqneri konvencian khakhtelu hamar (infografika). [Armenia Has Paid More than 1 mln Euros for Violations of the European Convention on Human Rights] *Hetq* (26 July 2018). Retrieved 21 August 2018 from http://hetq.am/arm/news/91662/1-mln-evroyic-avel-hayastany-vtcharel-e-mardu-iravunqneri-konvencian-khakhtelu-hamar-infografika.html.

Markedonov, Sergei. What Armenians Are Protesting (and What They're not). *openDemocracy* (24 June 2015). Retrieved 18 October 2018 from https://www.opendemocracy.net/sergei-markedonov/what-armenians-are-protesting-and-what-they%E2%80%99re-not-protesting.

Marshall, Anna-Maria. "Injustice Frames, Legality, and the Everyday Construction of Sexual Harassment," *Law and Social Inquiry* 28, no. 3 (2003): 659–689.

May, John D'Arcy. "Human Dignity, Human Rights, and Religious Pluralism: Buddhist and Christian Perspectives," *Buddhist-Christian Studies* 26, no. 1 (2006): 51–60.

Mayer, Ann Elizabeth. "Universal versus Islamic Human Rights: A Clash of Cultures or a Clash with a Construct?" *Michigan Journal of International Law* 15 (1993): 307.

McAdam, Doug. "Culture and Social Movements," In Buechler, Steven M. "New Social Movement Theories," *The Sociological Quarterly* 36, no. 3 (1995): 441–464.

McAdam, Doug. "Conceptual and Theoretical Issues." In Armaline, William T., Davita S. Glasberg, and Bandana Purkayastha, eds. *The Human Rights Enterprise: Political Sociology, State Power, and Social Movements*. Polity Press, 2015.

McCann, Michael W. "Rights at Work: Pay Equity Reform and the Politics of Legal Mobilization," In Silbey, Susan S. "After Legal Consciousness," *Annual Review of Law and Social Science* 1 (2005): 323–368.

McCann, Michael. "Law and Social Movements: Contemporary Perspectives," *Annual Review of Law and Social Science* 2 (2006): 17.

McCarthy, John D., and Mayer N. Zald. "Resource Mobilization and Social Movements: A Partial Theory," *American Journal of Sociology* 82, no. 6 (1977): 1212–1241.

McQuigg, Ronagh. "How Effective is the United Nations Committee against Torture?" *The European Journal of International Law* 22, no. 3 (2011): 813–828.

Mechlem, Kerstin. "Treaty Bodies and the Interpretation of Human Rights," *Vanderbilt Journal of Transnational Law* 42 (2009): 905.

Mejlumyan, Ani. Following Outcry, Armenian Government Steps Back on Controversial Mine Project. *eurasianet* (5 September 2019). https://eurasianet.org/following-outcry-armenian-government-steps-back-on-controversial-mine-project (accessed 17 January 2020).

Melkonian, Markar. No to Plunder, No to Maidan. *Hetq* (26 June 2015). Retrieved 18 October 2018 from http://hetq.am/eng/news/61154/.

Melucci, Alberto. "Getting Involved: Identity and Mobilization in Social Movements," In Buechler, Steven M. "New Social Movement Theories," *The Sociological Quarterly* 36, no. 3 (1995): 441–464.

Merry, Sally Engle. "Anthropology and Activism: Researching Human Rights across Porous Boundaries," *PoLAR* 28 (2005a): 240.

Merry, Sally Engle. "Concepts of Law and Justice among Working Class Americans: Ideology as Culture," In Silbey, Susan S. "After Legal Consciousness," *Annual Review of Law and Social Science* 1 (2005b): 323–368.

Merry, Sally Engle. "Human Rights and Transnational Culture: Regulating Gender Violence through Global Law," *Osgoode Hall Law Journal* 44, no. 1 (2006a): 53.

Merry, Sally Engle. "Transnational Human Rights and Local Activism: Mapping the Middle," *American Anthropologist* 108, no. 1 (2006b): 38–51.

Merry, Sally Engle. "Introduction: Conditions of Vulnerability." In Goodale, Mark, and Sally Engle Merry, eds. *The Practice of Human Rights: Tracking Law between the Global and the Local.* Cambridge University Press, 2007a.

Merry, Sally Engle. "Introduction: States of Violence," In Goodale, Mark, and Sally Engle Merry, eds. *The Practice of Human Rights: Tracking Law between the Global and the Local.* Cambridge University Press, 2007b.

Merry, Sally Engle. "Getting Justice and Getting Even: Legal Consciousness among Working Class Americans," In Somers, Margaret R., and Christopher NJ Roberts. "Toward a New Sociology of Rights: A Genealogy of "Buried Bodies" of Citizenship and Human Rights," *Annual Review of Law and Social Science* 4 (2008): 385–425.

Merry, Sally Engle. "Human Rights and Gender Violence: Translating International Law into Local Justice," In Aguilar, Gaby Oré. "The Local Relevance of Human Rights: A Methodological Approach," Institute of Development Policy and Management (IOB), Discussion Paper/2008.04.

Messer, Ellen. "Pluralist Approaches to Human Rights," *Journal of Anthropological Research* 53, no. 3 (1997): 293–317.

Messer, Ellen. "Anthropology, Human Rights, and Social Transformation." In Goodale, Mark, ed. *Human Rights: An Anthropological Reader.* Oxford: Blackwell, 2009.

Minasyan, Shushanik. "The Velvet Revolution – A New Path for Armenia," In Wolfram Hilz and Shushanik Minasyan, eds. *Armenian Developments: Perspectives of Democratization and the Role of the Civil Society.* Baden-Baden, 2019.

Mitchell, Neil J. and James M. McCormick. "Economic and Political Explanations of Human Rights Violations," *World Politics* 40, no. 4 (1988): 476–498.

Monshipouri, Mahmood and Claude E. Welch. “The Search for International Human Rights and Justice: Coming to Terms with the New Global Realities,” *Human Rights Quarterly* 23, no. 2 (2001): 370.

Morris, Lydia. *Rights: Sociological Perspectives*. Routledge, 2006.

Morris, Lydia. *Human Rights and Social Theory*. Macmillan International Higher Education, 2013.

Morse, Janice M. (1991). “Strategies for Sampling.” In Morse, Janice M. ed. *Qualitative Nursing Research: A Contemporary Dialogue*. Sage Publications, 1990.

Morsink, Johannes. *The Universal Declaration of Human Rights: Origins, Drafting, and Intent*. University of Pennsylvania Press, 1999.

Na'im, A. A. A., *Human Rights in Cross-Cultural Perspectives: A Quest for Consensus*. University of Pennsylvania Press, 1995.

Nadel, Laura. “Introduction: Registers of Power,” In Goodale, Mark, and Sally Engle Merry, eds. *The Practice of Human Rights: Tracking Law between the Global and the Local*. Cambridge University Press, 2007.

Nash, Kate. “Human Rights, Movements and Law: On not Researching Legitimacy,” *Sociology* 46, no. 5 (2012): 797–812.

Nathans, Benjamin. “The Dictatorship of Reason: Aleksandr Vol'pin and the Idea of Rights under “Developed Socialism”,” *Slavic Review* 66, no. 4 (2007): 630–663.

Nathans, Benjamin. “Soviet Rights-Talk in the Post-Stalin Era,” In Hoffman, Stefan-Ludwig, ed. *Human Rights in the Twentieth Century*. Cambridge University Press, 2010.

Nickel, James W. “Poverty and Rights,” *The Philosophical Quarterly* 55, no. 220 (2005): 385–402.

Nielsen, Richard A., and Beth A. Simmons. “Rewards for Ratification: Payoffs for Participating in the International Human Rights Regime?” *International Studies Quarterly* 59, no. 2 (2015): 197–208.

O'Brien, Thomas. “Shifting Patterns of Governance in Authoritarian Regimes,” *Australian Journal of Political Science* 52, no. 2 (2017): 303–316.

O'Byrne, Darren. “On the Sociology of Human Rights: Theorising the Language-Structure of Rights,” *Sociology* 46, no. 5 (2012): 829–843.

Ohanyan, Anna. A Very Potent Protest Movement is Emerging in Armenia. *Aljazeera* (21 April 2018). Retrieved 1 November 2018 from https://www.aljazeera.com/indepth/opinion/potent-protest-movement-emerging-armenia-180419135116999.html.

Ohlin, Jens David. “Is the Concept of the Person Necessary for Human Rights?” *Columbia Law Review* 105 (2005): 209.

Oliphant, Roland. Armenia's "Electric Yerevan" Protests Enter Seventh Day. *Telegraph* (25 June 2015). Retrieved 18 October 2018 from https://www.telegraph.co.uk/news/worldnews/europe/armenia/11699692/Armenias-Electric-Yerevan-protests-enter-seventh-day.html.

Orend, Brian. "Human Rights: Concept and context." In Christopher J. Anderson, Aida Paskeviciute, Maria Elena Sandovici and Yulia V. Tverdova. "In the Eye of the Beholder? The Foundations of Subjective Human Rights Conditions in East-Central Europe," *Comparative Political Studies* 38, no. 7 (2005): 771–798.

Osakwe, Christopher. "Soviet Human Rights Law under the USSR Constitution of 1977: Theories, Realities and Trends," *Tulane Law Review* 56 (1981): 249.

Owen, Nicholas J., ed. *Human Rights, Human Wrongs: The Oxford Amnesty Lectures 2001*. Oxford University Press on Demand, 2003.

Parekh, Serena. "Resisting Dull and Torpid Assent: Returning to the Debate over the Foundations of Human Rights." In Mooney, Annabelle. "Human Rights: Law, Language and the Bare Human Being," *Language & Communication* 32, no. 3 (2012): 169–181.

Parkin, Frank. "Durkheim." In Morris, Lydia, ed. *Sociological Perspectives*. Routledge, 2006.

Pati, Roza. "Rights and Their Limits: The Constitution for Europe in International and Comparative Legal Perspective," *Berkeley Journal of International Law* 23 (2005): 223.

Patton, Michael Quinn. *Qualitative Evaluation and Research Methods*. SAGE Publications, Inc., 1990.

Paturyan, Yevgenya. "(Dis)trusting People and Political Institutions in Armenia," *Caucasus Analytical Digest* 31 (2011): 6–10.

Paturyan, Yevgenya Jenny. "Armenian Civil Society: It is not All about NGOs," *Caucasus Analytical Digest*, No. 73 (26 May 2015): 1–5.

Paturyan Yevgenya Jenny, and Valentina Gevorgyan. Armenian NGOs and Civic Activists: Seeing Eye to Eye? *Póznan, Poland*. Retrieved 22 August 2018 from http://tcpa.aua.am/files/2016/08/Armenian-NGOs-and-Civic-Activists-Seeing-Eye-to-Eye.pdf (2016a).

Paturyan, Yevgenya Jenny, and Valentina Gevorgyan (2016b). Civic Activism as a Novel Component of Armenian Civil Society. Turpanjian Center for Policy Analysis. Yerevan, Armenia. Available at:https://tcpa.aua.am/files/2016/08/Civic-Activism-as-a-Novel-Component-of-Armenian-Civil-Society.pdf.

Paul Gordon, Lauren. *The Evolution of International Human Rights: Visions Seen*, 3rd edition. University of Pennsylvania Press, 2011.

Payaslian, Simon. *The Political Economy of Human Rights in Armenia: Authoritarianism and Democracy in a Former Soviet Republic.* London: I.B. Tauris, 2011.

Peerenboom, Randall. "Beyond Universalism and Relativism: The Evolving Debates about Values in Asia," *Indiana International & Comparative Law Review* 14 (2003): 1.

Perry, Michael J. "Are Human Rights Universal? The Relativist Challenge and Related Matters," *Human Rights Quarterly* 19, no. 3 (1997): 461–509.

Peters, Anne. Corruption as a Violation of International Human Rights (2016). [Online]. http://www.mpil.de/files/pdf4/Peters_Corruption_and_Human_Rights20151.pdf. [2018 November].

Pfaff, Steven, and Hyojoung Kim. "Exit-Voice Dynamics in Collective Action: An Analysis of Emigration and Protest in the East German Revolution," *American Journal of Sociology* 109, no. 2 (2003): 401–444.

Plummer, Ken. "Rights Work, Constructing Lesbian, Gay and Sexual Rights in Late Modern Times." In Morris, Lydia, ed. *Sociological Perspectives.* Routledge, 2006.

Poe, Steven C., and C. Neal Tate. "Repression of Human Rights to Personal Integrity in the 1980s: A Global Analysis." In Keith, Linda Camp. "The United Nations International Covenant on Civil and Political Rights: Does It Make a Difference in Human Rights Behavior?" *Journal of Peace Research* 36, no. 1 (1999): 95–118.

Prasad, Ajnesh. "Cultural Relativism in Human Rights Discourse," *Peace Review* 19, no. 4 (2007): 589–596.

Preis, Ann-Belinda S. "Human Rights as Cultural Practice: An Anthropological Critique," *Human Rights Quarterly* 18, no. 2 (1996): 286.

Přibáň, Jiří. "Political Dissent, Human Rights and Legal Transformations: Communist and post-Communist Experiences," *East European Politics and Societies* 19, no. 4 (2005): 553–572.

Protest Against Serzh Sargsyan's Prime-Ministership. *CIVILNET* (10 April 2018). Retrieved 22 August 2018 from https://www.civilnet.am/news/2018/04/10/Protest-Against-Serzh-Sargsyan%E2%80%99s-Prime-Ministership/333140.

Protesters, Armenian Riot Police Clash Over Nomination For Prime Minister. *RFE/RL's Armenian Service* (16 April 2018). Retrieved 20 October 2018 from https://www.rferl.org/a/armenia-opposition-activists-block-roads-bridge-subway-in-yerevan-protesting-sarkisian-expected-shift/29169981.html.

Rapley, Timothy John. "The Art(fulness) of Open-Ended Interviewing: Some Considerations on Analysing Interviews," *Qualitative Research* 1, no. 3 (2001): 303–323.

Rawls, John. "The Law of Peoples," In Shute, Stephen, and Susan L. Hurley, eds. *On Human Rights*. Basic Books, 1993.

Ray, Ranita, and Bandana Purkayastha. "Challenges in Localizing Global Human Rights," *Societies without Borders* 7, no. 1 (2012): 29–51.

Recknagel, Charles. Explainer: What Is Armenia's "Founding Parliament" Movement? *Radio Free Europe Radio Liberty* (18 July 2016). Retrieved 25 October 2018 from https://www.rferl.org/a/armenia-founding-parliament-explainer-sefilian/27865671.html.

Regional Studies Center. RSC Staff on Armenian Hostage Standoff (18 July 2016). Retrieved 30 October 2018 from https://regional-studies.org/news/media/548-180716.

Ress, Georg. "The Effect of Decisions and Judgments of the European Court of Human Rights in the Domestic Legal Order," *Texas International Law Journal* 40 (2004): 359.

Risse, Thomas, Stephen C. Ropp, and Kathryn Sikkink. *The Power of Human Rights: International Norms and Domestic Change*. Cambridge University Press, 1999.

Robinson, Mary. "Taking Stock of the Human Rights Agenda Sixty Years On," *Maryland Journal of International Law* 24 (2009): 1.

Robson, Elisabeth. "Media Freedom in Armenia: One Step Forward, Two Steps Back," In Hug, Adam, ed. *Spotlight on Armenia*. London: Foreign Policy Centre, 2011.

Rogobete, Silviu E. "Morality and Tradition in Postcommunist Orthodox Lands: On the Universality of Human Rights, with Special Reference to Romania," *Religion, State & Society* 32, no. 3 (2004): 275–297.

Roth, Andrew. Shock as Armenia's Prime Minister Steps Down after 11 Days of Protests. *The Guardian* (23 April 2018). Retrieved 1 November 2018 from https://www.theguardian.com/world/2018/apr/23/serzh-sargsyan-resigns-as-armenias-prime-minister-after-protests.

Rowley, David. "Interpretations of the End of the Soviet Union," *Kritika: Explorations in Russian and Eurasian History* 2, no. 2 (2001): 395–426.

Rucht, Dieter. "Themes, Logics and Arenas of Social Movements: A Structural Approach," In Buechler, Steven M. "New Social Movement Theories," *The Sociological Quarterly* 36, no. 3 (1995): 441–464.

Ruggie, John Gerard. "What Makes the World Hang Together? Neo-Utilitarianism and the Social Constructivist Challenge," *International Organization* 52, no. 4 (1998): 855–885.

Ryan, Gery W., and H. Russell Bernard. "Techniques to Identify Themes," *Field Methods* 15, no. 1 (2003): 85–109.

Sahakyan, Vahe, and Arthur Atanesyan. "Democratization in Armenia: Some Trends of Political Culture and Behavior," *Demokratizatsiya* 14, no. 3 (2006): 347–354.

Sakwa, Richard. *Soviet Politics: An Introduction*. Routledge, 1989.

Samson, Colin, and Damien Short. "The Sociology of Indigenous People's Rights," In Morris, Lydia, ed. *Sociological Perspectives*. Routledge, 2006.

Sanamyan, Emil. Saint Nick of Armenia: How Protest Leader Nikol Pashinyan "Rescued" Armenia and Made It Merry (5 May 2018). Retrieved 30 October 2018 from https://www.opendemocracy.net/od-russia/emil-sanamyan/saint-nick-of-armenia-how-nikol-pashinyan-rescued-armenia-and-made-it-merry.

Sandelowski, M. "Sample size in Qualitative Research." *Research in Nursing and Health* 18, no. 2 (1995): 179–183.

Sandford, Alasdair. How 11 Days of Protests Brought Down Armenia's Leader Serzh Sargsyan. *euronews* (23 April 2018). Retrieved 22 August 2018 from http://www.euronews.com/2018/04/23/how-11-days-of-protests-brought-down-armenia-s-leader-serzh-sargsyan.

Sarat, Austin. "The Law Is all Over: Power, Resistance and the Legal Consciousness of the Welfare Poor," *Yale Journal of Law & the Humanities* 2 (1990): 343.

Sargsyan, Tatevik. "Online Media in Armenia: A Taste of Free Expression," *Southeast European and Black Sea Studies* 14, no. 2 (2014): 283–300.

Saroyan, Gohar. Depoliticising Protests in Armenia. *openDemocracy* (6 June 2016). Retrieved 23 October 2018 from https://www.opendemocracy.net/od-russia/gohar-saroyan/depoliticising-protest-in-armenia.

Sarukhanyan, Vahe. Nikol Pashinyane 15-rd andzn e vore zbaxecnum e HH varchapeti pashtone. [Nikol Pashinyan Is the 15th Person that Is Occupying the Position of the RA Prime Minister] *Hetq* (8 May 2018). Retrieved 22 August 2018 from http://hetq.am/arm/news/88609/nikol-pashinyany-15-rd-andzn-e-ory-zbaxecnum-e-hh-varchapeti-pashtony.html.

Schifter, Richard. "Human Rights and the Helsinki Final Act: From USSR to Contemporary Russia," *Journal of Global Policy and Governance* 1, no. 2 (2013): 197–202.

Schmitz, Hans Peter. "Transnational Activism and Political Change in Kenya and Uganda." In Risse, Thomas, Steve Ropp, and Kathryn Sikkink, eds. *The Power of Human Rights: International Norms and Domestic Change*. Cambridge University Press, 1999.

Schoultz, Lars. *Human Rights and United States Policy toward Latin America*. Princeton: Princeton University Press, 1981.

Schwartz, Herman. "Economic and Social Rights," *American University International Law Review* 8 (1992): 551.

Serzh Sargsyan: From President to Prime Minister?. *CIVILNET* (28 March 2018). Retrieved 22 August 2018 from https://www.civilnet.am/news/2018/03/28/Serzh-Sargsyan-From-President-to-Prime-Minister/332448.

Sewell Jr, William H. "A Theory of Structure: Duality, Agency, and Transformation," *American Journal of Sociology* 98, no. 1 (1992): 1–29.

Shahnazarian, Nona. Here Is Not Maidan, Here Is Marshal Baghramian: The "Electric Yerevan" Protest Movement and Its Consequences. *PONARS Eurasia* (January 2016). Retrieved 17 October 2018 from http://www.ponarseurasia.org/memo/here-not-maidan-here-marshal-baghramian-electric-yerevan-protest.

Sharlet, Robert. "Party and Public Ideals in Conflict: Constitutionalism and Civil Rights in the USSR," *Cornell International Law Journal* 23 (1990): 341.

Shaw, Ibrahim Seaga. "Human Rights Journalism: A Critical Conceptual Framework." In Shaw, Ibrahim Seaga, ed. *Human Rights Journalism*, pp. 25–42. Palgrave Macmillan, London, 2012.

Shirinian, Tamar, and Nelli Sargsyan. The Armenian Violence Question: A Conversation on Means and Social Change. *Public Seminar* (13 December 2016). Retrieved 27 October 2018 from http://www.publicseminar.org/2016/12/the-armenian-violence-question/.

Shoemaker, M. Wesley. *Russia and The Commonwealth of Independent States 2014*. Rowman & Littlefield, 2014.

Silbey, Susan S. "After Legal Consciousness," *Annual Review of Law and Social Science* 1 (2005): 323–368.

Simmons, Beth A. *Mobilizing for Human Rights: International Law in Domestic Politics*. Cambridge University Press, 2009.

Smith, Mark. B. "Social Rights in the Soviet Dictatorship: The Constitutional Right to Welfare from Stalin to Brezhnev," *Humanity: An International Journal of Human Rights, Humanitarianism, and Development* 3, no. 3 (2012): 385–406.

Smith, William. "Civil Disobedience and the Public Sphere," *Journal of Political Philosophy* 19, no. 2 (2011): 145–166.

Smith-Cannoy, Heather. *Insincere Commitments: Human Rights Treaties, Abusive States, and Citizen Activism*. Georgetown University Press, 2012.

Socioscope Societal Research & Consultancy Center NGO (2017). Human Rights Defenders, Activism, and the Media: Cases, Challenges and Solutions.

Retrieved 26 October 2018 from http://socioscope.am/wp-content/uploads/2017/10/ACT17_pdf-for-internet.pdf.

Socioscope Societal Research & Consultancy Center NGO (2018). Analytical Report: From Shrinking Space to Post-Revolutionary Space: Reimagining the Role and Relations of Civil Society in Armenia. Retrieved 18 December 2019 from http://socioscope.am/wp-content/uploads/2019/01/Socioscope-report_15.01_spread-eng.pdf.

Somers, Margaret R., and Christopher NJ Roberts. "Toward a New Sociology of Rights: A Genealogy of "Buried Bodies" of Citizenship and Human Rights," *Annual Review of Law and Social Science* 4 (2008): 385–425.

Sparer, Ed. "Fundamental Human Rights, Legal Entitlements and the Social Struggle: A Friendly Critique of the Critical Legal Studies Movement," *Stanford Law Review* 36 (1984): 509–574.

Speed, Shannon. "Exercising Rights and Reconfiguring Resistance in the Zapatista Juntas De Buen Gobierno," In Goodale, Mark, and Sally Engle Merry, eds. *The Practice of Human Rights: Tracking Law between the Global and the Local*. Cambridge University Press, 2007.

Stammers, Neil. "Human Rights and Power," *Political Studies* 41, no. 1 (1993): 70–82.

Stammers, Neil. "A Critique of Social Approaches to Human Rights," *Human Rights Quarterly* 17, no. 3 (1995): 488.

Stammers, Neil. "Social Movements and the Social Construction of Human Rights," *Human Rights Quarterly* 21, no. 4 (1999): 980–1008.

Stammers, Neil. *Human Rights and Social Movements*. Pluto Press, 2009.

Stefes, Christoph H. and Katherine Weingartner. Environmental Crime in Armenia: A Case Study on Mining (January 2015) [Online]. https://efface.eu/sites/default/files/EFFACE_Environmental%20crime%20in%20Armenia_A%20case%20study%20on%20mining.pdf. [2019 February].

Steiner, Henry J. and Alston, Philip. *International Human Rights in Context: Law, Politics, Morals*. Clarendon Press, 1996.

Stern, Steve J. and Scott Straus, eds. *The Human Rights Paradox: Universality and Its Discontents*. University of Wisconsin Press, 2014.

Stones, Rob. "Rights, Social Theory, and Political Philosophy: A Framework for Case Study Research," In Lydia Morris, ed. *Rights: Sociological Perspectives*. Routledge, 2006.

Straus, Roger A. "The Theoretical Frame of Symbolic Interactions: A Contextualist, Social Science," *Symbolic Interaction* 4, no. 2 (1981): 261–272.

Stuck with Each other- Armenia and Russia. *The Economist* (20 March 2015). Retrieved 21 August 2018 from https://www.economist.com/europe/2015/03/20/stuck-with-each-other.

Swidler, Ann. "Culture in Action: Symbols and Strategies," *American Sociological Review* 51, no. 2 (1986): 273–286.

Sztompka, Piotr. "Agency and Progress: The Idea of Progress and Changing Theories of Change," In Stammers, Neil ed. *Human Rights and Social Movements*. Pluto Press, 2009.

Tarrow, Sidney. "Power in Movement: Social Movements, Collective Action and Politics." In Armaline, William T., Davita S. Glasberg, and Bandana Purkayastha, eds. *The Human Rights Enterprise: Political Sociology, State Power, and Social Movements*. Polity Press, 2015.

The Executive Board, American Anthropological Association. "Statement on Human Rights," *American Anthropologist* 49, no. 4 (1947): 539–543.

Thérien, Jean-Philippe, and Philippe Joly. "All Human Rights for All: The United Nations and Human Rights in the Post-Cold War Era," *Human Rights Quarterly* 36, no. 2 (2014): 373.

Thomas, Daniel C. *The Helsinki Effect: International Norms, Human Rights, and the Demise of Communism*. Princeton University Press, 2001.

Thomas, Daniel C. "Human Rights Ideas, the Demise of Communism, and the End of the Cold War," *Journal of Cold War Studies* 7, no. 2 (2005): 110–141.

Towe, Thomas E. "Fundamental Rights in the Soviet Union: A Comparative Approach," *University of Pennsylvania Law Review* 115 (1967): 1251.

Transparency International Anti-Corruption Center. Statement on the Effectiveness of the International Assistance in Police Sector Reforms (22 July 2016). Retrieved 28 October 2018 from https://transparency.am/en/news/view/1550.

Troebst, Stefan, "Sozialistisches Völkerrecht" und die sowjetische Menschenrechtsdoktrin. In: Norbert Frei/Annette Weinke (Hg.) *Toward a New Moral World Order? Menschenrechtspolitik und Völkerrecht seit 1945*, Göttingen: Wallstein 2013, S. 95 (= Jena Center Geschichte des 20. Jahrhunderts. Vorträge und Kolloquien, 15).

Trubek, David M. "Where the Action Is: Critical Legal Studies and Empiricism," In Silbey, Susan S. "After Legal Consciousness," *Annual Review of Law and Social Science* 1 (2005): 323–368.

Umroyan, Lilit, and Lucig Danielyan. "Human Rights Education in Armenia – A Base Line Study," In Mihr, Anja et al., ed. *Armenia: A Human Rights Perspective for Peace and Democracy. Human Rights Education and Minorities*. Universität Potsdam, 2005.

UN Committee on Economic, Social and Cultural Rights (CESCR). *General Comment No. 3: The Nature of States Parties' Obligations (Art. 2, Para. 1, of the Covnenant)*, 14 December 1990, E/1991/23, available at: https://www.refworld.org/docid/4538838e10.html [accessed 1 November 2018].

UN General Assembly. *Universal Declaration of Human Rights*, 217 A (III) (10 December 1948). Retrieved 21 August 2018 from http//www.refworld.org/docid/3ae6b3712c.html.

UN General Assembly. *Convention against Torture and Other Cruel, Inhuman or Degrading Treatment or Punishment*, 10 December 1984, United Nations, Treaty Series, vol. 1465, available at: https://www.refworld.org/docid/3ae6b3a94.html [accessed 15 January 2018].

UN General Assembly. *International Covenant on Civil and Political Rights*, 16 December 1966, United Nations, Treaty Series, vol. 999, available at: https://www.refworld.org/docid/3ae6b3aa0.html [accessed 19 January 2017].

UN Economic and Social Council, Forum Menschenrechte. *UN Report Shows Inadequate Implementation of Economic, Social and Cultural Rights by Germany (Concluding Observations by the UN Committee on Economic, Social and Cultural Rights on the Sixth Periodic Report by Germany)*, 31 October 2018, available at: https://www.forum-menschenrechte.de/wp-content/uploads/2017/10/List-of-Issues-FMR-GERMANY_TERRITORIAL_FINAL.pdf [accessed 9 December 2018].

Unarmed Soldiers Join Anti-Government Protests in Armenia. *Reuters* (23 April 2018). Retrieved 1 November 2018 from https://www.reuters.com/article/us-armenia-politics-protests-army/unarmed-soldiers-join-anti-government-protests-in-armenia-idUSKBN1HU15U?utm_campaign=trueAnthem%3A+Trending+Content&utm_content=5addc74504d3014ac94e325b&utm_medium=trueAnthem&utm_source=facebook.

United Nations. *Universal Recognition of Inalienable Right to Self-Determination Most Effective Way to Guaranteeing Fundamental Freedoms, Third Committee Told* (6 November 2012). Retrieved 21 August 2018 from https://www.un.org/press/en/2012/gashc4051.doc.htm.

United Nations Human Rights Office of the High Commissioner. The Core International Human Rights Treaties (2014) [Online]. https://www.ohchr.org/Documents/Publications/CoreInternationalHumanRightsTreaties_en.pdf. [2019 January].

United States Department of State. *Bureau of Democracy, Human Rights* and *Labor, Country Reports on Human Rights Practices for* 2008, ARMENIA (25 February 2009). Retrieved 10 June 2018 from https://www.state.gov/j/drl/rls/hrrpt/2008/eur/119066.htm.

United States Department of State. *Bureau* of *Democracy*, *Human Rights* and *Labor, Country Reports on Human Rights Practices for* 2015, ARMENIA. 2. Retrieved 21 August 2018 from https://photos.state.gov/libraries/armenia/231771/PDFs/hr2015.pdf.

United States Department of State. *Bureau of Democracy*, *Human Rights* and *Labor, Country Reports on Human Rights Practices for* 2016, ARMENIA. 2. Retrieved 10 June 2017 from https://www.state.gov/documents/organization/265604.pdf.

United States Department of State. *Bureau of Democracy*, *Human Rights* and *Labor, Country Reports on Human Rights Practices for* 2016, ARMENIA (3 March 2017). Retrieved 27 October 2018 from https://www.state.gov/j/drl/rls/hrrpt/2016/eur/265392.htm.

United States Department of State. *Bureau of Democracy*, *Human Rights* and *Labor, Country Reports on Human Rights Practices for* 2017, ARMENIA. 2. Retrieved 22 August 2018 from https://www.state.gov/documents/organization/277381.pdf.

Valentini, Laura. "Human Rights, Freedom, and Political Authority," *Political Theory* 40, no. 5 (2012): 573–601.

Vanderford, Marsha L. "Vilification and Social Movements: A Case Study of Pro-Life and Pro-Choice Rhetoric," In Jasper, James M. "The Emotions of Protest: Affective and Reactive Emotions in and around Social Movements," *Sociological Forum* 13, no. 3 (1998): 397–424.

Verdirame, Guglielmo. "Human Rights in Political and Legal Theory," *Routledge Handbook of International Human Rights Law*. Routledge, 2014. 41–64.

Vesa, Andreea. "International and Regional Standards for Protecting Victims of Domestic Violence," *Journal of Gender, Social Policy and the Law* 12, no. 2 (2004): 309–360.

"Vtcharum enq 100 dram" nakhadzernutyan haytararutyuny. [Announcement of "We Pay 100 Dram" Initiative]. *Hetq* (26 July 2013). Retrieved 21 October 2018 from http://hetq.am/arm/news/28378/vtcharum-enq-100-dram-nakhadzernutyan-haytararutyuny.html.

Wastell, Sari. "Being Swazi, Being Human: Custom, Constitutionalism and Human Rights in an African Polity." In Goodale, Mark, and Sally Engle Merry, eds. *The Practice of Human Rights: Tracking Law between the Global and the Local*. Cambridge University Press, 2007.

Wawra, Ernst. "The Helsinki Final Act and the Civil and Human Rights Movement in the Soviet Union," In Huhle, Rainer (Hg.). *Human Rights and History. A Challenge for Education*. Berlin: Stiftung "Erinnerung, Verantwortung und Zukunft", 2010.

Weber, Max. "Economy and Society: An Outline of Interpretive Sociology," In Benhabib, Seyla. "Political Geographies in a Global World: Arendtian Reflections," *Social Research* 69, no. 2 (2002): 539–566.

Weise, Zia. Armenia's Disputed Move toward True Democracy: Critics Worry a Parliamentary Shift Is Designed to Help President Serzh Sargsyan Maintain His Grip on Power. *POLITICO* (4 June 2018). Retrieved 22 August 2018 from https://www.politico.eu/article/armenia-true-democracy-disputed-move-eu-agreement-turkey/.

What Happened Today in Yerevan and Why (Developing). *CIVILNET* (17 July 2016). Retrieved 25 October 2018 from https://www.civilnet.am/news/2016/07/17/what-happened-today-in-yerevan-and-why-developing/296980.

What You Need to Know about Demonstrations in Yerevan. *CIVILNET* (14 April 2018). Retrieved 30 October 2018 from https://www.civilnet.am/news/2018/04/14/What-you-need-to-know-about-demonstrations-in-Yerevan/333498.

Wiles, Ellen. "Aspirational Principles or Enforceable Rights? The Future for Socio-Economic Rights in National Law," *American University International Law Review* 22 (2006): 35.

Williams, Craig. "International Human Rights and Confucianism," *Asia-Pacific Journal on Human Rights and the Law* 7, no. 1 (2006): 38.

Wilson, Richard. *Human Rights, Culture and Context: Anthropological Perspectives*. Pluto Press, 1997.

Wilson, Richard, A. "Tyrannosaurus Lex: The Anthropology of Human Rights and Transnational Law." In Goodale, Mark, and Sally Engle Merry, eds. *The Practice of Human Rights: Tracking Law between the Global and the Local*. Cambridge University Press, 2007.

Woodiwiss, Anthony. "Making Human Rights Work Globally." In Somers, Margaret R., and Christopher NJ Roberts. "Toward a New Sociology of Rights: A Genealogy of "Buried Bodies" of Citizenship and Human Rights," *Annual Review of Law and Social Science* 4 (2008): 385–425.

Wouters, Jan, et al. A Comparative Study of EU and US Approaches to Human Rights in External Relations [Online]. http://www.europarl.europa.eu/RegData/etudes/STUD/2014/534981/EXPO_STU(2014)534981_EN.pdf. [2019 January].

'"Ynddem kananc nkatmamb brnutyan koaliciayi" haytararutyuny.' [Announcement of the "Coalition to Stop Violence against Women"] (26 July 2016). *Hetq*. Retrieved 26 October 2018 from https://hetq.am/hy/article/69400.

Young, Iris Marion. "Justice and the Politics of Difference," In Somers, Margaret R., and Christopher NJ Roberts. "Toward a New Sociology of Rights: A Genealogy of 'Buried Bodies' of Citizenship and Human Rights," *Annual Review of Law and Social Science* 4 (2008): 385–425.

Zartner, Dana and Jennifer Ramos. "Human Rights as Reputation Builder: Compliance with the Convention against Torture," *Human Rights Review* 12, no. 1 (2011): 71–92.

Zerilli, Linda MG. "This Universalism Which Is Not One," *Diacritics* 28, no. 2 (1998): 3–20. *Project MUSE*, doi:10.1353/dia.1998.0013.

Zolyan, Mikayel. Armenia's "Permanent Revolution": Why Do the Protests Continue in Yerevan? *openDemocracy* (25 April 2018). Retrieved 1 November 2018 from https://www.opendemocracy.net/en/odr/armenia-s-permanent-revolution-why-do-protests-continue-in-yerevan/.

Gesellschaften und Staaten im Epochenwandel
Societies and States in Transformation

Herausgegeben von / Edited by
Dittmar Schorkowitz / Stefan Troebst

Mitbegründet von / Co-founded by
René Ahlberg / Lawrence Krader / Klaus Meyer

The series "Societies and States in Transformation" offers an interdisciplinary forum for contributions that focus on the radical changes in world history with their concomitant social, political, cultural, and economic upheavals. The focus is on people and societies both as actors in processes of transformation and as objects of the latter. These issues are addressed from a broader perspective which, reaching beyond the paradigm changes that have taken place in recent European history, puts an emphasis on current processes unfolding in an increasingly globalized world. The series thus deals with the various forms of expression in time and space that reflect the reactions to the challenges posed by epochal change by the societies and nations affected. In this interdisciplinary field, there is communication and interaction between analyses of historical and political science, sociology, social anthropology, and cultural studies.

Die Publikationsreihe "Gesellschaften und Staaten im Epochenwandel" bietet ein interdisziplinäres Forum für Beiträge, die auf die großen Umbrüche in der Weltgeschichte mit ihren sozialen, politischen, kulturellen und wirtschaftlichen Verwerfungen fokussieren. Mensch und Gesellschaften stehen hierbei sowohl als Handelnde als auch als Objekt von Transformationsprozessen im Mittelpunkt der Betrachtung, die über den Paradigmenwechsel in der jüngeren Vergangenheit Europas hinaus auch aktuelle Prozesse einer zunehmend global vernetzten Welt ins Blickfeld nimmt. Thema der Reihe sind damit die unterschiedlichen Ausdrucksformen in Raum und Zeit, in denen sich die Reaktionen der betroffenen Gesellschaften und Staaten auf die Herausforderungen epochalen Wandels zeigen. In diesem interdisziplinären Feld korrespondieren und interagieren Analysen der Geschichts- und Politikwissenschaft, von Soziologie, Ethnologie und Kulturwissenschaft.

Band 1 René Ahlberg: Sowjetgesellschaft im Epochenwandel. Studien zur Selbstaufklärung der sowjetischen Gesellschaft in der Zeit der Perestroika 1985-1990. 1992.

Band 2 Lawrence Krader: Die Anfänge des Kapitalismus in Mitteleuropa. 1993.

Band 3 Brigitte Heuer / Milan Prucha (Hrsg.): Der Umbruch in Osteuropa als Herausforderung für die Philosophie. 1995.

Band 4 Christian Kennert: Paul Cassirer und sein Kreis. Ein Berliner Wegbereiter der Moderne. 1996.

Band 5 Tatjana Eggeling / Wim van Meurs / Holm Sundhaussen (Hrsg.): Umbruch zur „Moderne". Studien zur Politik und Kultur in der osteuropäischen Transformation. 1997.

Band 6 Lev S. Klejn: Das Phänomen der sowjetischen Archäologie. Geschichte, Schulen, Protagonisten. Aus dem Russischen von D. Schorkowitz. 1997.

Band 7 Heinrich Härke (ed.): Archaeology, Ideology and Society: the German Experience. 2000. 2nd, revised edition. 2002.

Band 8 Dittmar Schorkowitz (Hrsg.): Transition - Erosion - Reaktion. Zehn Jahre Transformation in Osteuropa. 2002.

Band 9 Matthias Hardt / Christian Lübke / Dittmar Schorkowitz (Hrsg.): Inventing the Pasts in North Central Europe. The National Perception of Early Medieval History and Archaeology. 2003.

Band 10 Klemens Büscher: Transnationale Beziehungen der Russen in Moldova und der Ukraine. Ethnische Diaspora zwischen Residenz- und Referenzstaat. 2004.

Band 11 Stefan Troebst: Kulturstudien Ostmitteleuropas. Aufsätze und Essays. 2006.

Band 12 Tilman Musch: Nomadismus und Sesshaftigkeit bei den Burjaten. Gesellschaftlicher Wandel im Spiegel zeitgenössischer Folklore. 2006.

Band 13 Victoria Knebel: Preserve and Rebuild. Dresden during the Transformations of 1989–1990. Architecture, Citizens Initiatives and Local Identities. 2007.

Band 14 Przemysław Urbańczyk: Herrschaft und Politik im Frühen Mittelalter. Ein historisch-anthropologischer Essay über gesellschaftlichen Wandel und Integration in Mitteleuropa. 2007.

Band 15 Dittmar Schorkowitz: Postkommunismus und verordneter Nationalismus. Gedächtnis, Gewalt und Geschichtspolitik im nördlichen Schwarzmeergebiet. 2008.

Band 16 Monica Heintz (ed.): Weak State, Uncertain Citizenship: Moldova. 2008.

Band 17 Klaus Meyer: Rußland – Vertraute Fremde. Neues und Bleibendes in historischer Perspektive. 2008.

Band 18 Daniel Grabić: Montenegrizität. Sprache und Kirche im Spiegel des Identitätsdiskurses in der Republik Montenegro 1990–2007. 2010.

Band 19 Tetyana Kloubert: Aufarbeitung der Vergangenheit als Dimension der Erwachsenenbildung. Polnische, russländische und ukrainische Perspektiven. 2014.

Band 20 Artur Mkrtichyan (ed.): Armenians around the World: Migration and Transnationality. 2015.

Band 21 Anahit Babayan: Armenia on the Horizon of Europe. Successes and Shortcomings of Democratization Efforts by European Organizations in a Post-Soviet State. 2015.

Band 22 Dana Jirouš: Erinnerung als Mobilisierungsressource im Vorfeld ethnisierter Gewaltkonflikte. Das Beispiel Nordossetien – Inguschetien, 1989-1992. 2017.

Band 23 Peter Pichler: Zeitgeschichte als Lebensgeschichte. Überlegungen zu einer emanzipativen und aktuellen Zeithistoriographie. 2017.

Band 24 Liana Geghamyan: Exercising Human Rights in Armenia. Interactions between Governmental and Non-State Actors. 2020.

www.peterlang.com

www.ingramcontent.com/pod-product-compliance
Ingram Content Group UK Ltd.
Pitfield, Milton Keynes, MK11 3LW, UK
UKHW021829100926
8556IPUK00004B/238

9 783631 814598